Praise for *Cuba-U.S. Relations*

"Arnold August is one of the foremost experts on Cuba and the 1959 Revolution, which continues to shake the world. In this new book, August puts forth a valuable, detailed account of U.S.–Cuba relations dating back to 1783 and continuing to the present time. August shows that this relationship has centred on the U.S.'s attempts, sometimes successfully, to dominate Cuba and exploit it as its own playground and, in the case of Guantánamo, as a maximum security prison. As he shows, the 1959 Revolution broke the U.S. hold over Cuba, and the U.S. has tried desperately, and many times violently, to regain its control over the island. Obama opened diplomatic ties with Cuba for the first time in 50 years. August explains what this opening means for both countries, and where he sees U.S.–Cuba relations heading after the death of Fidel Castro at age 90 and the rise of U.S. President Donald Trump. For those who want a fresh and reasoned perspective on Cuba and U.S. relations — and with it a perspective very different from that which we get from the mainstream Western media — this book is a must-read."
— Daniel Kovalik, teacher of international human rights, University of Pittsburgh, School of Law

"In his third book, August highlights the many roadblocks on the way to normalization. Unlike many mainstream "cubanologists," who are blind to imperial arrogance, he places the onus squarely on U.S. prejudices. Regime change remains the ultimate objective under a new disguise. A cultural war has been targeting the younger generations. New Plattists [those in favour of annexation to the U.S.] are showing up. August's deft analysis, firmly grounded in a prolonged exposure to Cuban history and debates while mapping out the possible future developments, makes for an enlightening book."
— Claude Morin, professor (retired) of Latin American history, Université de Montréal

"Arnold August's new book on Cuba dispels the propaganda and myths perpetuated by both the U.S. corporate media and the Obama administration and provides valuable insights into what we might expect from a Trump government in the post-Fidel era. August lays bare the realities of Obama's policies toward Cuba by methodically revealing how his administration's engagement with the island constituted a shift in tactics while retaining Washington's decades-long objective of achieving regime change to bring the socialist nation back into the U.S. sphere of influence. It also highlights

our narrow definition of democracy by challenging the repeated assertions that Cuba is a dictatorship. This book is a must-read for understanding the constantly evolving imperialist strategies of the United States, not only in Cuba, but throughout the world in the 21st century."
— Garry Leech, independent journalist and teacher of
international politics, Cape Breton University

"Arnold August's bristling collection of interventions vigorously debunks U.S.-centric misrepresentations of Cuban society and of Obama's new 'regime change' strategy. It also engages critically with Cuban intellectuals and bloggers fighting in the 'Cultural War,' challenging the Revolution's cohesion since the 2014 'normalization' process began. With its withering anti-imperialism and comradely criticism of Cuban realities, this timely book will open many eyes and raise many hackles."
— Steve Ludlam, senior lecturer (retired), University of Sheffield,
and editorial board member, *International Journal of Cuban Studies*

"In *Cuba–U.S. Relations: Obama and Beyond*, Arnold August provides an incisive analysis of the process that led to the rapprochement between the United States and Cuba under the leadership of Raúl Castro and Barack Obama, as well as further developments since. The book is a timely and valuable source of clear analysis of Cuba–U.S. relations at the dawn of the Trump era, and an indispensable tome for activists and others interested in furthering normalized relations between Cuba and the U.S. and asserting Cuba's right to self-determination and sovereignty over all its territory."
— Pepe Ross, adjunct professor, University of Albany,
State University of New York

ARNOLD AUGUST has an M.A. in political science from McGill University, Montreal, where he resides. His most recent book is *Cuba and Its Neighbours: Democracy in Motion* (Fernwood Publishing/Zed Books, 2013). An accomplished journalist, he contributes articles in English and Spanish to websites in the United States, Canada, Cuba, Latin America and Europe. Since 1997, he has spent extended periods in Cuba pursuing his intensive investigations.

CUBA-U.S. RELATIONS

CUBA-U.S. RELATIONS

Obama and Beyond

ARNOLD AUGUST

FERNWOOD PUBLISHING
HALIFAX & WINNIPEG

Editing: Brenda Conroy
Cover design: John van der Woude
Printed and bound in Canada

Published by Fernwood Publishing
32 Oceanvista Lane, Black Point, Nova Scotia, B0J 1B0
and 748 Broadway Avenue, Winnipeg, Manitoba, R3G 0X3
www.fernwoodpublishing.ca

Fernwood Publishing Company Limited gratefully acknowledges the financial support of the Government of Canada through the Canada Book Fund, the Manitoba Department of Culture, Heritage and Tourism under the Manitoba Publishers Marketing Assistance Program, the Province of Manitoba, through the Book Publishing Tax Credit, the support of the Province of Nova Scotia through the Department of Communities, Culture and Heritage and the support of the Canada Council for the Arts.

Library and Archives Canada Cataloguing in Publication

August, Arnold, author
Cuba–U.S. relations: Obama and beyond / Arnold August.

Includes bibliographical references and index.
Issued in print and electronic formats.
ISBN 978-1-55266-965-5 (softcover).--ISBN 978-1-55266-966-2 (EPUB).--
ISBN 978-1-55266-967-9 (Kindle)

1. Cuba--Foreign relations--United States. 2. United States--
Foreign relations--Cuba. I. Title.

E183.8.C9A94 2017   327.7291073   C2016-908071-4
                          C2016-908072-2

CONTENTS

ABBREVIATIONS

ALBA-TCP	Alianza Bolivariana para los Pueblos de Nuestra América (Bolivarian Alliance for the Peoples of Our America)
ANAP	Asociación Nacional de Agricultores Pequeños (National Association of Small Farmers)
CACR	Cuban Assets Control Regulations
CANF	Cuban American National Foundation
CDA	Cuban Democracy Act
CDR	Comités de Defensa de la Revolución (Committees for the Defence of the Revolution)
CELAC	Community of Latin American and Caribbean States
CFR	Council on Foreign Relations
CSOS	civil society organizations
DRL	Bureau of Democracy, Human Rights, and Labor
EAR (or EAR99)	Export Administration Regulations (or Export Administration Regulation 99)
EEUU	Estados Unidos (United States of America)
FDA	U.S. Food and Drug Administration
FTAA	Free Trade Area of the Americas
GES	Global Entrepreneurship Summit
GTMO	Gitmo; Guantánamo Bay
ISRI	Instituto Superior de Relaciones Internacionales "Raúl Roa García" (Raúl Roa García Higher Institute of International Relations)
LASA	Latin American Studies Association
MINREX	Cuban Ministry of Foreign Relations
NED	National Endowment for Democracy
OAS	Organization of American States
OFAC	Office of Foreign Assets Control
PCC	Partido Comunista de Cuba (Communist Party of Cuba)
PRC	Partido Revolucionario Cubano (Cuban Revolutionary Party)
PSP	Partido Socialista Popular (People's Socialist Party)
SBA	Small Business Administration
TPP	Trans-Pacific Partnership
UNEAC	Unión de Escritores y Artistas de Cuba (Union of Writers and Artists of Cuba)
UNGA	United Nations General Assembly
UPEC	Unión de Periodistas de Cuba (Union of Cuban Journalists)
USAID	U.S. Agency for International Development

ACKNOWLEDGEMENTS

I am above all grateful to Fernwood Publishing. Errol Sharpe, who took up the responsibility as my editor, deserves special thanks. He accepted my proposal for the book without hesitation and found time in his busy schedule to review the earlier drafts of the manuscript. His suggestions led to fertile exchanges between us and the expansion of certain themes. It is assuring to work under conditions in which the author and editor are on the same political page.

Beverley Rach carried out her difficult role as production coordinator with aplomb, from the manuscript stage to copy editing, proofreading and artwork. Brenda Conroy was responsible for the final copy editing, which she carried out rapidly and efficiently so that we could meet our publishing deadline. She particularly did an admirable job in yet further improving the manuscript. I am grateful to Deb Mathers for preparing the manuscript for design. Marketing managers Curran Faris and Nancy Malek have already proved their skills in this area with the advance work they have done and I am looking forward to working with them on the promotion and marketing of this book. Designer John van der Woude created cover art that was beyond my expectations.

It was a great honour that Professor Emeritus Keith Ellis of University of Toronto agreed to write the foreword. He and his wife, Zilpha Ellis, were very supportive of my journalistic articles on Cuba–U.S. relations after December 17, 2014, into 2016. I am grateful to him for having executed a real *tour de force* by making use of his profound knowledge of Cuban culture and politics, as well as those of the U.S., in order to write a remarkable foreword.

Ricardo Alarcón is one of Cuba's most important experts on Cuba–U.S. relations and on the United States itself, taking into account his decades of direct experience and his ongoing sharp and principled analysis. No one can hope for a better person to introduce this book, especially for an English-speaking audience, which he knows so well. I thank him for taking the time from his busy schedule to write the introduction.

Gracias to Jesús Arboleya Cervera, Ph.D.; Esteban Morales Domínguez,

Ph.D.; Elier Ramírez Cañedo, Ph.D.; Iroel Sánchez Espinosa, Eng.; and Luis Toledo Sande, Ph.D. for granting me the interviews published in Chapter 3. Especially appreciated was their candour in the responses to my difficult and often sensitive questions and their confidence in my capacity to produce the interviews in English.

Veronica Schami, my main copy editor in Montreal, was once again a key ally in preparing the manuscript, as she did for my 2013 publication. In addition to copy editing the manuscript to the highest professional standards, she prepared the many sources and references. Veronica's devotion to constantly pushing me to make many points clearer has resulted in a reader-friendly book, both for academic circles as well as the general public. In all of this work, she was assisted by Jo Howard, her colleague. It was admirable to witness how they worked so well as a team. I sincerely thank Veronica and Jo.

Peter Feldstein, a Montreal-based professional Spanish-to-English translator, contributed substantially to the translation of the five Havana interviews. His profound knowledge of Spanish was essential, as Cuban writing is not easy to translate.

Finally, I would like to thank all those in Cuba who take a principled stand against the illusions emerging from U.S. Cuba policy while fully supporting the long-term goal of normalization. They inspired me throughout the writing of this book and will surely do so in the future.

"The greater war being waged on us is a war of ideas:
let us win it with our ideas."
— José Martí, 1895

Foreword

TOO INTERCONNECTED TO BE UNRAVELLED
by Keith Ellis

What does a Canadian progressive intellectual do when a revolution made by the people of Cuba has won, because of its spirit and its achievements, his admiration and his loyalty? What does he do when this revolution, which, he shows, is the authentic culmination of a process that has involved all the salient stages of Cuba's history, of its struggles, now finds itself in a time of unprecedented complexity and new difficulties, fed in part by the very successes of the Revolution? Arnold August brings to the task his finest gift, his superbly developed talent as a journalist, understanding this to mean the habit of assessing different aspects and representations of reality, so that he offers an ultimate fairness to the reasonable and humane reader. August constantly exhibits a related attribute: his remarkable power of analysis. The two together make the experience of reading him an enlightening one. His research work for this book, as for others on related topics, led him to live in Cuba for important periods of time, to live among Cubans and notice 1) how Fidel's extraordinary power of analysis has been reflected in the Cuban population and 2) the impact its diffusion throughout the society has had on producing the calm, pleasant affability that underpins

Keith Ellis (Jamaica 1935) is Professor Emeritus, Department of Spanish and Portuguese, University of Toronto, and Professor of Merit, the University of Havana. He taught Latin American poetry until his retirement, publishing many books and articles in this area. His own poetry has appeared in several journals in the Caribbean, North America and China. Among his awards are the Dulce María Loynaz International Prize (Cuba), the Andrés Bello Medal (Venezuela), Doctor honoris causa from the University of Havana and the Order of Distinction (cd) from the government of Jamaica. He is a Fellow of the Royal Society of Canada.

the stability of Cuba during times that could have been tempestuous. The people know how to think, and August has the superior skills, derived from his affinity for truth-telling, to produce a reliable picture of the complexities of their reaction to attempts to beguile them.

The paradox expressed by Fidel Castro, just after the military triumph of 1959, to Celia Sánchez — an iconic female revolutionary fighter, deeply patriotic in a multi-talented way — that the great contest of the Revolution, one in which the U.S. would show itself to be the main and persistent antagonist, would now begin. For while January 1, 1959, marked the defeat of and the liberation from Fulgencio Batista's dictatorship, Cuba's past history, its struggle against colonialism and slavery and for sovereignty and independence, indicated that the future held a complex and perilous trajectory, given the difficulty the U.S. would have in departing from its hegemonic and domineering behaviour toward weaker Latin American and other countries. This is the ongoing conflict that August studies in its many dimensions, with his keen awareness of how Fidel Castro's prediction of 1959 is linked to a historical Latin American problem, one recognized by José Martí in his essay "Congreso Internacional de Washington: Su historia, sus elementos y sus tendencias" (The Washington International Congress: Its History, Its Elements and Its Tendencies): "It is urgent to say, because it is the truth, that the time has come for Spanish America to declare its second independence" (Martí 1979b, 476; translations in this are mine).

The careful attention to language is a ubiquitous feature of this book. In the first place, there is the welcome clarity of August's writing, with its smooth syntax and its semantic precision. The clarity serves his trilingual awareness of the fact that his subject intimately concerns two language groups; and, even though he is writing in English, he must also be satisfied that his concepts are readily conveyable to a Cuban readership. He also writes to expose and counter a specific habit and tactic of imperial and colonial policy: that of using language to mislead.

In this case, August exposes a dual target: Cuba, which is pictured as the intended beneficiary of offers that, were they to be declined, would prove the country's unreasonableness or its secret satisfaction with the status quo. The ploy is even more effective as it is applied to a U.S. audience, which has been primed by its government and its media for more than half-a-century to see its side as occupying the space of the good guys. The Cuba–U.S. discussions regarding the U.S.-imposed blockade are replete with examples of this tactic. August points out, for example, how the U.S., vulnerable in the first place to criticism from people of moral rectitude, employs phrasing with such cunning ambiguity in reference to ostensible easings of some of the conditions under which U.S. currency may be used in international financial transactions involving Cuba that the apparent easings are in effect an elaborate trap. As a result, banks, companies (Cuban state enterprises included), international organizations such as the United Nations, and individuals have incurred unwarranted penalties of massive fines, seizures of property or loss of personal liberty. So the softening of the blockade remains, from the Cuban point of view, essentially an illusion and, from the U.S. point of view, an economic and propaganda benefit.

August recognizes that the core of Obama's strategy of the post December 17, 2014, period is the unleashing of a cultural war against Cuba's political and social system, against Cuba's socialism. He shows its tactics, in some of which the U.S. president takes an active, acting role, all with an eye to ensuring for himself the legacy of being the president who found the way to bring Cuba back to the fold of countries that remain loyal to the U.S. empire. As the months went by in 2016, Obama must have sensed that time was running out for taking advantage of the goodwill his acts of December 17, 2014, had won him in Cuba: namely, 1) his permitting the return to Cuba of the last three of the anti-terrorist Cuban Five, who had been cruelly imprisoned with long or interminable sentences and 2) his promise to normalize relations between the two countries.

Obama's attempt to devise tactics that would be effective with both targets at once, the U.S. one and the Cuban one, turns out to be an insurmountable challenge. Because he is tied to the assumption that, in all spheres of social life, the U.S. side reflects truly democratic values, he comes unprepared for the task of assessing Cuba correctly; and so, despite the considerable attention he has paid to certain cultural projects, they are foundering in their designed effect. Let us take, for example, the role of music, which August considers so perceptively in the context of the cultural war that Obama has unleashed on Cuba, targeting the youth with such weaponry as the Rolling Stones.

A measure of the desperate importance given to the cultural war against Cuba by the United States is the emphasis placed by Obama on rock music as highlighted by a free Rolling Stones concert staged in Havana on March 25, 2016, just three days after his historic visit to the island ended. From August's analysis we learn of the economic exploitation of Cuba's international desirability as a trendy locale, a perception also seized on by Rihanna and other stars. We learn too of the Obama ambition that the Cuban people, especially the youth, will come to develop a taste for this supposedly new music — with traditional Cuban music consequently loosening its hold on this important sector of the population — and make it open to ideological and political influences from the same source. This will mark an important victory by the Western team in the cultural war against Cuba. To this end, the West brings out its big guns to extract full value from the trip to Cuba: the charm of Obama himself, boosted on his visit by a younger and an older generation of his family and followed promptly by the spectacle of the Mick Jagger-led Stones concert. All of this is based on a usually reliable tactic of promotion: celebrity branding. The first celebrity is Barack Obama, the president of the United States, the world's most powerful country, throwing himself at every opportunity during his visit into the role of impresario for the upcoming concert by this rock and roll group. Tied to this hype is the self-promotion by Jagger, who drags the other Western potentate, her Majesty the Queen of Great Britain, into the picture, claiming ascendancy over her, without any complaint from the usually vigilant guardians of protocol and of her dignity. Cuba seems like a mighty fine prize when there is such stooping to conquer. Unfortunately, the "stooping" involves misleading, an almost obligatory contribution to a practice so rampant in Western journalism that the journalists themselves are speaking of a post-factual or post-truth world, terminology that has made its way into dictionaries of the English language.

Obama had implied that the coming of the Stones with their rock music signalled a new opening in Cuba to Western culture; and, in the course of his performance, as August notes, Jagger shouted that, with their visit, rock music had broken the ice. But while Jagger's and Obama's narrative is consistent with what is usually pictured for the North American public as denial of freedoms in Cuba, it suffers in the eyes of Cubans from a lack of veracity that enervates Obama's moral position and tends to invalidate the tactic. Visiting rock groups have been playing in Cuba over many decades, and Cuban rock bands have been performing in many scenarios, including on television.

The Beatles achieved great popularity in Cuba, even though they did not perform on the island. Their music was studied and played by such a leading Cuban and world-level composer, conductor and guitarist as Leo Brouwer. The expression of admiration peaked in the year 2000 when a statue of John Lennon was created by the renowned Cuban sculptor José Villa Soberón, with the British musician amiably and permanently seated on a bench in the Parque John Theodore Lennon, located centrally in Havana's Vedado district.[1] When Fidel Castro said in a television interview that he liked "rock," in addition to Cuban groups, he was perhaps thinking of the Beatles, perhaps specifically of "Give Peace a Chance," or "Imagine," perhaps of John Lennon's murder, a fate befalling so many others all over that country, on December 8, 1980, in the archway of the Dakota, the same building where another brilliant singer, Roberta Flack, of a different colour, had endured harassment by fellow residents.

There has been an unfortunate tendency on the part of some Cuban musicians to speak less than the truth, after they abandoned the country, about the freedom to practise their craft in Cuba. First-rate jazz musicians such as saxophonist and orchestra leader Paquito D'Rivera and trumpeter Arturo Sandoval helped to establish that pattern at the beginning of the last decade of the twentieth century. They allege that jazz was not allowed in Cuba. I have been among audiences of Cubans who listened to and vigorously applauded jazz performances in Cuba in the 1970s and 1980s. I noted the enthusiasm Cubans showed for Sandoval's music at the same time as they showed their revolutionary zeal

The strength of the popular musical traditions in Cuba fortified since the Revolution, by the higher levels of education attained by administrators and performers in the field and by the increasing sophistication of audiences for all of the genres, allows for scarce chances of success for outside forces to use music as a tool for subversion. Its vulnerabilities are essentially those shared by the economy of Cuba in general, which is subject to the effects of the blockade. The blockade has now meant more the fifty-five years of cruel suffering for Cubans. At the same time the blockade has heightened certain core aspects of conviviality among Cubans, making more pronounced certain tenets of ethics and morality, thus assisting in the Revolution's aim of strengthening the unity of the Cuban people. The fully democratic discussions described herein by August, which took place in 2016 of plans that go as far into the future as 2030, are an indication of the sensitivity of the administrators in Cuba to the need to maintain a society in which no group is left behind. All this will impede the effectiveness of measures that the Obama administration laid out in its plans for what they regard as normalizing relations with Cuba. August exposes these plans in such a way that readers will easily seize on their merits and demerits. Let us look at two tools that Obama planned to employ: 1) promoting aggressively the U.S. view of democracy and 2) popularizing the idea of entrepreneurship among young people.

It would seem that Obama, in his constant lecturing to the Cubans, in Cuba and elsewhere, about the inadequacy of their democracy, underestimates greatly the adequacy of the Cuban system of democracy to serve the needs and goals of the people. He would profit greatly from a reading of August's writings. At the same time, Obama greatly overstates the merits of his style of democracy as a model, and he underestimates the capacity of his Cuban audience, from leaders to school children, to judge accurately what he is saying. In response to his speech given at the Gran Teatro Alicia Alonso in March 2016 during his visit to Cuba, aspects of which were later contained in his presidential directive of October 14, 2016, not only did the leader of the Revolution, Fidel Castro, effectively deride him, but so did school children and women later marching through Havana. The contradictions on democracy are too glaring to be quietly tolerated by people who are schooled in or naturally possess ethics and morality and who are knowledgeable about "the history of our America from the Incas to the present" (Martí 1979b: 519), as Martí advised them to be.

The Cuban people know better than any other people, except the Venezuelan people themselves, that the U.S., under George W. Bush, attempted a coup d'état against Hugo Chávez's government in 2002. In addition to knowing it academically, thousands of them lived the tense days in Venezuela when the coup's success seemed likely. They know that Barack Obama carried out a coup, backing the military in Honduras in 2009; and that while doing so he displayed his special talent for ignoring his contradictions by speaking eloquently against the idea of coups d'état. They know, because many more thousands of Cubans are serving in missions in Venezuela and are now facing the hazards of a prolonged attempt at a coup d'état that has cost too many of them their lives. They know of the "parliamentary coup" of 2012 against the gentle President Fernando Lugo of Paraguay, who ascribed it to plotting by the U.S., whose only criticism of it was that the impeachment process was too rapid to seem truly democratic. The coup led to the suppression of Lugo's land reform program and the removal of his protection of peasants from pesticides that were doing great damage to their health (Lindsay 2013).

The Paraguayan model became favoured by the Obama administration. The word "parliamentary" sounds legitimate, and it is much easier to control a relatively small group of elected representatives than to go to the trouble of getting a new compliant parliament elected. Besides, Obama's preferred candidate to head the CIA in 2008 had been John O. Brennan, who needed the kind of terminological camouflage contained in the word "parliamentary" to cover his blatant defects, such as his friendliness to the idea of employing torture, which had led to his failure to be approved by the Senate Intelligence Committee as CIA director. When Obama presented him again in 2013, he won this approval. In one form or another the intelligence services of the United States have been taking advantage of what August identifies as U.S. style democracy, a system in which the survival of a government in countries such as Brazil may hang on how a small number of parliamentarians vote on a given issue. These voters, the system insists, are open to being approached by anyone, whether citizen or non-citizen, on any issue, however deeply, broadly and intimately it affects the country's people. From Honduras to the Ukraine, coups d'état have been effective for the Obama administration as a method of changing governments that is convenient to the U.S.'s imperialist designs. The coups and the sense of gratitude shared by their beneficiaries to the powerful enabler may assist in the perpetration of other coups. Honduras, Brazil, Paraguay and the Ukraine are expected to collude with the empire in making life as difficult as possible for Venezuela. They should do all they can, if not to expel this country from alliances such as Mercosur (a trading bloc of South American countries), at least to minimize the benefits the Bolivarian Republic gets from its membership, so that the success of the U.S. coup against Venezuela can be hastened.

In the face of such a prospect, how would the Cuban people behave? The primary image they have of Venezuelans is as continuers of the Bolívar-Chávez tradition, a mirror of their own Martí-Maceo-Fidel tradition, which makes the two people truly "two wings of the same bird." They know each other as well as they know themselves. Their leaders, Chávez or Fidel, Maduro or Raúl, have demonstrated their deep solidarity with each other, and together they have gifted unprecedented acts of goodness to their neighbours in Latin America and the Caribbean. Their youth have come to know each other in the cementing context of distributing this goodness. Will they ever accept defeat? Will U.S. style democracy prevail?

Will the U.S.'s enticements of entrepreneurship lead the youth of Cuba away from the Revolution? August describes how selected young people have been accepting scholarships to travel to the United States to learn how to be good entrepreneurs. Some of them have returned to Cuba to see that there are opportunities in small businesses that they can take up within the laws of the Revolution. Others can find examples of people who have skirted those laws and are successful entrepreneurs in the North American sense. This has made others wary of a conflict between entrepreneurship and the values of the Revolution which have become instilled in them and in their society. Those who live within the Revolution are undoubtedly the great majority.

How do these values manifest themselves? Essentially by putting people first, by showing the same love for people that led Martí and Fidel to fight for people's needs. Martí expressed it, among many other places, in the context of his reflections on scientific education, when he wrote in 1884: "In short, we need to begin a campaign of tenderness and science, and create for it a corps, which does not now exist, of missionary teachers" (Martí 1979a: 380). Nicolás Guillén subsequently wrote: "Martí promised it to you/and Fidel carried it out" (1964: 140).

The perception by Martí of the need to convey tenderness and science, which was shown as fulfilled by Fidel in Guillén's verses, is symbolic of the whole revolutionary process. The people are present in the concept as both participants and beneficiaries. In the medical field, for example, we see the concept playing out in the following way. Few doctors in Cuba have motor vehicles. A doctor serving in a polyclinic has a patient who needs hospital services. The doctor goes in a white gown to stand on the sidewalk in front of the polyclinic. Motorists passing by know that that is a signal that their transportation services are needed, which one, two or three of them may promptly stop to offer free of charge. The doctor will make the judgement about which offer to accept. The services of an ambulance would be reserved for contagious or critical cases. Another case. I am in a taxi. The driver stops at a red light. The light changes to green. He doesn't move. He keeps looking at a woman across the road who is looking at him too. He gets out and has a brief conversation with the woman. He comes back to the taxi and tells me: "That lady is suffering some distress. Is it okay with you if we take her to a nearby polyclinic?" I agree; and he does that, after stopping the meter. The taxi driver and I both feel good about what we have done. He doesn't show in any way that he has done something unusual, but there has no doubt been the fulfillment of a moral and ethical duty in both of these cases that overrides the efficiencies of entrepreneurship. Such efficiencies might also have dictated that an agreement by one country to work on eliminating illiteracy in the other country's population would be strictly an educational matter and not cross boundaries to be a medical one as well. And thus the ongoing gift to humanity that is Operación Milagro [Operation Miracle], a program initiated by Cuba and Venezuela for treating, free of charge, poor people in many countries who suffer from eye diseases, would never have become a cherished reality for more than three million people.

If U.S.-style entrepreneurship comes to prevail in Cuba and introduces a new system that places the emphasis on the efficient operation of the business, one will see a value system that doesn't carry the rewards of humanitarian service, that doesn't put people first; in other words, this would probably be the beginning of a process of disintegration. To accept Obama's offers will likely mean setting out on a road that, if not carefully navigated, will lead to Chicago, where Obama went to campaign strenuously for the successful re-election of its mayor and of an administration that presides over a city with rampant gang warfare, daily murders, police torture, poor schools and a host of other problems: in short, an environment that is concomitant with the economic thought of Milton Friedman. Cuban laws governing entrepreneurship are thoughtfully designed to preclude such failings. But the diehard promoters of laissez-fairism, the anti-regulationists, will always be pressing, encouraging from the outside, with a watchword of "freedom," which may come to be argued to include the human rights of ownership. Cuba will answer with those features of its culture that have reinforced its humane *cubanía* (deep Cuban identity), which has contributed so much to its stability.

There is a problem of instability on the U.S. side that looms when U.S.-Cuban relations are considered. This instability is not readily recognized, because instability is usually seen as characteristic of small, mismanaged countries. But it is becoming more and more obvious, when a sober examination of the functioning of the two societies and social systems is undertaken and in the light of the upheavals resulting from the recent elections in the U.S. These developments are undermining the basis for trust in agreements that might be reached in any negotiations that are undertaken between the two parties. This is more so because of the penchant for violence that is displayed by the U.S. both internally and externally, with the one inciting the other. The militarization of the police force in the U.S., as an answer to protests against police violence, is creating a cycle that perpetuates violence and also a willingness to turn to violent measures at the international level. The recourse to violence is so endemic to the United States that the surprise victory in the recent national elections of a candidate who speaks about making peace with Russia, a traditional, significant antagonist, is seen as a threat by even traditional victims of internal, institutionalized violence.

How much faith, then, can Cuba have in rational negotiations with such a country on matters such as the return of the occupied and degraded territory of Guantánamo Bay to its rightful owner? The military approach affected the issue of the taking of the territory from the very beginning because the Platt Amendment, which the United States holds to be the legal basis for its perpetual control, was itself a civilian disguise of a military initiative. The Amendment against which Cuban patriots such as Juan Gualberto Gómez argued so earnestly and skillfully, withstanding terrible racial insults, was in fact a civilian front for a firm military decision. A reading of the documents put forward by the United States to its administrators in Cuba and to the Cuban negotiators reveals that the terms of the Amendment were being presented by the United States Ministry of War in the person of its Secretary, Elihu Root, and only ostensibly by the Connecticut senator Orville Platt (*Documentos para la historia de Cuba* 1969: 102–05).

How does Cuba contend with this antagonist that is so mired in its war-like identity that its president, who won the Nobel Prize for Peace, at one point boasted that he was making war on seven countries? Surely there are advocates of peace and reasonable dialogue in that country who could come to the fore (I am writing this on Martin Luther King Jr. Day, Jan. 16, 2017). If Cuba could cultivate and encourage the finer instincts in the U.S. people, they may come to be informed of how it is that Cuba has achieved a stable and peaceful society. How since January 1, 1959, externally launched or supported terrorism, which included a military invasion of the island, has been the only significant disruptor of this peace. How there has been an absence of extrajudicial killings by the police and very few civilian murders. How the prioritization of education, culture and health care, in harmony with other essential areas of people's activities, has become a centripetal force that unites and elevates the people. The police are very much a part of this process, many of them having learned to read and write after January 1, 1959.

When it is said quickly that Cuba has good health care, people do not always have the chance to absorb and comprehend how integrative of many positive elements health care is in Cuban society. I give another example. I was visiting a friend in a Havana neighbourhood. He worked in the field of biotechnology. His wife was the family doctor for the neighbourhood. Shortly after I arrived at 8: 15 p.m. on a Sunday night, a man came to the clinic. She went downstairs to see him. She didn't return until about 9:30. I was concerned; her husband was calm. She came back to report that her patient was going through a time of dangerous stress because of his marital problems and she had needed to help him work through this crisis. I understood then the extent to which health care had been made accessible to the Cuban people and how this accessibility contributes to the peaceful temper of Cuban society and the many crucial connections that health care has to this peacefulness.

Obama, in his farewell speech to the nation, looked sad and worried and indeed expressed his concern about divisiveness in U.S. society and corrosiveness in its civil discourse. A step in remedying this might be to encourage the kind of relationship between the U.S. and Cuba in which journalists could play a constructive role and so give prestige to his legacy even though he is out of office. The five Cuban writers interviewed by August are serious, perceptive viewers of the state of affairs between Cuba and the United States and are naturally inclined to protect or defend Cuba from the obstinate haughtiness of its powerful northern neighbour. They could in the future mix their defensiveness with assertiveness, offer for emulation their social goodness and invite some of their promising U.S. peers to visit Cuba. The Cuban writers could show them how a society is made that is not divisive, not corrosive in its discourse, where there is civil peace.

Arnold August, the valiant and careful researcher, the limpid writer, the sensitive journalist, is a little bit worried, especially with the passing of Fidel. But we may tell him: Don't worry. The peerless protector by thought and deed has left us a structure too interconnected to be unravelled.

Note

1 This name replaced the name Parque Menocal or Parque García Menocal. Menocal was a Conservative political leader of the early neocolonial period. After the national elections of 1916, which his opponents thought he had lost, he refused to step down. His party tied the twenty-seven seats won by the Liberals, but the Liberals' allies, the Unionist Liberals and the Provincial Liberals, together won a further six seats. The stand-off resulted in a brief military skirmish that notably resulted in the death of the father of the then fourteen-year-old and future National Poet, Nicolás Guillén, a Liberal. See my book *Nicolás Guillén: Poetry and Ideology*.

THIS BOOK COMES INTO BEING

On December 17, 2014, Presidents Raúl Castro and Barack Obama stunned the world with their simultaneous announcements that Cuba and the U.S. would re-establish diplomatic relations. It was expected that this game-changing undertaking would lead to the complete normalization of the relationship.

I studied and reflected upon the White House statements and associated documents released on that memorable day; I was therefore not astonished by the fact that normalization (an ideal that I strongly support) would prove to be far more complicated and difficult than it may have first appeared. This has been especially true from the Cuban perspective.

Furthermore, the investigation I had carried out for my previous book, *Cuba and Its Neighbours: Democracy in Motion* (2013), attenuated my reaction to the declarations by the two heads of state. My analysis anticipated the nature of the new U.S. Cuba policy, if not the actual form of mutual diplomatic recognition, and highlighted its negative features. In particular, I foresaw that Obama would change tactics from ones that no longer worked to others designed to achieve the same goal in Cuba. Thus, as far as the *essence* of the new chapter in the relationship between the two neighbours was concerned, there was no surprise to me and others who may have carried out similar enquiries and reached the same conclusions. I had the advantage that my 2013 publication deals with the different political systems of Cuba and its neighbours, including the U.S. It also analyzes Cuba–U.S. relations in the context of traditional U.S. foreign policy, based on the seventeenth- and eighteenth-century Thirteen Colonies heritage up to the Obama era. It was no consolation to realize that my book foretold some of the key roadblocks that Cuba would have to confront in the course of the U.S. changing its policy toward Cuba. While difficulties were to be expected, I would have preferred a path devoid of major U.S.-induced impediments, as would have millions of people around the world, not to mention 11 million Cubans.

I must confess, however, that I am somewhat taken aback in analyzing today just how far the U.S. has actually advanced since December 17, 2014, in pursuing its interest in Cuba and, related to that quest, in Latin America. This book is about the methods and motives of this surprising American incursion, as well as the stunning Cuban resistance.

After the December 2014 statements, I began to write about the unfolding events and continued until the announcement on February 18, 2016, regarding Obama's visit to Cuba, planned for the following month. My journalistic work then focused on the period leading up to that event, and I was invited, along with Cuban specialists from the island, to Havana by TeleSUR television to analyze the March 20–22 visit. These three eventful days provided further insight into both the intentions of the U.S. and the varied Cuban responses.

I penned numerous articles in English and Spanish between December 2014 and April 2016 that covered the periods leading up to and following Obama's visit to Havana. The pieces were well received by both regular and new readers in North America, Europe, Latin America and Cuba. My TV appearance in Havana as an analyst was broadcast in Spanish in Cuba and other countries in Latin America, as well as live-streamed on TeleSUR's website to more countries in that region and elsewhere. The positive feedback on this special televised political affairs program and the suggestion of some readers that I compile my articles into a single work encouraged me to go in the direction of publishing another book. My proposal along these lines to Fernwood Publishing, which included fresh analyses of events in 2016 and prospects for the future, was promptly accepted, and so the book was on its way.

My website Democracy in the U.S. (August n.d.), a companion reference to my 2013 book, contains many articles that I wrote in 2011 and 2012 on the subject of Cuba–U.S. relations. Designed for readers of the 2013 volume, these have never been published anywhere except on my website. Given that many of the points I made proved to be accurate forecasts, I felt it would be helpful to share with readers of this book the evolution of my thinking going back to 2011. These articles therefore contribute to the depth and reasoning of the more recent ones and provide further insights about the current situation and what the future holds.

Within Cuba itself, critical realistic views of Cuba–U.S. relations are being developed that are not well known by non-Cubans, particularly the non-Spanish-speaking audience. To fill this gap, the book highlights my own documented analyses as well as indepth perspectives of Cubans writing from the island. Some of my analysis of the Cuban stance toward the new situation is geared toward shedding light on these Cubans' work mainly hitherto unpublished in English.

In addition, I concentrate on deconstructing the U.S. position. This is pursued with rigour and especially does not depend on U.S. mainstream media reports or cable news networks. The latter often sugar-coat and create illusions about U.S. Cuba policy. These portions of the book are based on analysis of original U.S. government and related documents. The influence of the U.S. media on Cuba–U.S. relations is also scrutinized by examining the media's own full transcriptions, rather than repeated sound bites.

This book contains six chapters that guide readers through the evolution of Cuba–U.S. relations to the current situation. It includes President-elect Donald Trump's transition period from November 2016 into the foreseeable future. It also contains important material on Fidel Castro regarding Cuba–U.S. relations written before his death on November 25, 2016. The book also includes an analysis of the impact of Fidel Castro's death on relations between the two neighbours and perspectives for 2017 and beyond.

Chapter 1, "Historical/Political Context: From the Thirteen Colonies to the Early Obama Era," draws on articles I wrote for my companion website in 2011–12. It provides the historical/political context, beginning with the first days of the Thirteen Colonies. A piece titled "Two Visions of Democracy: The U.S. vs. Fidel Castro" provides crucial background to the whirlwind of international controversy since the passing of Cuba's leader. In order to grasp the current situation and future perspectives, as with all international political phenomena, the circumstances must be anchored in history. This chapter comprises a selection of my previously published articles, edited and adapted for inclusion in this volume, as my original analyses have proven to be a harbinger of things to come. These pieces have been slightly modified to contextualize them, taking into account that they were written in 2011–12.

To each piece, I have added a short introduction to provide further background information. My research and that of others indicates that current American foreign policy finds its source and original inspiration, to a large extent, from the very foundation of the U.S. in the seventeenth and eighteenth centuries. The U.S. stance on Cuba is not exempt from this, and we will see how it is linked. The Obama era of foreign policy is one of the most controversial in recent U.S. history. Obama's decisive overture to Cuba constitutes an integral part of this contention, thus the importance of focusing on the period leading up to his 2008 election and the first few years of that first mandate.

Chapter 2, "Debate in Cuba Following Re-establishment of Diplomatic Relations, 2014–16," is based on articles I wrote in 2015–16 addressing the Obama-era Cuba policy since December 17, 2014. The articles were written from the vantage point of both pre- and post-visit periods surrounding Obama's March 2016 trip to Havana, a time of unprecedented polemics in Cuba. The pieces had the merit of emerging from my stay in Havana and frequent communications with Cuban colleagues. Indeed, there is currently even more widespread debate regarding Cuba–U.S. relations on the Cuban side of the straits. One is faced with the acute significance of analyzing current debates, because their outcome can determine the nature of Cuba–U.S. relations. An examination of the intense reflections flourishing in Cuba is of paramount importance because these are generally not known internationally, resulting in serious misinformation about the Cuban reality. The book strives to break through the virtual censorship by sharing with readers the Cuban reality from *within*. I draw on my fieldwork in Cuba carried out since 1997. This chapter therefore includes a selection of the articles I wrote for publication online from early January 2015 (in the wake of the December 17, 2014, joint presidential announcements) until April 2016. The analysis of Fidel Castro's views that could have an impact on Cuba–U.S. relations constitutes a full article as well as a theme in another one. His reception of former president Jimmy Carter when he visited Cuba is not only of interest in and of itself but sheds light on the controversial notion of "freedom of the press" and the Cuban leader's diplomatic efforts.

Chapter 3, "Interviews with Five of Cuba's Leading Experts on Cuba–U.S. Relations," presents original interviews with specialists who live and work in Cuba, where I interviewed them individually. The interviews provided the opportunity to formulate questions that might highlight concerns and interests of a non-Cuban audience. One of these queries, addressed to all five, was about their personal reactions regarding a controversial article written by Fidel that was directly related to Obama's visit to Havana in March 2016. The views of the five interviewees are their own and do not reflect a collective "Cuban" assessment. The result is a unique and varied insight into today's dynamic Cuban political culture. These five intellectuals are among many other outstanding writers on Cuba–U.S. relations who call Cuba home. It has been a humbling experience to be associated with them on this intimate publishing journey.

Chapter 4, "Challenges for Cuba in 2017 and Beyond," takes up the themes from the earlier chapters in order to examine them in the light of the events and debates that transpired between April and November 2016, including Trump's presidential election victory and initial transition period.

This chapter delves into Cuba's convulsive internal situation with regard to the U.S., a dynamic not well known outside of Cuba. This exercise is carried out especially in an effort to forecast the path that Cuba–U.S. relations will take. The topics analyzed include Obama's policies and views, as well as perspectives based on Trump's initial orientations. The subject matter includes Trump and Cuba; pluralism in Cuba; alternative media; foreign cultural incursions into the island and Cuban reactions; interaction between Cuban small businesses and the U.S.; individual and social human rights; Guantánamo Bay; Cuban political prisoners; U.S. democracy promotion; Cuba's approach to democracy; choosing Cuba's leaders, including Fidel Castro and Raúl Castro; U.S. immigration policy; Cuba and Latin America; and, finally, the U.S.-led cultural war against Cuba's socialist system, which is also dealt with elsewhere in this chapter and indeed throughout much of the book.

Chapter 5 is dedicated to the Cuba–U.S. conflict over the blockade. The most important issues related to this controversy are updated from April 2016 to November 2016. This analysis, also dealing with the prospects for 2017 and beyond, necessarily strives to envisage the future of this contentious issue during the first Trump mandate. One of the challenges he faces is the powerful anti-blockade forces in the country. The chapter also provides some insight into how the blockade operates with the case study of Cuban coffee exports to the U.S. Beyond the headlines on cigars and rum, what is the real nature of American amendments to the blockade and how do they affect the Cuban private sector? Despite the impression often given that the blockade is being made more "flexible," do leverage and a cover for democracy promotion and subversion still remain its cornerstones?

Chapter 6 deals with the situation in Cuba after the passing of Fidel Castro on November 25, 2016. Immediately afterwards, the U.S. establishment media led an unprecedented disinformation campaign regarding the persona of the iconic leader and the Cuban political system. The subtle introduction into the international public opinion of similar falsehoods from unexpected quarters is likewise brought to light. Based on the experience in the streets and homes of Cuba, the chapter offers a unique inside view of the vast majority of Cuban people's reactions to his death. The scrutiny in this chapter is carried out with the goal of evaluating the effects of these events on current and future Cuba–U.S. relations.

This publication deals with the four most significant recent events in Cuba–U.S. relations that have shaped its present and will frame its future: the simultaneous announcements by Presidents Castro and Obama on December 17, 2014; Obama's visit to Havana on March 21–22, 2016; Obama's

"Presidential Policy Directive — United States–Cuba Normalization," released on October 14, 2016; and the impact of Fidel Castro's death on November 25, 2016, on Cuba–U.S. relations. These four together lay the foundation (with variations potentially negative or positive, from the Cuban perspective) of expectations for the Trump 2017 mandate and the American media regarding U.S. Cuba policy.

The volume is written to be accessible to university students and is also a convenient text for the general public inasmuch as there is an increasingly widespread interest in the subject matter. Since the number of American visitors to Cuba for cultural and other reasons is on the rise, this book can also serve as a reader before departure.

In order to maintain contact with students, professors and others, and with the goal of encouraging debate, readers are invited to leave their comments on my Facebook page "Cuba–U.S. Relations," which is dedicated to the exchange of views on the content of this book.

Translations from Spanish to English are my own and indicated in the References after each source. Unless specified in this way, all other sources are in their original English.

The writing of the book required that I take a hiatus from regularly penning articles on Cuba–U.S. relations for several months that even spanned Obama's October 14, 2016, Presidential Policy Directive. This was a difficult decision for me, as it felt as though I were abandoning my loyal readers in both the English- and Spanish-speaking worlds, who followed my views on this topic with interest. However, I trust that this new book will make up for the interruption.

NOT ONE IOTA

by Ricardo Alarcón de Quesada

Can a country be said to be democratic when it possesses colonies, practices imperialism, and dominates and oppresses others outside its borders? Can one have democracy at home while tyrannizing the neighbourhood? The answer to these questions would seem to be obvious. Yet the country that has, since its inception, lived by attacking, exploiting and depriving others of their rights has also, paradoxically, and for a long time, claimed as its own a concept to which it has always been a stranger: government by and for the people. It has wielded this concept, and still does today, as one more weapon in its arsenal of domination.

The true history of the United States of America provides irrefutable proof that its trajectory since separating from the British Crown in the late eighteenth century constitutes a total negation of the ideals of freedom and democracy, which its governing elites have always claimed to embody and defend.

It has been this way since the long-ago days when a group of large landowners, including slave owners and traders, revolted with the aim of preserving and expanding their privileges, extending their dominion westward, expelling or subduing indigenous populations and grabbing their land — objectives hitherto held in check by London. The independence of the Thirteen Colonies, a historic event almost universally associated with the "revolutionary"

Ricardo Alarcón de Quesada was a member of the leadership of the 26th of July Movement in the clandestine struggle against the Batista dictatorship; Vice-President and President, Federation of University Students, 1959–62; Director, United States Desk, Ministry of Foreign Affairs, 1962–65; Permanent Representative of Cuba to the United Nations, 1965–78 and 1990–92; Vice-Minister of Foreign Affairs, 1978–90; Minister of Foreign Affairs, 1992–93; Deputy and President, National Assembly of People's Power, 1993–2013.

insurgency of the bourgeoisie, was intrinsically contradictory: the goal was liberation from the authority of the European monarchy because this was a prerequisite to territorial expansion and subjugation of other peoples. It is no exaggeration, in fact, to call this episode what it was: a counterrevolution.

From the outset, the rebels were concerned with keeping the craftspeople, wage workers, small farmers and businesspeople who inhabited the original Thirteen Colonies at bay. Instead of a democracy, in which these others would have had a predominant place, the elites established an imperial republic of which the large landowners would be lord and master. To predetermine this outcome, they invented a system of government whose norms, institutions and mechanisms ensured that those who controlled wealth would enjoy political hegemony.

The founding fathers made no bones about their intentions — indeed, these are clearly set out in the Federalist Papers of Madison, Hamilton and Jay. The new nation would have little to do with the Athenian agora and nothing whatever with the ideals of people's sovereignty. The Constitution and its fundamental institutions and mechanisms —an apparent separation of powers, federalism, restrictions on suffrage, presidential elections mediated by an electoral college and so on — were designed to exclude the masses from the genuine exercise of power. Still, the elites made sure to erect a façade for their newly minted system, presenting it as the only legitimately representative form of government. This idea was turned into a self-evident dogma by means of unending, mass-scale propaganda.

To put an end to the deception, rehabilitate the truth and help others understand the issues is a challenge that must be taken up with academic rigour and intellectual integrity, and this book by Arnold August makes a key contribution to the task. It is one of several bold and enlightening works he has written about the Cuban system and how it compares with those of its neighbours, including the United States. August's works set him apart from the majority of authors who have covered these subjects, primarily because, in contrast with the typical approach of the so-called "Cubanologists," he has declined to conform to a certain narrow vision that espouses U.S.-centric falsehoods and half-truths as dogma; and also because he has analyzed the Cuban experience from within, living in Cuba like just another Cuban and taking part in the daily life of the country — something that other observers have not even attempted. August comes to this task free of the prejudice and braggadocio that encumber the thinking of many who claim to interpret and judge Cuba from afar, without delving into its history.

In contrast to what occurred in the United States and with other emancipatory processes, the Cuban struggle for liberation from Spain was inextricably bound up with abolitionism and movements for equality and social justice. Inevitably, the independence movement also entailed a radical social transformation. Thus, the Cuban Revolution that finally triumphed in 1959 had actually begun on October 10, 1868. Between these two dates, the Cuban people had to wage innumerable battles and confront the enormous challenge of a powerful neighbour that never stopped thinking of the island as its rightful prey.

These designs on the part of the empire explain the developments that have taken place over the half-century and more since Fidel Castro entered Havana in triumph after overthrowing that servile pawn of Washington, the Batista dictatorship. In its determination to regain what it had lost, the empire resorted to every imaginable stratagem: economic warfare, mercenary invasion, terrorist attacks, sabotage, diplomatic isolation and a colossal propaganda effort consisting of slanders and lies. The list of aggressions — prominent among them hundreds of plans to assassinate Fidel Castro and other revolutionary leaders — is interminable.

This was the context in which Cubans strove to develop People's Power, a unique system of government arising out of the country's own history and based on the idea of participatory democracy. Given the adverse circumstances of its genesis, it is a system which, alongside undeniable strengths, shows deficiencies and weaknesses that must be overcome. August devotes honest and objective analysis to these problems.

The book covers this process up until the moment when Barack Obama acknowledged the failure of U.S. policy while giving it a new twist, embarking upon what might well have been an attempt to achieve the old goal with new, putatively more sophisticated methods. The discussion and debate provoked by this "new" policy is likewise given in-depth consideration in this book. Can there be normal relations between the rebel island and those who never stopped trying to dominate it? If so, what path might lead to such an outcome? How can the inevitable risks and contradictions be confronted?

As this important book went to press, a new administration had taken control of the White House. The process that led to Donald Trump becoming president of the United States brought the most negative elements in U.S. society out of the woodwork, laying bare the true nature of a political system that has nothing to do with democracy. This is not the place to analyze "Trumpism" or its causes and consequences. What can be affirmed is that with the current state of U.S. politics, a large majority of the country's citizens no longer view its system of government as democratic, or regard it as a model for anyone. It was Che Guevara who said, "never trust imperialism — not one iota," and his warning remains as relevant as ever.

Chapter 1

HISTORICAL/POLITICAL CONTEXT
From the Thirteen Colonies to the Early Obama Era

This chapter is based on six articles that I wrote in 2011 and 2012. The first four deal with pre-Obama American foreign policy toward the region south of the Rio Grande and especially Cuba. The articles trace the U.S. vision of external affairs from its origins in the seventeenth century (as the Thirteen Colonies) and subsequent development to the 1960s, including the January 1, 1959, Cuban Revolution. The pieces provide the historical and political background to the Obama era, which ushered in the new Cuba policy, whose essence will probably continue with variations in form under the Trump presidency, as discussed in Chapters 4 and 5.

The last two articles are directly related to the first Obama mandate (2008–12). They provide insights into two controversies that emerged during the second mandate, highlighted by the Obama visit to Cuba in March 2016. First, there is Obama's alleged use of the "race card," and second, his selective use of Cuban–U.S. history. The latter has created an ongoing polemic that includes denying the negative historical experience that Cuba suffered as a result of the relations between the two neighbours.

THE ORIGINS AND DEVELOPMENT OF U.S. DEMOCRACY PROMOTION[1]

In the words of William Shakespeare, "What's past is prologue," and when it comes to U.S. policy toward Latin America and Cuba, the American past does indeed hold the key to evaluating in a balanced manner the new U.S. Cuba policy initiated by Barack Obama. Moreover, when we speak of this "past" in the case of the U.S., the antecedents extend all the way back to the period of the Thirteen Colonies. The U.S. policy of growing its empire arose even while the Thirteen Colonies were still in battle for independence against the older empire, England. The first U.S. president, George Washington, took up the empire dream, soon to be focused on Cuba by the second president, John Adams. This article goes on to trace the U.S. policy toward Latin America and Cuba carried out by both Democrats and Republicans until 1969.

Once the Thirteen Colonies broke from England, the new chess player in the international arena had a major advantage. It was established in the New World. Its capitalism was unfettered by European stratification; it could use the open spaces and beckoning spheres of endeavours for the spirit of innovation, so important for expansion.

Even the very conservative U.S.-based think-tank Council of Foreign Relations (CFR), in a 2010 essay titled "Empire Without End" in its journal *Foreign Affairs*, traces the beginnings of the dreams of a new empire to its roots. In 1778, while the U.S. War of Independence was still raging and almost ten years before the adoption of the U.S. Constitution (1787), which set the basis of the new state, David Ramsey (South Carolina's delegate to the Continental Congress) expressed the sentiment that originated from the initial days of the Thirteen Colonies. He wrote that the "grandeur of the American continent provided the basis for a realm that would make 'the Macedonian, the Roman, and the British sink into insignificance'" (Maier 2010). Even while the Council of Foreign Relations distances itself from those serious, critical U.S. historians who claim the capitalist search for markets motivates U.S. imperialism, it also admits that the "Empire could not exist without its intellectuals, who take up the task of explaining that goals pursued for self-interest are in fact justified for progress." This elucidates the role of U.S.-centrism and the section of academia and political actors in its service. They provide and elaborate on pretexts, such as "democracy promotion," as a ploy for imperialism.

It is perhaps one of the strangest twists of history that Europe, the birthplace of "Eurocentrism" in the sixteenth century, had to cede its pre-eminence to its growing offspring. The U.S. expanded into the western frontiers and then to the south, where Cuba was a prime target. George Washington's "rising empire" vision for the Thirteen Colonies was declared during the War of Independence. The second president, John Adams, whose son, U.S. Secretary of State John Quincy Adams, proclaimed that Cuba will fall into the grips of the U.S. as a ripe fruit, amplified this vision. Thomas Jefferson, the third president, followed suit on Cuba, as did the fourth, James Madison.

The Monroe Doctrine, proclaimed in 1823, served as a political pretext for the 1898 U.S. intervention in Cuba. The U.S. neo-colonial domination of Cuba after 1898 featured, among other things, the imposition of U.S.-style democracy and elections. Other U.S. military interventions in Latin America and the Caribbean served as the sword to appropriate Eurocentrism for the U.S. to the detriment of Europe. During this long period, U.S. capitalism developed and, with it, the need for expansion. Simultaneously, the U.S. political system consolidated, ridding itself of one of its most grotesque features — slavery. It made U.S. democracy increasingly appropriate, in the eyes of its beholders, for exportation to the countries in the South (August 2012e).

The Monroe Doctrine continued in different forms, such as the Roosevelt Corollary to the Monroe Doctrine (1904), for more than a century, until World War ii. President William Howard Taft's (1909–13) pretext for expansion throughout Latin America and the Caribbean, in his own words, "by virtue of our superiority of race," was an outgrowth of the previous doctrines (Bowden 2009: 154). Woodrow Wilson's presidency (1913–21) coincided with, among other events, the October Revolution in Russia and his motto called for "making the world safe for democracy."

President Franklin D. Roosevelt's (FDR) (1933–45) Good Neighbor Policy toward Latin America did not hinder further U.S. interference and violent repression in that area. Notable as well is the initial U.S. support for fascism. For example, U.S. Ambassador to Italy Henry Fletcher (1924–29) expressed the view that was to oversee U.S. guidelines for many years, not only toward Italy but in other areas, such as with regard to Germany: "Italy faced a stark choice … either 'Mussolini and Fascism' or Giolitti [a leading Italian progressive personality] and Socialism." This support for fascism was at the very least "acceptable," if not fully endorsed, until such time as Germany and Italy contested the interest of the U.S. and the U.K. (Chomsky 2003: 64–68). When the U.S. finally entered World War ii, FDR articulated the ambition for the U.S. being "the Great Arsenal of Democracy" (Roosevelt 1940). This was to be used as an instrument for U.S. policy after the war (August 2011b).

U.S. intervention in World War ii took place only when and as far as it served its imperial interests. Its participation was embedded in the policy of self-interest and expansion as the very nature of U.S. foreign strategy. This strategy was initiated following its inception as a former colony and was accelerated after World War ii, when the U.S. scheme of foreign expansion exploded onto the world scene. It has continued without let-up.

An indication of the two parties' (Republican and Democratic) similarities is the role of the U.S. in foreign military interventions. *ReVista: Harvard Review of Latin America* provides information regarding U.S. direct and indirect military interventions in Latin America from 1898 to

1989 (Coatsworth 2005: 8). Tables 1-1 and 1-2 collate the Harvard data with the records indicating which political party was in power at the time of each intervention; the results speak for themselves.

Irrespective of which party was in power, the same policies of military intervention were followed. The Harvard list, moreover, is somewhat conservative. For example, "the 41 cases [of direct intervention] do not include incidents in which the United States sought to depose a Latin American government, but failed in the attempt. The most famous such case was the failed Bay of Pigs [Playa Girón] invasion of April 1961" (Coatsworth 2005: 6).

Table 1-1: U.S. Direct Interventions:
Military–CIA Activity That Changed Governments

Country	Year	U.S. Political Party in Office
Cuba	1898–1902	Republican
	1906–09	Republican
	1917–23	Democratic
Dominican Republic	1916–24	Democratic
	1961	Democratic
	1965	Democratic
Grenada	1983	Republican
Guatemala	1954	Republican
Haiti	1915–34	Democratic, Republican and again Democratic
	1994	Democratic
Mexico	1914	Democratic
Nicaragua	1910	Republican
	1912–25	Democratic and Republican
	1926–33	Republican and Democratic
	1981–90	Republican
Panama	1903–14	Republican and Democratic
	1989	Republican

Table 1-2: U.S. Indirect Interventions:
Government-Regime Changes Wherein the U.S. Was Decisive

Country	Year	U.S. Political Party in Office
Bolivia	1944	Democratic
	1963	Democratic
	1971	Republican
Brazil	1964	Democratic
Chile	1973	Republican
	1989–90	Republican
Cuba	1933	Democratic
	1934	Democratic
Dominican Republic	1914	Democratic
	1963	Democratic
El Salvador	1961	Democratic
	1979	Democratic
	1980	Democratic
Guatemala	1963	Democratic
	1982	Republican
	1983	Republican
Guyana	1953	Republican
Honduras	1963	Democratic
Mexico	1913	Democratic
Nicaragua	1909	Republican
	1979	Democratic
Panama	1941	Democratic
	1949	Democratic
	1969	Republican

Sources: Coatsworth 2005: 8; Leip 2011; White House n.d.-b

In addition, it is not explicitly divulged that Cuba is absent from the list
of victims that suffered from the *indirect* intervention of the 1952 Batista
coup d'état. It is true that the U.S. military forces did not intervene directly
and that the coup was formally the work of Batista himself and other offic-
ers. Yet, his army was completely armed and trained by the U.S., which
immediately recognized the Batista military coup regime. Important for the
focus of this book is that both the Democratic Party and Republican Party
had taken part in these interventions. In fact, the Democratics presided over
more interventions than the Republicans (twenty-seven versus nineteen).

U.S. CUBA POLICY: 1783–1820s[2]

As we will see in subsequent chapters, there is an ongoing polemic in Cuba against the American long-term goal toward the island. This article deals explicitly with the U.S. policy with regard to Cuba in the late eighteenth and early nineteenth centuries, providing further historical information on the official American outlook.

George Washington, the leader of the U.S. War of Independence and later the first president of the U.S., wrote as early as March 1783 that the U.S. was a "rising empire" (Van Alstyne 1960: 1). Cuba was included as part of this expansion project and, indeed, placed high on the list. On June 23, 1783, also *before* the formal end of the war with England, John Adams, who later became the second president of the U.S.,

> articulated the U.S. attitude toward Cuba that would endure until the end of the nineteenth century. Depicting Cuba as a natural extension of the North American continent, he argued that the continuation of the United States required annexing Cuba. He calculated that Cuba should remain under Spanish rule until the United States could directly seize it and that Cuba would never be independent. (Carlisle and Golson 2007: 53)

In 1786, George Washington, during the period when procedures for a constitution were just beginning to be elaborated by him and others, wrote: "However unimportant America may be considered at present, ... there will assuredly come a day when this country will have some weight in the scale of Empires.... As the member of an infant empire ... I cannot help turning my attention sometimes to this subject" (Van Alstyne 1960: 69).

The third president of the U.S., Thomas Jefferson (one of the Founding Fathers of the Constitution), stressed a key desire in his first inaugural address on March 4, 1801. He highlighted the importance of "possessing a chosen country, with room enough for our descendents [sic] to the thousandth and thousandth generation" (Jefferson 1975: 292).

Two years later, Jefferson translated these words into reality by approximately doubling the size of the original Thirteen Colonies with the Louisiana Purchase from France. From Louisiana, Jefferson looked further south and sent one of his generals to Cuba to find out whether the Spanish were ready to cede Cuba to the U.S., a proposition rejected by Spain. In 1809, as former president Jefferson wrote to his successor, President James Madison,

"I candidly confess that I have [for] ever looked upon Cuba as the most interesting addition that can be made to our system of States." With Cuba and Canada, he says, "We should have such an empire for liberty as she has never surveyed since the creation." In 1810, Madison let it be known to Great Britain that the U.S. would not tolerate any attempt by Britain to gain possession of Cuba (Franklin 1997: 2–3).

In 1819, the U.S. took possession of East Florida, closing in yet further on Cuba. On April 28, 1823, U.S. Secretary of State John Quincy Adams (son of former president John Adams) wrote to his minister responsible for Spain, Hugh Nelson, enunciating his now famous "ripe fruit" theory:

> There are laws of political as well as of physical gravitation; and if an apple severed by the tempest from its native tree cannot choose but fall to the ground, Cuba, forcibly disjointed from its own unnatural connections with Spain, and incapable of self-support, can gravitate only towards the North American Union, which by the same law of nature cannot cast her off from its bosom. (Adams 1823: 7)

However, often overlooked is Adams's preamble to this "ripe fruit" concept. In the same letter, he highlights Cuba's strategic importance and explains much about the current U.S. policy toward Cuba underlined by "democracy promotion" and other pretexts:

> These islands [Cuba and Puerto Rico], from their natural local position, are natural appendages of the North American continent; and one of them, Cuba, almost in sight of our shores, from a multitude of considerations has become the object of transcendent importance to the political and commercial interests of the Union. [A consideration is its] commanding position with reference to the Gulf of Mexico and the West Indies ... its safe and capacious harbor ... the nature of its productions and wants.... It is scarcely possible to resist the conviction that the annexation of Cuba to our federal Republic will be indispensable to the continuity and integrity of the Union itself. (6)

The American Dream of an empire translated itself into repeated military interventions around the world. According to the U.S. Congress House Committee on Foreign Relations, between 1798 (only fifteen years after the establishment of the Constitution) and World War II, the U.S. carried out worldwide 166 military interventions. In the first decades until 1846–48 (the U.S. war to annex Mexico), most of the military interventions took place as part of the forceful absorption of other territories into what is the present-day U.S. (a period in which many Indigenous people were massacred). Most of the military interventions were against countries in the South, just a few examples being: Mexico, ten times; Cuba, eight (1822, 1823, 1824, 1825, 1906–09, 1912, 1917–22, 1933); Honduras, seven; Haiti, four (U.S. Congress 1975).

Let us take some other examples, beginning with the earliest statements of the Founding Fathers with regard to Latin America and Cuba. The context was the 1810s and 1820s, when countries in Latin America were freeing themselves from Spain and Portugal. On December 2, 1823, U.S. President John Monroe, during his State of the Union Address, made a barely veiled threat to Europe, especially Spain, to stay away from Latin America, which the U.S. staked out as its own exclusive territory (known as the Monroe Doctrine):

> The American continents [North and South America], by the free and independent condition which they have assumed and maintain, are henceforth not to be considered as subjects for future colonization by any European powers.... In the wars of the European powers in matters relating to themselves we have never taken any part, nor does it comport with our policy to do so.... We owe it, therefore, to candor and to the amicable relations existing between the United States and those powers to declare that we should consider any attempt on their part to extend their system to any portion of this hemisphere as dangerous to our peace and safety.... But with the Governments [in Latin America] who have declared their independence and maintain it, and whose independence we have, on great consideration and on just principles, acknowledged, we could not view any interposition for the purpose of oppressing them, or controlling in any other manner their destiny, by any European power in any other light than as the manifestation of an unfriendly disposition toward the United States. (Monroe 1823)

IMPERIALISM AND DEMOCRACY IN CUBA[3]

In 1898, the USS *Maine Navy ship was anchored in the Bay of Havana. It mysteriously blew up, killing three-quarters of its crew. The U.S. mainstream press blamed it on Spain despite the lack of proof. Nevertheless, the tragedy served as a pretext for the U.S. to enter into the war between the Cuban patriots and the Spanish colonizers, in order to prevent Cuba from winning its independence. Spain was on the verge of defeat by the Cuban independence fighters, but the U.S. hijacked that upcoming victory and appropriated the liberation to bring Cuba under U.S. control. The U.S. promptly proceeded to replace Spain in Cuba.*

Once it had succeeded in occupying Cuba, the U.S. immediately began to insert its own approach to democracy in an attempt to replace the rudimentary anti-U.S.-centric Cuban model of democracy, especially as it had developed under José Martí.

In the 1868–98 Wars of Independence, Cubans developed their own political system, the Republic in Arms, within the Spanish colony. It featured the development of constituent assemblies, constitutions and even electoral laws written by the Cubans themselves. Another characteristic was the expansion of suffrage irrespective of wealth and property to all males over the age of sixteen. The Cuban tradition was also based on popular participation at the grassroots level (August 2013: 77–78).

And yet, what happened after the U.S. took control of Cuba in 1898? In *Leonard Wood: Rough Rider, Surgeon, Architect of American Imperialism,* Jack McCallum (2006) paints a relatively favourable picture of Wood as the principal envoy of the U.S. His mandate was to convert the virtual Cuban victory over Spain into a defeat for Cuba and thus appropriate Cuba as the U.S.'s own neo-colony.

In opposition to the growing Cuban experience in democracy, the U.S. policy that Wood carried out consisted of several important elements inspired by the U.S. approach to democracy. This included promoting U.S. democracy under the aegis of imperialism, as McCallum himself terms this policy. Wood was thus promoting the U.S. approach to democracy in Cuba as part of U.S. imperialism.

The first strategy was the restriction of suffrage in line with U.S. tradition. This was carried out alongside the manipulation of elections so that the results would be favourable to the U.S. Second, the U.S. co-opted those elements in the Cuban political system that were considered friendly to the U.S. domination of Cuba. These individuals had to have a certain level of credibility in the eyes of the Cubans. This was important, given the omnipresent danger of a resurgence of the nineteenth-century independence war, which the U.S. wanted to avoid at all costs. Also it required the collaboration of individuals willing to be co-opted for presidential office in order to serve their own personal profit and motivations. The policy of co-opting those who would favour the U.S. had its origins in the policies adopted by Wood and his collaborators in order to defeat the Indigenous peoples in the U.S. itself. Wood also drew from his experience of isolating the U.S. Indigenous resistance from its economic and social base in order to weaken it. In McCallum's own words,

> Wood and [U.S. Secretary of War] Root were convinced that any long-term relationship between Cuba and the United States had to be based on the willing cooperation of the Cuban people. Both men believed in [American-style elite] democracy, but the general and the secretary were also firmly convinced that universal suffrage was a recipe for disaster.
>
> ... [In preparation for the first municipal elections,] although Root and Wood were convinced an educated populace was [a] prerequisite to full democracy, they felt obligated to take a few steps toward limited self-government.... .
>
> The first decision was who should be allowed to vote. Masó [a former *mambí* independence fighter] and the [other] insurrectionist leaders favored universal (male) suffrage, a prospect that terrified the Cuban upper classes.... The Americans found the upper classes, especially the Iberians, easier to relate to than native Cubans. The municipal election's outcome would most certainly be determined by who voted, and Wood and Root did not want the poor and illiterate at the polls.
>
> ... [In preparation for the Constituent Assembly] he [Wood] meant for the elected convention to discuss and presumably approve a document he would submit. He told Root, "I am going to work on a Constitution for the Island similar to our own and embody in the organic act certain definite relations and agreements between the United States and Cuba [the eventual Platt Amendment, which gave the right to the U.S. to militarily intervene in Cuba]." (2006: 157–58, 181)

U.S. Cuba policy regarding democracy and people's participation varied from 1898 to 1958. It at times somewhat increased people's participation, even if only in form, being forced to take into account pressure from the grassroots. It also morphed into open dictatorship on several occasions. The last was the Batista tyranny starting in March 1952. However, irrespective of the form, the underlying ideological political outlook remained as expressed in Wood's own words. In fact, this mindset is still the key today for fathoming U.S. policy before, during, since the Obama visit and beyond.

TWO VISIONS OF DEMOCRACY: THE U.S. VS. FIDEL CASTRO[4]

Fidel Castro and his movement rose to power under the following conditions. Presidential and legislative elections had been scheduled for 1952. The polls showed that the opposing Orthodox Party presidential candidate was heading for a victory, while the pro-U.S. Batista candidate was a distant third. Fidel Castro was running for a Congressional seat as an Orthodox Party candidate. Even historians who are relatively critical of the Cuban revolutionary process write that Batista's running "a distant third [was] a likely reason for his staging a coup" (Domínguez 1978: 113). It was widely speculated, both in Cuba and the U.S., that Batista's forces could not even come close to winning the election. As a result, Batista executed the coup d'état in the early morning of March 10, 1952.

Technically speaking, the U.S. did not organize the March 10, 1952, military coup by Batista and did not even immediately recognize it. However, a mere seventeen days after the coup, on March 27, the U.S. recognized the Batista regime because its goals were in complete alignment with U.S. policy for Cuba at the time. The U.S. assured this alliance before extending formal recognition. At the heart of the U.S.-Batista agreement was Batista's program to eliminate the revolutionary forces.

> Documented evidence from original U.S. sources shows this very clearly. For example, in a formerly secret U.S. State Department Memorandum written by U.S. Ambassador in Cuba Willard Beaulac, on March 22, 1952 (twelve days after the coup), based on a conversation in Havana with Dr. Miguel Ángel de la Campa, minister of state of the Batista regime, Campa asked the U.S. Ambassador, as recorded by the latter, why the United States hadn't recognized Cuba.... He said that an intolerable situation had developed in Cuba. Graft, gangsterism, and favoritism had made *a travesty of democracy....* Batista once before had brought *order out of chaos* and Dr. Campa thought he was going to do it again.... I reminded Dr. Campa that our Government had not been consulted about the *coup d'état* and that Cuba could not expect automatic recognition from us.... I told Dr. Campa that I would transcribe faithfully what he said to the Department of State in Washington. I was sure our conversation would be helpful to my Government, and I hoped it would be to his. (*Latin American Studies* 1952, emphasis added)

In short, the coup spokesperson declared in the statement above that the raison d'être of the coup was the lack of democracy in Cuba and that Batista had the talent to recover a state of order or, by implication, democracy.

On March 25, 1952, during Democratic President Harry Truman's administration, in the following formerly secret memorandum on the subject of continuing diplomatic relations with Cuba, Secretary of State Dean Acheson wrote:

> I recommend ... the continuation of diplomatic relations with the Batista Government in Cuba [for March 27].... On the early morning of Monday, March 10, General Fulgencio Batista with the support of a group of officers of the Cuban Army overthrew the duly constituted Government of President Carlos Prío Socarrás. Batista's revolution came as a complete surprise both in Cuba and in this country ... *with remarkable ease and over virtually no resistance....* The Batista regime has formally requested our recognition and has made satisfactory public and private statements with regard to ... *its attitude towards private capital*; its intentions to take steps *to curtail international communist activities in Cuba.... We have no reason to believe that Batista will not be strongly anti-communist....* The Department of State naturally deplored *the way in which the Batista coup was brought [about]....* [I] request your authorization to announce the continuation of diplomatic relations with Cuba on March 27. (Acheson 1952, emphasis added)

Note that the U.S. opposed "the way in which the Batista coup was brought [about]," but not the coup itself.

The U.S. had to make sure that Batista was really in favour of private capital and, above all, opposed to the communists and the revolutionary movement. It should be recalled that, as part of the U.S. co-optation policy in the 1930s and 1940s, Batista fully collaborated with the U.S. to decorate U.S. domination with a "new face," even to the extent of tolerating the Communist Party and allowing the progressive 1940 Constitution to be adopted.

It is also noteworthy that the memorandum asserts that the coup took place with "virtually no resistance." However, in the early hours of the coup in the dead of night, all transportation, radio transmitters, radios and banks fell under army control, and Batista's military closed off access to and from Havana. U.S. historian Louis A. Pérez, Jr. reveals: "Sites of potential protest demonstrations against the coup passed under military control" (1995: 288–89).

Offices and headquarters of the opposition forces, anti-Batista unions and the Communist Party were occupied. Union leaders and political opponents were detained and arrested. The emblematic University of Havana was shut down and Congress dissolved. It should be noted that the PSP, the name by which the Communist Party was known at the time, had nine seats in the lower house (288–89).

The U.S. press, even the most "liberal," played their historical role of assisting the government in covering up this repression and thus justifying its actions, such as supporting the Batista dictatorship. For example, *Time,* in a front-page April 1952 article (showing a cheerfully smiling Batista with the Cuban flag as backdrop), embellished Batista in its headline as "Dictator with the People." *Time* wrote:

> Relaxing on the awning deck in shorts, the Strong Man was in his best bluff humor. Once again he was undisputed dictator of Cuba.... Power and prestige are two things Batista understands and values. It has been said of him that he has *limitless ambition,* plenty of ability and no respect for his fellow men.... With or against the people, the Strong Man, at any rate, came from them. *The son of a poor farmer of mixed blood [mulato],* he was born in 1901, while his country was still under U.S. occupation, at the eastern sugar town of Banes. Quitting Banes' Quaker School at twelve, he worked as a tailor's apprentice, bartender, barber, banana picker, cane cutter and railroad hand.... *Democracy must come from within, not from without.* It is up to Cubans, not the U.S., to make military coups obsolete. Meanwhile, so far as Latin America is concerned, the U.S. can only be the *Good Neighbor,* avoid undue interference.... The making of democracy takes, among other things, time. (emphasis added)

What stands out is co-optation (even to the extent of recruiting a willing *mulato* in overtly racist, pre-1959 Cuban society) combined with the use of an individual of "limitless ambitions" such as Batista. We can also discern the real nature of FDR's Good Neighbor Policy with its desire to avoid "undue" interference. In this case, it meant to "avoid interfering in Cuba's affairs" by recognizing Batista.

Fidel Castro presented a brief (as a lawyer) to the Court of Appeals on March 24, 1952, regarding the Batista coup, at that time about to be diplomatically recognized by Washington. Castro said:

> The nation, unable to act, witnessed a flood of military actions which demolished the Constitution, putting lives and property at

the whims of bayonets.... The chief of the insurrectionists, assuming absolute power and arrogating to himself omnipotent functions, ordered the immediate suspension of the elections scheduled for the first of June.... When Congress tried to meet in the usual fashion, it was dissolved by gunfire.... At present the total transformation of the republican system is being carried out, and they plan [on] substituting the national constitution, a product of the people's will, with a juridical farce created in the barracks behind the back of popular opinion. (1972: 149–50)

The stage was being set for a democratic and social revolution against the dictatorship, rekindled by Fidel Castro and the movement he initiated and led in 1953, continuing through to January 1, 1959. During this period, attempts to blunt the inevitable through more fraudulent elections could not hold back the revolt against the economic and political system.

Presidential elections were to be held in 1954. Two issues can be examined: the roll of candidates as well as voter turnout, that is, the percentage of registered voters going to the polls. Registration was already very low in proportion to the population due to the disenfranchisement policy of the U.S. since the time of Wood in 1898. Jorge Domínguez, among the most skeptical, even writes that, in 1954 "Batista was 'elected' president without opposition" because the other candidate pulled out due to a lack of confidence in the electoral system at the time. In addition, voter turnout of registered voters dropped from 79.5 percent in 1948 to 52.6 percent in 1954 (1978: 124).

Another election was scheduled for 1958. Domínguez, who is critical of the Cuban Revolution, further states: "The presidential elections of 1958, a few months before Batista's fall, had two opposition candidates, but the elections were so obviously fraudulent that they served, once again, to undermine the government rather than to strengthen it" (124).

BRAZIL: DEMOCRACY, LIBYA, SELECTIVE HISTORY AND THE AFRICAN-AMERICAN PRESIDENT[5]

The Cuban Revolution succeeded on January 1, 1959. From that time until Barack Obama's first mandate in 2008, U.S. Cuba policy followed a path, to different degrees, of open hostility to the Revolution. This situation began to change at the dawn of the Obama era. Nevertheless, there is far more to this adjustment than meets the eye. This article traces the origins of this shift leading up to the Obama presidency, followed by an example of how he went into action to apply his new calling during his 2011 visit to Brazil.

In 2006–08, there were a number of indications by representatives of the U.S. ruling circles that their country had a serious problem. The obstacles involved, among others, its international credibility, especially after the Bush years. Zbigniew Brzezinski (2007), a former National Security adviser to President Jimmy Carter, wrote in his book Second Chance: Three Presidents and the Crisis of American Superpower about the "global alienation from America and worldwide doubts about Bush's leadership." He also expressed a preoccupation with the "increasing linkage in Latin America between the rise of democracy [in reference to countries such as Venezuela] and the rise in anti-American sentiments." Brzezinski went on to write about how George W. Bush "misunderstood the historical moment … and undermined America's geopolitical position." Brzezinski was also apprehensive about Europe being "increasingly alienated." Latin America was "becoming populist and anti-American." He highlighted the "intensifying hostility to the West throughout the world of Islam [and] an explosive Middle East" (2007: 175–77, 208).

During the Democratic primaries in 2007, Brzezinski, one of the most influential foreign-policy experts in the Democratic Party, threw his support behind Obama's presidential candidacy, saying the Illinois senator had a better global grasp than his chief rival, Hillary Clinton. Obama "recognizes that the challenge is a new face, a new sense of direction, a new definition of America's role in the world," Brzezinski said in an interview on Bloomberg Television's Political Capital with Al Hunt. "Obama is clearly more effective and has the upper hand," Brzezinski said. "He has a sense of what is historically relevant, and what is needed from the United States in relationship to the world" (Zacharia 2007, emphasis added).

Brzezinski, 79, dismissed the notion that Clinton, 59, a New York senator and the wife of former President Bill Clinton, was more seasoned than Obama, 46: "Being a former first lady doesn't prepare you to be president." Clinton's foreign-policy approach is "very conventional," Brzezinski said, "I don't think the country needs to go back to what we had eight years ago." He added, "There is a need for a fundamental rethinking of how we conduct world affairs. And Obama seems to me to have both the guts and the intelligence to address that issue and to change the nature of America's relationship with the world" (Zacharia 2007, emphasis added).

There was wide-scale fear regarding U.S. credibility abroad. It was expressed, for example, at a high-profile panel in November 2008 featuring the establishment's think-tank, the Council on Foreign Relations, whose representative declared: "The election of an African-American had effectively countered propaganda about U.S. racism." As readers will see in the interviews in Chapter 3, Cuba–U.S. experts assert that Obama used the "race card" when *dealing with his March 20–22, 2016, visit to Havana. It is thus important to explore the origins of this approach by Obama as part of U.S. Cuba policy and to analyze the manipulation of the "race card" during the Cuba visit. As a precursor to that trip, we have his 2011 sojourn to Brazil.*

Thus, the March 2016 Cuba visit was not the African-American president's first to Latin America and the Caribbean. Obama had travelled to Brazil, Chile and El Salvador from March 19 to 23, 2011, which was his first trip to Central and South America as a public official. It is instructive, therefore, to examine his visit to Brazil in 2011 in order to evaluate the use of race to further U.S. interests.

In Brazil, the first leg of a March 2011 Latin American trip, Obama stressed his opinion that the U.S. and Brazil are "the hemisphere's two largest democracies and the two largest economies" (Obama 2011d). Exactly two hours and forty-five minutes later, Obama organized a press conference in Brasília, where he announced: "Today I authorized the Armed Forces of the United States to begin a limited military action in Libya in support of an international effort to protect Libyan civilians. The action has now begun" (2011e).

The next day, March 20, in Rio de Janeiro, Obama was afforded the opportunity to address the entire Brazilian population. He said the U.S. and Brazil "began in similar ways ... home to ancient and indigenous peoples.... The Americas were discovered by men who sought a New World ... settled by pioneers who pushed westward.... We became colonies claimed by distant crowns, but soon declared our independence" (2011c).

The question remains of how it is possible to compare Brazil to a country like the U.S., whose settled inhabitants pushed westward and committed genocide against the Indigenous peoples. Were the settlers not the ones who actively encouraged slavery and began its striving to dominate Latin America as part of the manifest destiny of a chosen people, the beacon on the hill for the whole world, stemming from the very foundation of the Thirteen Colonies in 1620?

Brazil is part of this Latin America and a victim like the other countries in the region, after Portuguese colonialism, of U.S. domination and exploitation. Brazil also took a strong stance against the 2009 military coup d'état in Honduras, which was supported by Obama. These are two different worlds, the First World and the Third World, each with its own traditions, values and international stands, a history completely distorted by Obama.

Obama spoke about how Brazil fought against "two decades of dictatorship," referring to the 1964 coup, to move toward a democracy (2011c).

However, who sponsored and supported the 1964 military coup in Brazil? It was the U.S. under none other than the Democratic Party presidents John F. Kennedy and Lyndon B. Johnson. As later came to light through a perusal of the Presidential Libraries and Museums, which contain vast archives of documents, these presidents were in favour of using the military to oppose "communist" and "left-wing dangers." Moreover, it was the U.S. military attaché Vernon Walters, a CIA veteran troubleshooter and later President Ronald Reagan's UN ambassador, who coordinated matters with the Brazilian military (Cockcroft 1996: 641–53). This is one example of how Obama tried to falsify history in order to distance himself not only from his country's role but also from that of his own Democratic Party. Obama's omission of the U.S. involvement in Brazil should not come as a surprise, given his barely veiled admiration for Ronald Reagan, whose UN ambassador-to-be was instrumental in carrying out the coup. For example, in his second book, *The Audacity of Hope: Thoughts on Reclaiming the American Dream* (2006: 341–42), after decrying some of Reagan's policies such as support for apartheid regime in South Africa, Obama wrote:

> But at times, in arguments with some of my friends on the left, I would find myself in the curious position of defending aspects of Reagan's worldview. I didn't understand why, for example, progressives should be less concerned about oppression behind the Iron Curtain than they were about brutality in Chile.
>
> I might have arguments with the size of Reagan's military buildup, but given the Soviet invasion of Afghanistan, staying ahead of the Soviet's military seemed a sensible thing to do. Pride in our country, respect for our armed services, a healthy appreciation for the dangers beyond our borders, an insistence that there was no easy equivalence between East and West — in all this I had no quarrel with Reagan.

Obama's evolving precept of "leaving the past behind" was also revealed in the following manner. Eduardo Galeano's famous book *Open Veins of Latin America* was given to Obama as a gift by Hugo Chávez during the 2009 Trinidad and Tobago Summit. In this classic, among other important events, the Uruguayan author details how U.S. mining interests were directly involved in the Brazilian military coup and the dictatorship that followed (1997: 135–36). Regarding this book, Obama's main adviser for the 2009 Summit and his 2011 Latin America trip, Daniel Restrepo, said: "He has not read it and I doubt that I will read it ... and I doubt if the President has time to focus on the book ... but obviously it is a book out of a past which we would like to leave behind us" (Vásquez 2009).

In addition to striving toward obliterating history, Obama also deftly played the African-American card in Brazil. A carefully orchestrated media visit to the *favelas* (the poorest shantytowns in Rio) was organized, with photo-ops concentrating on the Obama family kicking around a soccer ball with African-Brazilians. A review of a sample of the major press in Spanish and English based in Latin America, the U.S. and the U.K., the latter two with international repercussions, proves to be instructive. Only a few mentioned, in passing, that there were demonstrations in Brazil against Obama's presence and his interest in the oil reserves and other resources. Virtually all the rest of the press made exclusive use of the *favela* visit "with the pictures and videos [the Obama trip] needed" to demonstrate that Obama is different, representing change. This was illustrated with quotes from Brazilians sporting Obama 2008 presidential campaign "Vote Obama" T-shirts, shouting his "Yes We Can" slogan, expressing how proud they were to have one of "their own" as president of the U.S. (Taylor 2011; Cabral 2011; *ABC Color* 2011; *Voz de América* 2011; *Globovisión* 2011; de Moura 2011).

In his speech from Rio, Obama stated, quoting a resident: "People have to look at favelas not with pity, but as a source of presidents and lawyers" (Obama 2011c). Applying the American Dream to Brazil is nothing short of cruel. Not only is it a fantasy in U.S. society but it applies even less so to a Third World country, especially its *favelas*. This example glaringly illustrates that the idea of the American Dream serves as an alternative to progressive ideas and forms of struggle by the majority, whether in the U.S. or in Brazil.

Brazilian President Dilma Rousseff went out of her way to be diplomatic, toasting Obama in the following way: "We should celebrate that the first woman president of Brazil will receive today and host the first president of Afro descent of the United States of America" (Taylor 2011). However, the U.S. "new face" did not reciprocate as diplomatically. On the contrary, Obama could not hide the arrogance of the interests he was representing. He announced the war against Libya in Brazil — the very country that had taken a stand against U.S. interference and bullying in the hemisphere and the world since Luis Ignácio da Silva, or Lula, as he is commonly known, became president. Brazil was also one of the key countries that opposed the U.S. incursion into Libya by abstaining in the 2011 U.S.-sponsored United Nations Security Council Resolution initiating the war into that North African country.

OBAMA IN CHILE: PINOCHET AND CUBA[6]

During Obama's 2016 visit to Havana, which was followed by a trip to Argentina, he created a polemic. He reiterated his standard position that peoples should forget their past and look to the future. This view was already in the making in 2011. After two days in Brasília and Rio de Janeiro, the president travelled to Santiago, Chile.

Chile was the second stop on Obama's trip to Latin America. For the vast majority of people in Latin America, as well as many in North America and Europe, Chile invokes the extremely negative memory of September 11, 1973. There is general agreement worldwide that this was a military coup carried out by U.S.-backed forces. It was directed against the democratically elected socialist government of Salvador Allende. As a result of the coup, tens of thousands of people were imprisoned, tortured, killed, forced into exile or disappeared. All left-wing socialist and communist organizations were violently suppressed. Allende, one of the icons of Latin American socialist and revolutionary personalities, himself died on that day in the Moneda Palace (government building).

On March 21, 2011, in the Moneda, Obama, along with his host, Chilean President Sebastián Piñera, addressed invited guests and some journalists at a press conference. In his opening remarks, Obama did not refer to the 1973 military coup nor, of course, to U.S. responsibility, but he did mention that Chile has "built a robust democracy."

The first question asked by a journalist addressing Obama, despite his comments about transition to democracy, was:

> In Chile ... there are some open wounds of the dictatorship of General Pinochet. And so in that sense, leaders, political leaders, leaders of the world, of human rights, even MPs ... have said that many of those wounds have to do with the United States.... In that new speech ... do you include that the U.S. is willing to collaborate with those judicial investigations, even that the United States is willing to ask for forgiveness for what it did in those very difficult years in the '70s in Chile? (Obama 2011a)

Obama, the same person who wrote and spoke on several occasions quoting or paraphrasing William Faulkner's motto "The past is never dead" (Obama 2009: 63; Obama 2004: x), responded to the correspondent's question by referring to the coup only as evidence of an "extremely rocky" relationship between the U.S. and Chile. He followed with the statement that we should not be "trapped by our history," that he "can't speak to all of the policies of the past" and repeated once again the importance of "understand[ing] our history, but not be[ing] trapped by it" (Obama 2009: 63; Obama 2004: x).

He was forced to make a vague reference to it in the same vein — that of avoiding the role of the U.S. in the 1973 coup — during another address in the Moneda several hours later. He referred to the Moneda as the place where "Chile lost its democracy decades ago." He also used the opportunity to direct a frontal attack on Cuba. He ignored the U.S. anti-communist orientation that motivated the 1973 coup against the Allende socialist government supported by the Chilean communists. Cuba and Chile, while the latter was being led by Allende, had a fraternal, mutual relationship. Nevertheless, Obama vowed "support for the rights of people to determine their own future — and, yes, that includes the people of Cuba" (Obama 2011b).

People should not be surprised by Obama's selective use of history regarding the 1973 coup in Chile. Obama noted in his second book (2006), for those who were interested to know, where he stands on the issue of military coups versus progressive or socialist thought and action when he wondered why progressives should be less concerned about repression in the U.S.S.R. and Eastern Europe than in Chile.

It is important to reflect seriously on Obama's use of the past to manipulate history and political content. It explains the manner in which Obama and the U.S.-type of multi-party, competitive democracy use selective history with the goal of distancing themselves to a certain degree from previous administrations and, indeed, the entire history of U.S. military interventions in the hemisphere.

This process is carried out in order to provide a "new face" to U.S. intrusion. This action even goes so far as to co-opt *opposition* to the decades-long U.S. policy so that this resistance is retrieved in order to applaud the new U.S. image under Obama. He goes to the Moneda, where the U.S. was responsible for the death of Allende. He then uses the hostility against the U.S.-organized coup and the pro-Allende sentiment, by attempting to convert it in *favour* of the U.S. and by giving the impression that the U.S. is turning the page and that the Chilean people can rely on him. In addition, as mentioned above, Obama's comment in his second book regarding his frustration about progressives and the left standing up against the coup in Chile, juxtaposed with the repression behind the Iron Curtain. Obama's view on the "Iron Curtain" versus Chile reflects a pre-eminent traditional stance of U.S. foreign policy.

Irrespective of the opinions people hold about the former U.S.S.R. and Eastern Europe of the 1970s and 1980s, what has been the age-long policy of the U.S. since the 1917 October Revolution? The course of action has been to support anything that opposes socialist, progressive and revolutionary ideas and actions. Taking the twentieth century alone, there was the initial support for the fascists in Germany and Italy leading up to World War II (because they had in their crosshairs the U.S.S.R.).

There were also the innumerable, bloody undertakings in Latin America throughout the century (El Salvador, Guatemala, Cuba, Nicaragua, Brazil, Argentina, Grenada, etc.). Obama's opportunistic use of history endorses this policy of foreign domination but mollifies it for domestic and foreign consumption.

Notes

1   August 2012c.
2   August 2012e (original title "Appropriating U.S.-Centrism for Itself").
3   August 2012b.
4   August 2012d.
5   August 2011a.
6   August 2011c.

Chapter 2

DEBATE IN CUBA FOLLOWING RE-ESTABLISHMENT OF DIPLOMATIC RELATIONS, 2014-16

This chapter features a selection of my articles that were published between January 2015, when the interview below was published, and April 2016, in the wake of simultaneous surprise announcements by Presidents Raúl Castro and Barack Obama on December 17, 2014. On that date, they made known their plan to re-establish diplomatic relations and open embassies in their respective countries, after more than five decades of the U.S. refusing to recognize Cuba.

WHERE ARE CUBA-U.S. RELATIONS HEADING?[1]

KIM PETERSON (*DISSIDENT VOICE*): What is your take on the seeming rapprochement between the United States and Cuba [announced on December 17, 2014]?

ARNOLD AUGUST: I was overjoyed to hear that the three Cuban Five who remained in U.S. prisons were released as part of a prisoner swap. On that aspect of the December 17, 2014, Cuba–U.S. agreements, I immediately wrote an article. That was the easy part. Also relatively simple was a shout of victory: at long last, the unconditional establishment of diplomatic ties and embassies was assured for the first time since the U.S. had broken off diplomatic relations with Havana in 1961. In addition, Cuba is to be removed from the U.S. arbitrary list of countries sponsoring terrorism. These decisions represent a clear victory for Cuba.

The policies that President Obama is to introduce as part of the common accord consist of encouraging and widely expanding business investments, commerce, tourism and remittances to family in Cuba. Half a million self-employed Cuban individuals are targeted as among the main beneficiaries of some of these policies. The new Obama policies are to flourish side by side with the U.S. democracy promotion programs that remain intact; their continuation is emphasized by the fact that, in his December 17 announcement, Obama mentioned "democracy" in relationship to Cuba four times and alluded to political freedom and human rights several other times (Obama 2014b). This statement was accompanied by another document released by the White House on December 17 that spelled out even further their plans for democracy promotion in Cuba (White House n.d.-a). In both these statements quoted above, the White House notes that the "Castros and the Communist Party still govern Cuba." Taken together, these converging yet conflicting factors create a very complex situation for Cuba.

On that December 17, the situation caused me to think of a statement Fidel Castro made to his followers on January 8, 1959, just eight days after the triumph of the Revolution: "This is a decisive moment in our history: The tyranny has been overthrown, there is immense joy. However, there is still much to be done. Let us not fool ourselves into believing that the future will be easy; perhaps everything will be more difficult in the future" (Castro Ruz [Fidel] 1959). I realize that there is no comparison between the January 1, 1959, victory and the one on December 17, 2014; likewise, there is no analogy between the tenuous context of 1959 and the early 1960s, characterized by open U.S.-sponsored terrorist attacks and the Playa Girón [Bay of Pigs] invasion, and the post-December 17 situation as it is unfolding so far.

However, I continue to follow events and reactions from all over the world and the full political spectrum from left to right. And I am thus forced to remember the statement by Fidel Castro that initially and spontaneously sprung to mind on December 17, 2014. That day ushered in an "immense joy" in Cuba and among many people in the world, and rightly so, as David was finally rewarded after more than five decades of persistent and heroic struggle against Goliath. However, this "immense joy" camouflages adversities that, in principle, are supposed to have been alleviated but in fact contain the seeds of even more difficult challenges to the extent that perhaps the situation will be more complex in the future. Watersheds in the history of a country can be contradictory.

While the U.S. has changed its tactics, the objective remains the same: to bring Cuba into the U.S. sphere of influence, which includes governments that the U.S. deems acceptable. These "tolerable" governments are characterized as being capitalist, even semi-feudal, and notably anti-socialist.

Since December 17, 2014, I have been in communication with some of my social science colleagues in Cuba to receive input from them both as professionals and as people who are based in the grassroots. One of the most frequent reactions has been proclaiming, somewhat warily, that "we have to keep our eyes open." In other words, they warn that there is more than meets the eye to the U.S.'s vastly increased resumption of diplomatic and commercial penetration.

It cannot be overstated that the change is in the *tactics,* not the goals. At the same time, Raúl Castro and the Cuban government are absolutely right in striving to take advantage of this change in tactics, as they so brilliantly did through the December 17 events.

When Raúl Castro and the government saw some differences between the old tactics and the new ones, it would have been foolhardy not to take advantage of the situation. In fact, the Cubans were the ones who had been proposing these changes all along. Relations are improving to the extent that the measures taken by both sides involve tactics but not long-range principles or strategy. The U.S. still wants to usher in change in Cuba that involves a different type of regime but more softly and smoothly than before, when the use of force and chaos was never ruled out. For its part, Cuba has not given in one iota to its right to self-determination and sovereignty. This was reiterated by Raúl Castro on December 17 (Castro Ruz [Raúl] 2014c) and again on December 20, when he added that there is no possibility at all that the main means of production will ever be privatized, but will remain in the hands of the state (Castro Ruz [Raúl] 2014b). Thus, both sides are entrenched in their respective principles and long-term strategies. The complicated and more difficult future will be faced mainly by Cuba. Almost all the changes are unidirectional, from the U.S. into Cuba.

The first difficulty to be faced is the cultural intrusion by the expected large number of American visitors through the wide-ranging types of visits now allowed thanks to the Obama executive orders. I have always noticed in Cuba that there is a soft spot among not insignificant sections of the youth, intellectuals and artists in favour of U.S. culture and virtually all things "American." This fatal attraction is bound to be amplified as the visitors carry out Obama's program of increased numbers of travellers who he *hopes* will be the best ambassadors for the American way of life, as they, according to the U.S. president, "represent America's values" (Obama 2014b). This is one example of how a *change in tactics* is geared to bring about the *objective* of doing away with revolutionary Cuba as we know it today.

One has to take into account objectives and principles. This cultural blindness in Cuba, referred to above as the pernicious fascination with American culture, is politically based on the festering illusion that the U.S. two-party system ushered in an entirely new era with Obama. This misconception serves as a smokescreen that facilitates to a certain extent the infiltration of the culture and values from the North. (See the section titled "From Tropical

Hell to Trendy Hot Spot for Westerners" in Chapter 4 to discover how some Western stars landed in Havana to a great deal of fanfare.) In conversation with my Cuban colleagues, one jokingly asked (perhaps with some justified apprehension) whether the streets of Havana will be filled with people carrying placards of Obama. Argentinean political scientist Atilio Borón echoed this foreboding when he declared, in reference to the U.S. change in tactics, that Latin America does not need another "Obama-mania." Borón concludes his outstanding article (2014, which to date has been published only in Spanish on the Cuban website *Cubadebate*) by saying that we cannot — as Che Guevara had declared — trust imperialism "even one iota, not at all!"

And this is the path Raúl Castro is following; while being flexible on tactics, he and his government and the vast majority of people are not conceding one single iota to the U.S. on questions of principle. My experience in Cuba tells me that this orientation is being pursued by the vast majority of the Cuban people, who are politically conscious and cultivated. They will not fall for the American way of life nor thus respond positively to the plans of the U.S. to turn back the clock on Cuban history. Notice that I say the "vast majority." Does this mean that a small minority has a penchant for the American way of life, including capitalism? Yes, and this is bound to increase under the new conditions and thus act as fertile ground among some youth, intellectuals and artists for the realization of the U.S. objective. This is a danger that can be thwarted only by the political action of the majority.

The second difficulty that I foresee is rooted in a tactic used by the Obama Administration. It comprises singling out the half million people involved in the burgeoning private business sector as an excellent target of capital through the U.S. government and businesses as well as Cuban-American families. (This issue is dealt with further in this chapter and in Chapter 4.)

DEMOCRACY AND THE RESTORATION OF CUBA-U.S. DIPLOMATIC RELATIONS: EMBASSIES IN HAVANA AND WASHINGTON ON JULY 20, 2015[2]

The re-establishment of diplomatic relations between Cuba and the U.S. and the opening of embassies in Havana and Washington, D.C., is a victory for Cuba. Negotiations between the two countries had been taking place secretly for eighteen months before being made public on December 17, 2014. On July 1, 2015, the agreement was sealed through the announcement of a formal opening date of July 20 for the embassies. It is important to note that, over the course of this two-year process, Cuba did not give up its principles. Two primary examples of this pertain to the contentious issues of democracy/human rights and of Venezuela.

In the first instance, the two neighbours agreed that democracy/human rights should be part of the discussion. Cuba has long declared that it is willing to put it on the table but only insofar as the issue of democracy/human rights in the U.S. is also open for debate. This should be on the condition that Cuba's right to discuss this with the U.S. as a sovereign independent country be recognized on the basis of mutual respect and equality. Thus, this portion of the agreement was actually a demand by Cuba with a view to ending the long impasse of more than five decades since the U.S. cut off diplomatic relations with Cuba. In fact, talks on this subject of democracy/human rights between the two parties took place between December 17, 2014, and July 1, 2015. Cuba did not give up any of its principles and is continuing on its own path to bring about changes according to its own needs and evaluations.

Cuba's second potential challenge in upholding its principles is one of the most contentious issues in Latin America and the Caribbean: the Bolivarian Revolution in Venezuela and the legitimacy of President Nicolás Maduro. Coincidence or not, during the heat of the negotiations from December 2014 to July 1, 2015, between Cuba and the U.S., the latter took open and provocative steps that could have led to destabilizing Venezuela and the eventual overthrow of the Maduro government through a "slow-motion coup." Cuba nonetheless continued to support the Venezuelan government and reject U.S. attempts at regime change in Venezuela. Cuba did not abandon its principle of internationalist solidarity, which has become one of its hallmarks, just to curry favour with the U.S. during their efforts to build diplomatic relations.

In addition to the above two examples of upholding principles, we cannot overlook the fact that the three remaining prisoners of the Cuban Five were returned to Cuba on December 17, 2014, after more than sixteen years in prison. There was no way Cuba would have agreed to even the first step of diplomatic relations without the return of these three prisoners.

The July 20 date means diplomatic relations and the opening of embassies but nothing more. It represents a first phase that has the potential to lead toward the long path of normalizing relations. There remain many issues to be settled as part of normalization, such as lifting the blockade, returning Guantánamo to Cuba, ending discriminatory legislation on immigration and putting an end to U.S. internal subversion and destabilization in Cuba in the name of democracy and human rights.

I would like to address one of these disputes: how U.S. democracy promotion in Cuba relates to the blockade. Among other pieces of legislation, the two principal Congressional building blocks underlying the blockade consist of the 1992 *Torricelli Act* and the 1996 *Helms-Burton Act*. The former, whose real title is the *Cuban Democracy Act*, stipulates: "Assistance to support democracy in Cuba. The United States Government may provide assistance, through appropriate nongovernmental organizations, for the support of individuals and organizations to promote nonviolent democratic change in Cuba" (U.S. Department of Treasury 1992). The second legal framework is the 1996 legislation, whose full title is the *Cuban Liberty and Democratic Solidarity (Libertad) Act*. Section 109 is titled "Authorization of support for democratic and human rights groups and international observers." It stipulates:

> The President is authorized to furnish assistance and provide other support for individuals and independent nongovernmental organizations to support democracy-building efforts for Cuba, including the following:
>
> (1) Published and informational matter, such as books, videos, and cassettes, on transitions to democracy, human rights, and market economies, to be made available to independent democratic groups in Cuba.
> (2) Humanitarian assistance to victims of political repression, and their families.
> (3) Support for democratic and human rights groups in Cuba. (U.S. Department of Treasury 1996)

Based on this legislation, in June 2015, the *State, Foreign Operations, and Related Programs Appropriations Bill* proposed by the House of Representatives for 2016 includes funding for the National Endowment for Democracy (NED). Regarding Cuba, "the Committee recommendation includes $30,000,000 (an increase compared with 2015) for programs to promote democracy and strengthen civil society in Cuba, of which not less than $8,000,000 shall be for NED" (U.S. House of Representatives Committees on Appropriations 2015). The rest of this $30 million is earmarked for other organizations, such as USAID. The funding is clearly indicated as being part of blockade legislation:

> The Committee directs that funds shall only be used for programs and activities … of the Cuban Liberty and Democratic Solidarity (Libertad) Act of 1996 and … the Cuban Democracy Act (CDA) of 1992, and shall not be used for business promotion, economic reform, entrepreneurship or any other assistance that is not democracy-building. (U.S. House of Representatives Committees on Appropriations 2015)

The "Congressional Budget Justification, Foreign Operations, Appendix 3" for fiscal year 2016 spells out the objective of democracy promotion for Cuba since December 17, 2014:

> The President noted during his December 17, 2014 policy speech that the promotion of democratic principles and human rights remains the core goal of U.S. assistance to Cuba.... The United States will continue robust democracy assistance to Cuba to support civil society and greater human rights for the Cuban people.... The United States continues to provide support for democracy and human rights in challenging operating environments, including Cuba and Venezuela. (U.S. Department of State n.d.)

The single most important point about democracy in Cuba is that its approach is entirely up to the Cuban people and its government. It is Cuba's sovereign right as an independent nation to take the path it desires. No other country can dictate the type of democracy that should exist in Cuba.

The U.S. has its own brand of democracy. Cuba does not have a program to undermine and subvert the status quo in the U.S., even though Cuba's views on the political and economic system in the U.S. are public and well known. The fact that Cuba is a small Third World country does not grant the right to any powerful nation in the North to impose its system. This, however, is the bottom line of U.S. democracy promotion. A careful reading of the main U.S. legislation cited above reveals an open declaration by the U.S. that its multi-party election style and free market capitalism are the goals of democracy promotion in Cuba.

Cuba has its own history and tradition when it comes to democracy. Ironically, the negative impact of U.S.-style democracy is part of this heritage. In the second half of the nineteenth century, in the course of waging its independence wars against Spain, Cuba was confronted with challenges of social and political priorities and organization. In the areas liberated from Spanish domination, this led the Cuban patriots to experiment with organizing their own constituent assemblies and constitutions. In these constitutions were enshrined what we would now call human rights.

However, this course of action and set of evolving values were interrupted by U.S. intervention in the war against the Spanish in which the U.S. replaced the Spanish as the colonizer. During the period of U.S. domination from 1898 to 1958, the U.S. rolled back the embryonic yet positive benefits of democracy and human rights. For most of this period during the twentieth century, the

Cubans suffered under a political and socio-economic system that resembled, in very general terms, U.S. democracy and its market economy.

The Cuban transition to democracy was rekindled with the triumph of the Cuban Revolution on January 1, 1959. From that period until now, it has undergone, and continues to undergo, many changes. Are changes in fact ever brought about in the Cuban political system? Yes, but not in the direction that U.S. official policy would like. For example, from 1959 to 1974–76, Cuba exercised political power in the absence of elections and a new constitution. However, during this period, participation in the Cuban political process was at its peak; today, many Cubans remain nostalgic about that time. In 1974–76, Cubans participated in drafting a constitution, voting upon it in a referendum and initiating elections. In 1992, reforms were made to the political and electoral system. Now there is talk about a new electoral law and other political changes. These new efforts are in response to Cuban analysis and needs and not to those of the U.S. In other words, Cuba is a democracy in motion, a democracy that changes and adapts to meet ever-changing conditions.

What about the U.S.? Does its political system bring about changes? Yes, but it does so only in the context of its own political system and within the boundaries and limitations that these impose. For example, there have been changes to party financing that do not at all negate the main feature of party politics and funding based on wealth and privilege. There are also amendments to the right to vote, but they cannot go beyond the context of the socio-economic/political system, which is based on racial discrimination and inequality coupled with apathy.

Thus, Cuban democracy and U.S. democracy each have their own features embedding their respective values and traditions. U.S. democracy promotion in Cuba will continue even after July 20. Does this mean that the establishment of diplomatic relations and embassies remains an important victory for Cuba? Yes, it does. The situation has changed radically. Before July 20, there was no convenient official channel with the U.S. for Cuba to register its opposition to these programs. Now that diplomatic relations have been established with embassies in both countries, Cuba can put its cards on the table with its American counterparts in Havana and Washington and state its case face to face with facts and proof. Does this mean that the American side will listen to reason and take into account the Cuban version of the facts? Not necessarily.

Nevertheless, the situation has improved in another way. Since December 17, 2014, Cuba has taken centre stage on the international political scene under the leadership of President Raúl Castro. While there are many interpretations of this December 17 event, what basically comes across is that "Cuba was right" all along, for more than five decades. Its heroic resistance in the face of the Empire paid off. Before December 17, 2014, Cuba was marginalized in international politics (aside from much of Latin America and the Caribbean and the South). Cuba's voice has now stretched not only to the U.S. and Europe but to the whole world. It can no longer be viewed contemptuously.

Obama's prestige also improved with his accomplishments internationally — including Cuba — and domestically. However, U.S. presidents are always at the forefront on the international scene; for example, in Berlin, Obama gave one of his first campaign speeches for the 2008 U.S. presidential elections, tailored for both domestic and international consumption.

Cuba has not had the luxury of automatic access to the limelight, apart from some sporadic and distorted international reporting on Fidel Castro. Going forward, as issues arise, the world will have to take notice of what the Cuban government says with regard to the subversive and destabilizing effects of U.S. democracy promotion programs. Cuba–U.S. relations will factor in mainstream international public opinion.

In an ideal world, this open international debate may further push Obama and his successor to work toward lifting the blockade, among other things, in Congress, whose legislation is the basis of their democracy promotion programs. Would it be a stretch for presidents to consider bypassing a hostile Congress by using their executive powers in order to divert these programs? These programs may destabilize Cuba to a certain extent, which would serve to undermine smooth diplomatic relations. Would it be naive to posit that this may put the U.S. in an awkward position, while Cuba may seem to come up clean?

There is a new reality in the U.S. More and more visitors from all walks of life are travelling to Cuba, including students, professors, artists and others in a position of influence, such as journalists. Once they are familiar with Cuba, how will they react if it were to become widely known that the U.S. is using funds to destabilize Cuba?

In addition, strange as it may seem, the American business community that is increasingly converging on Cuba may well prefer to maintain its investments in, and trade with, a stable Cuban political system headed by the revolutionary government rather than with a society that is in chaos because a handful of individuals with the assistance of U.S. democracy promotion programs challenge the evolving status quo and upset the applecart. After all, it is Cuba as it currently exists that has been attracting business people to invest in and trade with. At this time, it seems that the

U.S. tourist industry is one of the most active of the businesses. It is taking advantage of Americans' desire to visit a safe and calm present-day Cuba as it goes through the process of updating its socio-economic system. This is what visitors want to see, not a Cuba as a Caribbean mirror image of the U.S. Things can change in the U.S. over the course of the many years that it will take to lift the blockade and end subversive democracy promotion activities in Cuba. Who would have thought before December 17, 2014, that this historic step would take place?

CUBA–U.S. RELATIONS AND FREEDOM OF THE PRESS[3]

At the August 14, 2015, flag-raising ceremony in Havana to formally open the U.S. Interests Section as the U.S. Embassy, Secretary of State John Kerry stated: "We remain convinced the people of Cuba would be best served by genuine democracy." This U.S. promotion of democracy for Cuba is explicitly or implicitly referring to freedom of the press, among other features. Nonetheless, Kerry's comment on democracy was not the main focus of his remarks; rather, he spoke primarily about the Administration's policy on Cuba–U.S. relations, about the recognition of the Cuban government and of the establishment of diplomatic relations and embassies as a step toward the possibility of normalizing relations as neighbours rather than enemies or rivals.

But how did the U.S. press deal with Kerry's speech and his other formal engagements in Havana that day? Let us take as an example CNN USA, which sent one of its star anchors, Jake Tapper, to Havana for the occasion. What spin did he provide to the Kerry speech? The CNN host declared: "But it is not as though, you know, snap, all of a sudden there is democracy and freedom of the press" (2015c). At another time that same day, he reported: "This is a country that does not have freedom of the press, does not have the right of assembly. You can go on and on" (2015d). Tapper broadcast on yet another CNN television spot that same day: "One American flag does not solve every problem or release the Castro brothers' grip on the people here … President Eisenhower said then — quote — 'Our sympathy goes out to the people of Cuba now suffering under the yoke of a dictator.' The dictator and his yoke now enforced [by] his brother, Raúl" (2015b).

By his own account, Tapper actively sought out Cuban dissidents, among others, to interview. He hung on to every word they uttered in their opposition to the unconditional re-establishment of diplomatic relations between the two countries. He summarized that "critics claim that today [August 14] only will give legitimacy to a dictator who has no interest in true change" (2015b). Tapper went further by playing a July 2007 presidential debate video clip in which then Senator Barack Obama, according to Tapper, was "laying out his rationale for engaging a rogue regime such as Cuba" (2015a). However, according to CNN (2007) transcripts, the question in July 2007 was whether the presidential candidates favoured meeting "separately, without precondition, during the first year of your administration, in Washington or anywhere else, with the leaders of Iran, Syria, Venezuela, Cuba and North Korea, in order to bridge the gap that divides our countries." The question and Obama's response did not employ the term "rogue regime."

Thus, to summarize, while CNN did broadcast in its entirety the flag-raising ceremony and Kerry's statement, whose main feature was the promotion of diplomatic relations as neighbours, CNN did its own editing. The cable news network jumped on Kerry's remarks about democracy for Cuba and one of its correlations, freedom of the press. During the entire day and on practically every program going into the late evening, TV viewers were bombarded by the sound bites of "freedom of the press," "dictatorship" and "rogue regime."

What is also significant, and serving as a corollary to the treatment of Kerry's remarks, was what CNN *omitted*. In addition to the flag-raising ceremony, there was a second momentous activity. Kerry was welcomed by his counterpart, Cuban Foreign Minister Bruno Rodríguez, at the Ministry of Foreign Affairs building. The meeting behind closed doors was followed by public availability to the press at the Hotel Nacional. This event included remarks by both Kerry and Rodríguez followed by an open question-and-answer period. The entire activity was virtually censored by CNN. It is unfortunate, because the U.S. audience and others around the English-speaking world served by CNN USA missed the opportunity to hear what the Cuban side had to say about "democracy for Cuba."

During the question period, AP journalist Andrea Rodríguez addressed Bruno Rodríguez: "Secretary Kerry today mentioned that he hopes to see in Cuba a genuine democracy. I would like to know your comments on this." The Cuban foreign minister's response never reached the U.S. public via CNN. Here is what he said:

> I feel that we should work very actively in order to build confidence, mutual confidence, and to develop contacts in the areas where we have a very close approach or those areas where our ideas could come closer, and to be able to discuss in a respectful way about our respective differences. In some areas, it is true that differences are

profound. However, I can say that some of these issues have been subject to an intensive international debate.... I feel very comfortable with the Cuban democracy, and at the same time there are things that could be further perfected.

Today we are working actively as part of the processes related to the updating of our economic and social, socialist model.... There are attempts to increase international cooperation to solve problems related to civil and political liberties, which, in our opinion, should be guaranteed, such as the right to food, the right to gender equality, the right to life, the right to education, and health care. (U.S. Department of State 2015b)

One can guess why these comments were suppressed by CNN. One conclusion is that the Cuban foreign minister enunciated, as expected, some views that fly in the face of the CNN sound bites. On the question of democracy, he turned the attention toward a concern shared by many people in the U.S. and elsewhere in the West regarding the quality of democracy and the electoral processes in these advanced industrial countries. This Cuban interjection throws a wrench in the CNN narrative regarding democracy, which hammers Cuba but leaves the U.S. unscathed or even as the model.

The minister's remarks in defence of Cuban democracy were qualified with the important caveat that it has to be improved. This logic of combining sovereign decisions with the recognition of improvements within the Cuban traditions and values also flies in the face of the U.S. mainstream press such as CNN.

Finally, the minister threw the ball back into the court of the U.S. in a diplomatic manner by indicating that Cuba highly regards, for all countries, the guarantee for civil and political liberties, such as the right to food, to gender equality, to life, to education and to health care. Cuba's accomplishments in these fields are well known and internationally recognized, while the lack of these guarantees in the U.S. is increasingly notorious in the country itself and internationally.

How did the Cuban press deal with August 14? Did it carry out censorship and misinformation? No. On the contrary, the entire day was broadcast live on Cuban TV and radio. This began with the arrival by Kerry at the airport in Havana and an informational biography of the secretary of state that was not at all tinged by derogatory statements or qualifications. The entire ceremony and Kerry's remarks at the U.S. Embassy were transmitted. The full press availability mentioned above was equally on Cuban TV. The next day, the Cuban official press carried the full transcripts in Spanish of the flag-raising ceremony (Consejo de Estado 2015b) and the press availability (Consejo de Estado 2015a).

This aversion to censorship is part of the Cuban tradition when it comes to striving to normalize relations with the U.S. For example, in 2002, former president Jimmy Carter visited President Fidel Castro in Cuba. On this occasion, Carter's speech in Spanish was broadcast in its entirety by Cuban TV and radio, even though it contained comments regarding democracy for Cuba similar to Kerry's remarks in August 2015. In his own report on the visit, Carter wrote:

> That evening at the University of Havana I made a speech and then answered questions that, as promised, was carried live on television and radio. It was later rebroadcast, and the entire transcript was published in the two Cuban newspapers. Subsequently, we could not find anyone on the streets or in the markets who had not heard it. (Carter 2002)

The diametrically opposed approaches of the Cuban press and of CNN in covering August 14 indicate that CNN does not have any grounds to criticize Cuba for the lack of freedom of the press. In fact, it was Cuba that gave a lesson to CNN about opposing censorship and misinformation. Cuba turned the tables on the U.S.

In the U.S., "freedom of the press," like "democracy" itself, is presented in the abstract. They are buzzwords that are designed to make people in the U.S. and abroad kneel down in homage to the U.S. as the model. The First Amendment to the U.S. Constitution (1791) proscribes that "Congress shall make no law respecting an establishment of religion, or prohibiting the free exercise thereof; or abridging the freedom of speech, or of the press; or the right of the people peaceably to assemble, and to petition the Government for a redress of grievances" (U.S. Office of the Secretary of the Senate n.d.). The amendment gives the impression that there are no restrictions by abstracting the press from the socio-economic context in which it operates. Thus, supposedly, anybody can write and say anything.

In Cuba, on the other hand, as the U.S. logic goes, there are restrictions. Article 53 of the Cuban Constitution indicates that "citizens have freedom of speech and of the press in keeping with the objectives of socialist society" (Ministry of Foreign Affairs of Cuba 2003). The U.S.-centric framework dictates that, in Cuba, there is no real freedom of the press, as there are constraints, while in the U.S. there are supposedly no conditions.

Does pure freedom of the press exist in the U.S.? Let us take CNN's reporting on August 14, 2015, as our ongoing example. How did host Jake Tapper and the other CNN anchors come to spin their story and reporting? It is possible that no one instructed them on exactly what angle to take. However, there was no need to, as they know that in order to advance their careers certain concepts have to be promoted, while others have to be omitted or distorted. All of these contortions are broadcast in order to make their story coincide with the preconceived notions and interests of the ruling circles.

Noam Chomsky unravelled the role of the U.S. media as part of the establishment in his classic book *Manufacturing Consent*. He and his co-author wrote that the "media serve, and propagandize on behalf of, the powerful societal interests that control and finance them" (Chomsky and Herman 2002). Chomsky goes on to unveil the inner workings of this phenomenon by indicating that the constraint the establishment exercises over the media "is normally not accomplished by crude intervention, but by the selection of right-thinking personnel and by the editors' and working journalists' internalization of priorities and definitions of newsworthiness that conform to the institution's policy" (xi). Yet it is well known that "crude intervention" also takes place (Tracy 2015).

Considering Chomsky's view on the U.S. media as it relates to CNN and Jake Tapper, we can give the cable news outlet the benefit of the doubt that "crude intervention" was not carried out for the August 14 angle on Cuba–U.S. relations. However, following the Chomsky thesis, let us take into account that, in December 2012, Tapper was first selected by CNN based on his career as a "right-thinking" person. On August 14, 2015, in Havana, he "internalized" or embodied the angle that CNN desired. In other words, by incarnating the U.S. long-term view on Cuba held by some sections in the establishment, Tapper knew perfectly well what he was doing. It is part of building a career with the monetary rewards that accompany climbing the ladder.

Tapper is a rising star in CNN and thus was chosen to moderate the September 16, 2015, Republican presidential debate. There is a serious struggle between Fox News and CNN to capture more and increasingly higher-priced ads and expand their ratings as part of these Republican presidential debates (Trujillo 2015). CNN is banking on Tapper to contribute toward attaining its goals.

The corporate "freedom of the press" situation in the U.S. is further emphasized when contrasted with the Cuban approach. Article 53 of its Constitution stipulates that the "mass media are state or social property and can never be private property" (Ministry of Foreign Affairs of Cuba

2003). This is not a restriction but rather a liberating factor, especially if one compares it to the U.S. corporate-controlled press.

However, as indicated above, Cuba, for its part, has an explicit constraint on freedom of the press: the press must coincide with the objectives of socialist society. There is no hypocritical attempt to hide it. The objectives of the Cuban socialist society and its principles with regard to Cuba–U.S. relations require that diplomacy be fostered to the utmost as a crucial input toward bringing about improvements to Cuba's socialist model. This Cuban diplomatic effort included full press coverage of Kerry's visit, irrespective of his declarations. For Cuba, it is also a question of principle to treat its U.S. guests in that way, as did Fidel Castro with President Carter.

Did CNN's reporting on the August 14 activities in Havana contradict the current official U.S. policy on Cuba? Did it represent one section of the ruling circles that is not favourable to the thawing of relations between the two neighbours against another faction of the U.S. establishment that is inclined to the normalizing option? The situation is complex.

We have to keep in mind that on December 17, 2014, when Presidents Obama and Castro made the surprising simultaneous announcement of the new U.S. policy, both the White House and the State Department made — and continue to make — one point clear. The new U.S. approach represents only a change of tactics, while the objective of the U.S. remains in place. U.S. officials continue to promote the U.S. version of democracy for Cuba. This ultimate goal, couched in a more diplomatic manner and thus not as boorish as CNN, requires ongoing propaganda that Cuba is not democratic, that there is no freedom of the press and so on.

There remains the question of why CNN did not contribute to the evolution of the two countries' diplomatic efforts by professionally informing the U.S. public as did the Cuban press with its people. CNN's crass reporting serves as another reminder of this new situation with its positive perspectives for both Cubans and Americans, as well as the dangers for Cuba.

Cubans are keenly aware of this. Its press and journalists' blogs presently serve as a forum for a mature and lively debate on the significance of the new U.S. approach. This debate is a result of the attempts by the leadership and the journalists to improve the Cuban press as part of the wide-ranging changes going on in Cuba.

CUBA-U.S. RELATIONS AND THE PERSPICACITY OF FIDEL CASTRO'S THINKING[4]

In the online interview with alternative U.S.-based website *Dissident Voice* (August 2015e), reprinted at the beginning of this chapter, I was asked about my take on the seeming rapprochement between the U.S. and Cuba. With regard to the December 17, 2014, announcement, I responded that the situation caused me to think of Fidel Castro's statement just eight days after the triumph of the Revolution: "Perhaps everything will be more difficult in the future" (August 2015e).

Only days after that interview was published, I began to have second thoughts about my assertions. Even though I was careful to indicate the obvious — that we cannot compare the contexts of 1959 with 17D (as the Cubans refer to December 17, 2014), my main point was to have readers appreciate the perspicacity of Fidel Castro's thinking, as applied to today's entirely different situation. In his customary astuteness, he was able to peer into the future in order to provide a sober long-term context for the new Cuban Revolution. The remarkable insight he exhibited on January 8, 1959, allowed him to analyze dialectically how immense problems on the horizon can be camouflaged by the equally immense joy exhibited right after the triumph of the Revolution.

Despite providing the caveat that conditions in both periods are completely dissimilar, I wondered if I stated my message clearly enough regarding applying his 1959 pronouncement to the current situation? This uncertainty began to dissipate as I read with my usual keen interest what Cuban academics, researchers and journalists were writing. A few wrote pieces essentially similar to mine. For example, Elier Ramírez, the young researcher and co-author along with Esteban Morales of a 2015 watershed book on Cuba–U.S. relations, wrote a two-part article on his area of expertise (see Chapter 3 for my interviews with these two specialists). The second part of his article was published on his own blog on January 28, 2015, reprinted the same day on Iroel Sánchez's blog *La pupila insomne*, followed by a reprint on February 7, 2015, in *Cubadebate* and the Communist Youth League daily *Juventud Rebelde*. Elier Ramírez wrote how Fidel Castro declared on January 8, 1959, that "it is possible that in the future everything would be more difficult.... especially in the realm of the ideological and cultural confrontation with imperialism."

The well-known journalist Rosa Miriam Elizalde penned an article on July 21, 2015, in *Cubadebate* with the telling title "Cuba–U.S.: The Difficulty Is Coming Now" ("Cuba–EEUU: Lo difícil viene ahora"). Of interest is a reader's online comment made on that article about the significance of the

January 8 declaration by Fidel Castro that states "maybe everything in the future will be more difficult."

In October 2015, journalist Rafael Cruz Ramos expressed in a post on his blog, which was reprinted in *CubaSí,* his concern, among other things, about the current situation: "Fidel was right when he said that the current battles are more complex than those in the Sierra Maestra." Others have written similar articles.

It seems that my initial reference to Fidel Castro's thinking was not out of place, given the similar assertions from some of the Cuban media and in light of the events that transpired since then (i.e., from 17D to fall 2015), which I have followed closely. This conclusion constituted a mixed blessing, since it is not comforting to acknowledge that an ongoing Revolution since 1959 can still confront a situation that "may be" more difficult now than the period leading up to it. One can also counter my position by indicating there are not that many journalists or public figures who share this opinion. However, this apparent lack of widespread attention is another reason for ratifying the view on Fidel Castro's thinking. The current manifest scarcity of caution among some may in fact reflect a certain amount of "immense joy" in pushing the stark reality of U.S. imperialism's intentions to the background.

Elier Ramírez makes an extremely important qualification that the more difficult time now is to be found "especially in the realm of the ideological and cultural confrontation with imperialism." While it is a broad topic, one example stands out. When visiting Havana not long after 17D, I could not help but notice the American flag being widely exhibited as clothing apparel on virtually all body parts, on taxis and cars, and in shops.

As a Canadian, this struck me as a not too subtle warning. Canada is the closest ally of the U.S. in the West, and Canadians are frequent visitors to their neighbour to the south. However, we do not see such a virtual carnival-like display of the U.S. flag in Canada. In fact, many Canadians would abhor such fanfare as the nationalist anti-U.S. imperialist sentiment in Canada, while not the highest in the world, is enough to draw the line.

The proliferation of the U.S. flag in Havana was confirmed and highlighted by journalist Luis Toledo Sande's series on the flag issue in three articles complete with photos, published in *Cubadebate* and blogs. (See my interview with Luis Toledo Sande in Chapter 3, where we deal with the "flag issue" and other U.S. cultural incursions.) These trends and many others corroborate Elier Ramírez's concern about the complicated "ideological and cultural confrontation with imperialism" as a consequence of 17D.

The U.S. blockade against Cuba is now more than ever a subject of debate in Cuba and elsewhere, especially in the U.S. On October 27, 2015, in the United Nations General Assembly (UNGA), the U.S. was decidedly defeated in a record vote of 191 in favour of the Cuban resolution to lift the blockade and only two — the U.S. and its closest political and military ally, Israel — in favour of maintaining it, with no abstentions. However, a vote the following year was even more dramatic. On October 26, 2016, the UNGA voted to approve the Cuban resolution expressing the need to put an end to the blockade imposed by the U.S. on the island for more than fifty years. For the first time since 1991, when the resolution and then the annual vote began, the U.S. and Israel, rather than voting against the resolution, abstained. A total of 191 countries voted in favour of the resolution, with none voting against, and only the two abstentions (*Granma* 2016a).

Much has been written in Cuba and the U.S. on the blockade by the two governments and by experts on both sides. These debates concern primarily those measures that have been — and can still be — carried out by President Obama. The blockade, in reality, is upheld by both his executive wing and the legislative body (Congress) of the U.S. government. The main conditions of the blockade are the prerogative of Congress. Some commentators, however, indicate that there are contradictions in the Obama Administration's policy with regard to the blockade. Based on his *apparent* opposition to the blockade, he can — but does not — use his executive prerogatives to restrict as much as possible the effects of the blockade.

The official documents show that the White House and Department of State seem to protect themselves by leaving the door open to the continuation of the blockade and restricting Washington's action to a minimum. The U.S. statements speak for themselves. Whether or not the Administration is really even in words in favour of lifting the blockade is at best not clear. It may be preferable to err on the side of safety by not harbouring illusions but also to pressure the Administration on that basis.

In Obama's December 17, 2014, declaration, he listed a series of issues that he wants to address regarding Cuba, such as democracy and human rights, people-to-people travel and remittances from Americans to the "emerging Cuban private sector," that is, 500,000 self-employed workers. He concludes: "As these changes unfold, I look forward to engaging Congress in an honest and serious debate about lifting the embargo" (Obama 2014b). In other words, it seems that a condition for confronting the majority Republican Congress is the evolution of change in Cuba according to U.S. standards. His stand does not appear to be a principled unconditional demand that Congress lift the blockade. Secretary of State John Kerry expounded on this angle:

Look, I can't tell you when the embargo will be lifted, because it really depends, to a large degree, on the *decisions and choices made by Cubans. They have to make it possible to lift the embargo.* And the Congress of the United States appropriately is very concerned about human rights, about democracy, about the ability of people to speak their mind, and to meet, and to do things. And we'd like to see — we're not asking for everything to change overnight, but we want to see Cuba moving in the right direction, and our hope is that it will. (U.S. Department of State 2015a, emphasis added)

The impression was given in some media around the world that Obama called for the lifting of the blockade in his speech to the United Nations General Assembly on September 28, 2015. In fact, what he said, in talking about human rights in Cuba and Cuba–U.S. people-to-people contacts, was, "*as these contacts yield progress,* I'm confident that our Congress will inevitably lift an embargo that should not be in place anymore" (Obama 2015a, emphasis added).

Words and semantics are used deceivingly by U.S. imperialism. The U.S. employs words that seemingly take a just position but in fact camouflage the real nature of U.S. tactics and strategy. Take as an example the 2009 U.S.-orchestrated military coup d'état in Honduras and the expulsion of the constitutionally elected President Mel Zelaya. At first, both Obama and Secretary of State Hillary Clinton did not use the word *coup.* Facing the outrage of all of Latin America, they finally used the word *coup* but not *military coup d'état.* To employ this latter term would provide the legal basis for the restriction of military aid to the putschists, which Washington did not wish to do. In a similar fashion, facing international pressure, Obama and Clinton said they favoured the return of Zelaya to Honduras. However, on both occasions in which he attempted to enter the country, the U.S. opposed it, claiming that this return had to be carried out with the full involvement of the U.S. and its allies. Thus, the words favouring the "return of Zelaya" in fact carried no meaning, as did the so-called opposition to the coup.

Similarly, the semantics of supporting the lifting of the blockade carry little weight, given that they seem to be conditional to Cuba "doing more," "opening up" and so on. The older pre-17D crude diplomacy has changed to "soft power" attempts to influence from within. This is carried out to a certain extent as "democracy promotion" programs still funded by the U.S. Obama said with regard to Cuba that the U.S. is no longer in the business of regime change; however, the regime change programs are continuing.

Thus, words from the mouth of the imperial power cannot be taken at face value and must be scrutinized.

It is now well known — and made explicit by the Obama Administration — that the U.S. stance toward Cuba in the 17D situation is only a change in tactics, such as the re-establishment of diplomatic relations and the reopening of embassies in both countries. However, the U.S. main strategy remains the overthrow of the Revolution or changing it from within so that it has no resemblance to its pre-17D years.

It is necessary to expand on the concept of strategy. It can be recalled that Obama came to his new position on Cuba because, among other points, as he and others have admitted on several occasions, U.S. Cuba policy was isolating the U.S. from Latin America and the Caribbean. The Summit of the Americas, led by the U.S. and held every few years, in principle includes all the countries of South and Central America, the Caribbean and North America. However, Cuba has been systematically excluded.

At the Sixth Summit of the Americas held in Cartagena, Colombia, in April 2012, when Cuba was still not included, the conflict between the South and the North had reached the breaking point. The entire South demanded the inclusion of Cuba, threatening a de facto collapse of the next summit if it did not incorporate the island. The Seventh Summit was to be held in April 2015 in Panama. If Obama had not changed tactics immediately, the U.S. — and not Cuba — would have been blamed for the breakdown of the Panama Summit.

A corollary to the Obama strategy for Cuba is the U.S. strategy for Latin America to defeat the new progressive and left-wing movements and governments, such as in Venezuela, Bolivia, Ecuador and even the more moderate ones, such as in Argentina and Brazil. In fact, the U.S. Cuba strategy is part and parcel of the strategy for Latin America. It is thus no accident that, while the impression is given that the U.S. has softened up on Cuba and finally come to its senses, there have been U.S.-assisted and -supported destabilizing efforts in all of the above-mentioned countries. If they succeed in part or in whole, it would be a major setback for the entire region, including Cuba. It would also be a defeat for the world, as Latin America and the Caribbean is the most promising region for socio-economic/political progress. The region is now a concrete foundation for developing a multi-polar world that would leave behind the U.S. hegemony-based unipolar globe.

Thus, Fidel Castro's statement on January 8, 1959, takes on relevance today, that is, that the situation may be more difficult in the future. This may be challenged by some, and understandably so, by pointing out that in 1959 Cuba was alone, while Cuba is now part of this new regional bloc whose members in general support each other.

However, this new Latin America has been established with many sacrifices and struggles, such as in the case of Venezuela since the 1998 election of Hugo Chávez as president. Any significant defeat in Latin America may have, as the U.S. desires, a domino effect in the region. The situation today is more difficult than in 1959, seeing as the peoples have so much more to lose. However, I think that the U.S. will lose again. For example, in Venezuela, even if there is a temporary defeat or stalemate in elections, the Bolivarian Revolution has become, and is growing as, a material force in Venezuelan society. Once people are consciously and actively participating in their own ongoing empowerment and defence of their national sovereignty, this material force can in the long run defeat even the most formidable enemy.

Both the U.S. and Spain harbour and promote anti-Castro bloggers in those countries. They act as "advisors" to some bloggers, especially among those youth in Cuba who share a similar inclination or gravitate toward it. In Cuba itself, there also exist blogger "consultants" whose goal is to detour Cubans from the path of Revolution. Thus, the image of the dissidents is changing from one that has been discredited as mercenaries of the U.S. to another, younger sort. The new crop gives the impression that they are not interested in regime change funds. They are not easy to detect. Dissidence is being renovated in the context of 17D and is a cancer that strives to eat away at Cuban society from within, targeting especially youth, artists, intellectuals and journalists.

The acumen of Fidel Castro's statement as applied to 17D is ratified in light of both the foregoing discussion and the fact that Cuban society has accumulated problems over the last decades.

The Congress of the Communist Youth League was held in July 2015. Contrary to the disinformation from the mainstream U.S. media about censorship and the press in Cuba, Cuban TV broadcast practically all the proceedings and debates in this Congress of 600 delegates. Never have I been so impressed by so many spontaneous and unwritten statements, profound in content, by Cubans at these types of events. It strikes me that any of them could be future leaders of Cuba. Even though the conditions now are very different and may be more difficult and especially more complicated than the period leading up to the Revolution, new generations prepare to continue the legacy, in the context of defying the current situation. The new generation of dissidents, whose "dissidence" is being been recycled to match the 17D conditions, is no match for the young Cuban revolutionaries.

Furthermore, those in the U.S. who are banking on self-employed workers to drain Cuba from the inside completely underestimate the political/

ideological consciousness and patriotism of the vast majority of Cubans. Cubans are steeped in this tradition. President Raúl Castro made it clear in his remarks on December 17, 2014. He opened by stating right from the beginning:

> Since my election as President of the State Council and Council of Ministers I have reiterated on many occasions our willingness to hold a respectful dialogue with the United States on the basis of sovereign equality, in order to deal reciprocally with a wide variety of topics without detriment to the national Independence and self-determination of our people.
>
> This stance was conveyed to the U.S. Government both publicly and privately by Comrade Fidel on several occasions during our long standing struggle, stating the willingness to discuss and solve our differences without renouncing any of our principles. (2014c)

Cuba has gone though many years of revolutionary and patriotic struggles. One such period took place between 1868 and 1898, during the patriotic wars against Spanish colonialism and in favour of independence and a more just society. A second historic period was the negative one of U.S. domination from 1898 to 1959. A third era, which is ongoing, was initiated on January 1, 1959, is steeped in the 1953 Moncada action and ensuing program as the basis of the Revolution. December 17 is not historic in that sense but, rather, is another chapter in the current period, with its promises as well as perhaps even more difficulties and challenges, under entirely different circumstances than the period leading up to the January 1, 1959, victory.

WHAT OBAMA REALLY SAID ABOUT CUBA, FOREIGN AFFAIRS AND THE U.S.[5]

During the annual State of the Union address on January 13, 2016, President Obama reiterated his policy regarding Cuba–U.S. relations: "Fifty years of isolating Cuba had failed to promote democracy, and set us back in Latin America. That's why we restored diplomatic relations — (applause) — opened the door to travel and commerce, positioned ourselves to improve the lives of the Cuban people. (Applause)."[6] Obama conveyed this sentiment several years ago in the course of developing his Cuba policy, and also a series of *New York Times* editorials reflected upon and elaborated the Obama plan. All of this helped pave the way for the December 17, 2014, joint statement by Presidents Barack Obama and Raúl Castro to restore diplomatic relations, a victory for Cuba. There has been no change in the U.S. position. As Obama expressed previously in other ways, the old policy of isolating Cuba failed to bring "democracy" to Cuba, a euphemism for overthrowing the constitutional order and the Revolution.

Obama expressed that his new Cuba policy "opened the door to travel and commerce." While this is true, it is not very much more than a one-way effort that favours the U.S. It does not open doors equally, on a mutual basis, for Cubans to do business with the U.S. and internationally.

What did he mean when he stated that the White House and the Administration "positioned ourselves to improve the lives of the Cuban people"? A crucial objective of the policies designed to improve the "lives of the people" is geared toward the 500,000 people in the expanding self-employed sector of the Cuban economy. The immediate tactical goal of the Administration is to strengthen this sector, with its made-in-the-U.S. branding. If Obama were really interested in the goal of improving the lives of the Cuban people, he could use his executive powers to gut vital parts of the blockade that Congress cannot block. So what did Obama really say to the Congress about the blockade: "If you want to consolidate our leadership and credibility in the hemisphere, recognize that the Cold War is over — lift the embargo. (Applause)."

Let us forgo for a moment the fact that he favours the lifting of the genocidal blockade not for moral reasons but rather to reach the goal of improving the U.S. image in Latin America. If he is so much against the blockade, why divert the focus toward the majority Republican U.S. Congress? As mentioned, there is much he can do using his executive prerogatives. Blaming Congress for blocking the Executive Branch is a ruse. His lack of real opposition to the blockade was likewise illustrated when, in 2014, under Obama's tutelage, a German bank was fined $1 billion for dealing with Cuba. Why should the Cuban people wait for U.S. Congress, when the blockade has been the principal obstacle to Cuba's sustainable development?

Obama flamboyantly bragged: "I will keep working to shut down the prison at Guantánamo. (Applause) It is expensive, it is unnecessary, and it only serves as a recruitment brochure for our enemies (Applause)." He does not want to shut down the prison because it is a torture chamber, a blot on humanity, but because it is expensive and unnecessary. He has been promising this since he was elected. Why has he not done it? There is no need for Congressional approval. After all, Bush opened the notorious prison on his own without Congressional approval. Blaming Congress is once again part of U.S. opportunist politics. Moreover, what about returning Guantánamo to the Cuban people? Not a word was mentioned, even though the U.S. naval base is part of Cuba. Just before playing the Guantánamo card, Obama said: "That's American strength. That's American leadership. And that kind of leadership depends on the power of our example." The example offered immediately afterwards is the one of shutting down the Guantánamo prison. However, the example is not exactly persuasive since it is still open, notwithstanding his legal right to close it on his own.

Despite the statements with regard to Cuba, he never acknowledged the following problem faced by his administration. The Cuban government is acutely aware that the U.S. has only changed its tactics while maintaining its long-term strategic goal to subvert the Cuban Revolution, and they are valiantly opposing U.S. interference in Cuban affairs. President Raúl Castro and the Cuban Ministry of Foreign Affairs publicly cautioned the U.S. that it will never sell out on its principles and will always steadfastly defend its sovereignty and dignity. The Cubans are striving to make as much headway as possible in the context of the change in U.S. tactics for the good of the Cuban and American peoples.

That is all Obama said — and did not say — in the State of the Union address about Cuba. However, what he said about other foreign relations affects not only Cuba but also the rest of the world. For example, he took dead aim at China and Russia, which form an important part of the foundation of a new multi-polar world in a growing alliance with Latin America and the Caribbean regional blocs: "When it comes to every important international issue, people of the world do not look to Beijing or Moscow to lead — they call us. (Applause)." During the course of his speech and buoyed by the traditional applause, Obama went on to perhaps unintentionally reveal the ferocious competition that U.S. world hegemony faces from China and Russia. For example, he took jabs at Russia for what the U.S. sees as an unjust policy toward Crimea. With regard to China, he indicated how China was supposedly outmanoeuvred by the U.S. through the Trans-Pacific Partnership (TPP) trade agreement. The TPP is a trade agreement among twelve Pacific Rim countries concerning a variety of matters of economic policy that was reached on October 5, 2015, after seven years of negotiations. The members include Chile, Mexico and Peru. It is being rammed through Congress with the representatives barely knowing what it is all about. Obama said: "With TPP, China does not set the rules in that region; we do. You want to show our strength in this new century? Approve this agreement. Give us the tools to enforce it. It's the right thing to do. (Applause)."

Cuba depends on itself for its own sovereignty and independence. Even when it allied itself with the former Soviet Union, Cuba kept its distance and never became a satellite. Nevertheless, a growing multi-polar world favours Cuba. In this situation, the island can more effectively develop economic and political relations, as is the case now, with such countries as China and

Russia, which have freed themselves from U.S. domination. The striving of the U.S. for world domination cannot be underestimated. Any success in this direction will also affect Cuba.

Not only is the concept and policy of U.S. imperialism still applicable but, more than ever, it is necessary to remain vigilant, as it camouflages itself in order to carry out the same policies. Its chameleon nature is all the more dangerous as its goes through its Obama phase. World domination has not ceased to be the objective of U.S. imperialism. World supremacy is its very nature. Latin America and the Caribbean, including Cuba, is one of its targets in achieving this goal.

THE WHITE HOUSE NATIONAL SECURITY AGENDA FOR OBAMA'S VISIT TO CUBA[7]

Ben Rhodes, Assistant to Obama and Deputy National Security Advisor, provides crucial input into the new tactical road map for Cuba–U.S. relations. Rhodes, who is also officially the speechwriter for Obama, is to be commended, along with the president himself, for the new Cuba policy, including the decision concerning the president's visit to Cuba.

One of the most important documents serving as the basis of this visit is the February 18, 2016, transcript of a press briefing (Obama 2016g) by Rhodes and White House Press Secretary Josh Earnest. Unfortunately, it has not been widely disseminated. During the course of the briefing, Rhodes had to answer questions from journalists, which forced him to elaborate on the plan for the president's visit.

The briefing indicates that the U.S. is on the offensive with regard to Latin America and the Caribbean. However, Rhodes had to candidly admit and partially recognize that Cuba has its principled stand. Actually, it is more than that. The Cuban government, far from letting its guard down, is also on the offensive regarding Cuba–U.S. relations. Although many issues were raised during the briefing, I deal with only a few here.

Dissidents

After a summary of the visit to Cuba with a short mention of a second leg of that trip to Argentina, Rhodes entertained questions from correspondents. The first question concerned dissidents:

> Q: Will the President meet with dissidents when he's in Cuba? And would you negotiate that with the Cuban government?
>
> Rhodes: Yes, he'll be meeting with dissidents, with members of civil

society, including those who certainly oppose the Cuban government's policies.

The issue came up again. Another reporter asked: "Who determines which dissidents the President will meet with?" Rhodes answered: "We determine … and we've certainly indicated to the Cubans." In another query on the same theme, which compared Cuba with other countries where the U.S. works with an established opposition, Rhodes had to admit that "you have a one-party system [in Cuba], and then you have elements of opposition but it's not analogous [to other countries]." Later on, in defending the Administration's decision to reopen the U.S. Embassy in Havana, he said that the "embassy allows us to better represent our interests, to better engage civil society."

Blockade

One of the correspondents mentioned the following: "The trade minister [Cuba's Minister of Foreign Trade and Investment Rodrigo Malmierca], earlier this week, prescribed things that he thinks the White House can do without the lifting of the embargo — allowing the dollar to be used in a third country, and permitting U.S. import of rum and cigars."

Only Congress can fully lift the blockade because it is codified into legislation; however, important aspects of the blockade can indeed be mitigated by White House executive orders. Regarding the journalist's question on the international use of the dollar, one also has to take into account the Cuban demand: the Cuban government wants to be able to use the dollar for international transactions not only in countries other than the U.S. but also in trade and commerce with the U.S. itself. The Cuban delegation headed by Malmierca visited Washington in mid-February 2016 for several days. Malmierca went much further than mildly "prescribing things." He strongly stressed the Cuban government's position in this meeting and went on the offensive against the blockade. The Cuban minister also stressed the need for the Obama Administration to use all the executive powers at its disposal to effectively gut it. Rather than responding to the examples provided by the questioning, such as allowing the dollar to be used, Rhodes said: "Our judgment is that the embargo should be lifted. Short of that, we want to look at what are the areas where we can open up space that can promote the greatest travel and commercial activity that ultimately benefits the Cuban people." In response to persistent questions about the blockade, Rhodes said: "This is a government that was very comfortable for over five decades with the embargo in place and with the United States as essentially the source of legitimacy that they drew upon because of what we were trying to do to Cuba."

How can the Cuban government be described as "comfortable" when in fact it has fought courageously against the blockade for five decades? However, Rhodes's last words indicate that his road map is still quite convoluted when it comes to the use of executive powers to render much of the blockade ineffective. The Cuban government is forced to be in assault mode with regard to this executive option comfortably in the hands of Obama. Will Obama's visit to Cuba make a decisive dent in the blockade?

Travel Ban

A journalist asked if the Obama Administration will use an "executive order to lift the travel ban to the extent that [he] can." Rhodes response was evasive: "What we've aimed to do is promote additional travel, commerce and economic activity in Cuba that, again, we believe benefits the Cuban people." In response to another question on the blockade and in that context lifting the travel ban, once again travel is circumscribed by Rhodes. He said that the Administration is continuing to allow travel only for "Americans who want to travel to Cuba to engage the Cuban people, or American businesses that want to engage in Cuba, but also, frankly, in helping ordinary Cubans."

Are Americans who want to visit Canada or the U.K. obligated to "engage" Canadians or the British? Or if they wish to travel to other countries in the Third World, are they restricted to "helping ordinary people" there? Why is there a double standard? The use of an executive order to lift the travel ban as much as possible is definitely a step that can be taken in the period leading up to the Obama visit.

Guantánamo Bay

In response to a query about Guantánamo Bay, Rhodes stated:

> I'm sure that will be part of the discussion. I know that because I've had that discussion many times with my Cuban counterparts. They are insisting, obviously, that our presence there is not legitimate and that the facility be returned to them. But again, that is not on the table as a part of our discussions. We're focused on the range of issues that I discussed. But I'm sure that they will raise it. It continues to be an issue of concern to them.

To say that the Cubans are "insisting" that it be returned is an understatement. The Cubans have been fighting tooth and nail on all international tribunes for the return of the territory to Cuba. This demand is a mark of national pride and dignity for the Cuban people, and it constitutes a major roadblock to normalizing Cuba–U.S. relations. With regard to U.S. Cuba policy, why is this thorny issue — one that can be solved by a stroke of the presidential pen — not "on the table"?

Wet-Foot, Dry-Foot Policy

On August 19, 1994, President Bill Clinton announced his "wet-foot, dry-foot" policy: Cubans who land on U.S. soil ("dry-foot") could remain in the U.S., even if they did not enter the country through the standard legal immigration channels. However, migrants who were intercepted by the U.S. Coast Guard at sea ("wet-foot") would be returned to Cuba. This policy applies only to Cubans, thus encouraging illegal emigration and a pool of people to be used as a political tool against the Cuban socio-economic/political system. The change of this Cuba policy is something that the Executive Branch can do in the same way that Clinton initiated it.

A question went right to the point. While in Cuba, is the "wet-foot, dry-foot policy … something that the President is going to address?" Rhodes's response was disappointing but clear: "We are not planning to institute change with respect to wet-foot, dry-foot.… Our focus is on how conditions can improve in Cuba so that over time there's more economic opportunity and less of a need, frankly, for Cubans to have to pursue opportunity elsewhere."[8]

The Argentine Leg of the Obama Visit

In the November 2014 Argentine presidential election, after more than a decade of left-wing governments, the right wing won the vote. During his electoral campaign, the new president, Mauricio Macri, promised to realign Argentina's foreign policy away from Venezuela and closer to the U.S.

Even though the subject of the Rhodes's press briefing was the Cuba trip, he also said in his opening remarks:

> Following the trip to Cuba, I'd just note the President will be traveling to Argentina. The Cuba opening also has to be seen as part of an effort by the United States to significantly increase our engagement in the hemisphere. This is a region that had long rejected our Cuba policy. Our Cuba policy had, in fact, isolated the United States

more than it had isolated Cuba in the hemisphere. Argentina is a country that, until recently, had a President who had, I'll say, problematic relations with the United States. The new President there has indicated his interest in beginning and restoring and renewing U.S.–Argentina relations.

Rhodes is frank about the new Cuba policy being linked to the U.S. prestige in Latin America. Even though the Argentine sojourn was relegated to a secondary position in the opening briefing, it did provoke two questions.

The first concerned "whether they [new Argentine government] can be an ally. And what kind of reception do you expect the President to get, especially considering the one that President Bush received when he went down there?" The Bush reception refers to the Fourth Summit of the Americas, which was held November 4–5, 2005, at Mar del Plata, about 400 kilometres (250 miles) southeast of Buenos Aires. This summit gathered the leaders of all the countries of the American continent, except Cuba. President George W. Bush's plan to push through the Free Trade Area of the Americas (FTAA) was a debacle. The charge against it was led by the host, President Néstor Kirchner of Argentina, President Hugo Chávez of Venezuela and President Lula da Silva of Brazil. The response by Rhodes to the query is perhaps indicative of where his road map is intended to lead:

> With respect to Argentina, we definitely anticipate that they'll be a closer partner on a range of issues.... He [new President Mauricio Macri has] signaled that he'd like to have closer economic and diplomatic cooperation with the United States. So we believe this is really a new beginning and a new era in our relationship with Argentina, and it mirrors the sentiment we see across the region, particularly since our Cuba opening, where there's much more receptivity to working with the United States.

According to Rhodes, the U.S. is, as planned, already reaping the fruit of the Cuba opening in Latin America.

In response to a question requesting further elaboration on the Argentine visit, Rhodes said that the goal of the Obama Administration is to "demonstrate that a cornerstone of the President's legacy is his approach to Latin America [that] involves the Cuba opening."

Cuba Sticks to Its Principles

By playing the Cuba card, the U.S. offensive in Latin America seeks to drive a wedge between Argentina and countries such as Cuba, Venezuela, Bolivia and Ecuador. The U.S. game plan is to force differences between Cuba and the other left-wing countries. However, the Cuban Revolutionary Government fully supports the revolutionary processes in these countries. Cuba is also one of the main stalwarts of regional integration through the Community of Latin American and Caribbean States (CELAC, for its Spanish initials). It includes all countries in the Americas except the U.S. and Canada.

The U.S. is using its Cuba policy to make progress along the path of diplomacy, such as with the Obama visit to Argentina. However, the U.S. is limiting its approach to this relatively peaceful road: it is simultaneously interfering in the internal affairs of Venezuela, Bolivia and Ecuador in order to bring about regime change.

WHY DOESN'T OBAMA USE HIS EXECUTIVE POWER TO CLOSE GUANTÁNAMO PRISON?[9]

The closing of Guantánamo prison and the return of Guantánamo Bay to Cuba is one of the most heated subjects of Cuba–U.S. relations. It is taking on even more significance as Obama's trip to Cuba on March 21–22 approaches.

On February 23, 2016, President Barack Obama announced, in a prepared statement to the press, that he is taking measures to close the notorious Guantánamo facility through Congress (Obama 2016f). However, he did not mention the possibility of using his executive power to do so, nor did he entertain questions from journalists, who perhaps may have raised this issue.

Thomas B. Wilner is one of the pre-eminent lawyers in the U.S. dealing with the Guantánamo issue. A timely interview with Wilner by Cuban journalist Rosa Miriam Elizalde was published on February 23, 2016, in *Cubadebate*. In response to her question as to whether Obama can use executive power to finally shut down the prison even if Congress opposes the plan, Wilner said: "I am not absolutely clear if he will do this. I think he has the power, as President, to close the Guantánamo prison and transfer detainees to the U.S., even if Congress opposes. I think he has this power."

Gregory B. Craig is a prestigious lawyer who served as White House counsel to Obama in 2009. Cliff Sloan was the special envoy for Guantánamo closure in 2013 and 2014. In a co-authored article published on November 6, 2015, in the *Washington Post,* they wrote:

Some maintain that the congressional ban on transfers from Guantánamo to the United States prevents closure without congressional approval. But that is wrong. Under Article II of the Constitution [National Constitution Center n.d.], the president has exclusive authority to determine the facilities in which military detainees are held. Obama has the authority to move forward. He should use it.... The question is whether Congress can tell the president where military detainees must be held. The answer is an emphatic no. One need not accept a particularly broad view of executive authority — let alone the Bush administration's sweeping view that the president has "exclusive and virtually unfettered control over the disposition of enemy soldiers and agents captured in time of war" (an extravagant assertion with which we disagree) — to see that the restrictions Congress has imposed are unconstitutional.

There are different views at this time as to why Obama does not use his power to close Gitmo. One possible consideration relates to domestic politics. Let us put aside for the moment the notion of Obama's legacy as seen negatively by others. Perhaps not enough emphasis is placed on the importance to Obama of a Democratic Party victory in the November 2016 presidential election. This is an absolute condition in assuring the credibility of a positive endowment as a Republican victory would call into question his legacy. If his policies and actions do not result in his party electing the next president, then what value would his heritage hold in the broader political spectrum of U.S. politics?

For example, George W. Bush's Republican Party lost the presidential elections in 2008. As a result, even though the potential of a positive legacy was far inferior to Obama's, any chance for that was eliminated. George W. Bush was left with his brother, candidate Jeb Bush, repeating in the last phase of his 2016 presidential campaign that "George W. Bush has 'been a great president' and that his father, George H. W. Bush, 'is the greatest man alive'" (Weiss n.d.). Shortly after that, Jeb Bush had to abandon the campaign because of a complete lack of support among the Republicans.

The Republican-controlled Congress strongly opposes the closing of the Guantánamo prison, even though some Republicans are in favour. By refusing to use his power to close Gitmo and relying instead entirely on the GOP majority in the Congress, Obama can blame Congress for blocking it. This would, according to logic, place the eventual Democratic presidential candidate in a positive light while reflecting poorly on the Republican candidate.

The second possible angle regarding his refusal to close Guantánamo prison relates to the trip to Cuba, followed by his visit to Argentina. Obama has stated on many occasions, from 2014 to present, that his Cuba policy is designed to improve relations with Latin America. Immediately following the Cuba visit, the Argentine leg of his March 2016 trip to Latin America is a key element in this plan. This was confirmed by Ben Rhodes, as indicated in the previous section.

One cannot underestimate the damage Guantánamo has done to U.S. credibility on human rights, especially in Latin America, a politically conscious region. Many countries there have suffered under U.S.-imposed military dictators' use of torture and assassinations to remain in power. One of these countries is Argentina. Perhaps the White House has to consider this. Already the Plaza de Mayo grandmothers — family victims of these atrocities — are planning a demonstration against the Obama visit. The prestige of this Plaza de Mayo movement is so high that President Macri had to meet with the organizers on February 23, 2016, to deal with their complaints about his dictatorial methods.

These types of activities in Buenos Aires can have repercussions in other countries of Latin America, whose people also have a very negative opinion about U.S. respect for human rights. Obama's visit to Argentina with the dead weight of Guantánamo on his shoulders will definitely not help his standing as far as Argentines are concerned, even though the newly elected right-wing Argentine President Macri does not have any issues regarding Guantánamo. Perhaps Obama believes he can arrive in Argentina with his head high, carrying the February 23, 2016, statement as a badge: his attempt to close Guantánamo prison despite Congressional opposition.

OBAMA'S VISIT TO CUBA AND HUMAN RIGHTS[10]

The issue of human rights in the context of Cuba–U.S. relations erupted once again on the eve of Obama's visit to the island. In Geneva on March 2, the U.S. deputy secretary of state, Antony J. Blinken, issued the National Statement at the Human Rights Council. He dealt with several countries that are the usual targets of U.S. accusations of supposed human rights violations, such as China, Russia and Venezuela. As is always the case, Cuba was also singled out:

> In Cuba, we are increasingly concerned about the government's use of short-term detentions of peaceful activists, which reached record numbers in January. We call on the Cuban government to stop this tactic as a means of quelling peaceful protest. President

Obama will make a historic visit to Cuba in a few weeks and will emphasize that the Cuban people are best served by an environment where people are free to choose their political parties and their leaders, express their ideas, and where civil society is independent and allowed to flourish.

The head of the Cuban delegation to the Council, Pedro Núñez Mosquera, who is general director of the Division on Multilateral Affairs and International Law at the Ministry of Foreign Affairs of Cuba, was not at all intimidated by the superpower. Since 1959, Cuba has had a history of defending its interests in all international forums. Cuba is a small country, but it has a voice that is respected internationally. In Geneva, Núñez Mosquera turned the tables on the U.S. by calling it out for the gross violations of human rights that the U.S. itself is responsible for, including racial discrimination, police violence, persecution of immigrants and torture that takes place in the Guantánamo prison. In addition, he insisted, the U.S. is responsible for violations of the human rights of the Cuban people because of the blockade against the island (Redacción Internacional 2016).

Blinken's statement on behalf of the Obama Administration is notable for being yet another gross attempt at interfering in the internal affairs of Cuba. However, let us leave this aside for the moment and deal with his accusations against Cuba. Blinken charges Cuba with temporarily arresting peaceful activists as part of a strategy of "quelling peaceful protest." The term "peaceful" is arbitrary. In the U.S., for example, when African-Americans and their allies in the U.S. revolt against police assassinations of African-Americans, they are called violent and referred to as thugs. However, in January and February 2016, when armed right-wing individuals in Oregon occupied a federal agency, the government and media politely labelled the occupiers "protesters" and "militia," a term that provided legitimacy to these armed people. They were never categorized in any derogatory way as being violent.

Turning south to Latin America, the same double standard applies. In the National Statement, the U.S. State Department demands the release of two imprisoned pro-American individuals in Venezuela. It respectfully refers to them as "opposition leaders." However, they were responsible for violent terrorist acts against the constitutional order in which forty-three people were killed and over 800 were injured. The U.S., therefore, is far from being a reference point in dealing with peaceful or violent protests.

In the Cuban context, the individuals to which the U.S. refers cannot be seen as merely peaceful protesters. Mainly, they are directly or indirectly paid mercenaries of the U.S. Their publicly stated goal is regime change in

Cuba. The very essence of the objective is to smother the Cuban Revolution as the basis of Cuban sovereignty. This means turning Cuba once again into a de facto neo-colony of the U.S., making it safe for capitalism. Cuban independence, in turn, is the safeguard of the Cuban Revolution, whose mission is to continuously strive to develop and improve its socialism.

Thus, the reactionary change that the "peaceful protesters" seek is a rupture from the Cuban constitutional order to satisfy U.S. interests. By its very nature, this goal is violent, as it translates into a fork in the road that the overwhelming majority of Cuba people have taken since 1959. Whether, at the time of their detention, these individuals were or were not violent is irrelevant. Cuba has every right to defend itself from the coordinated efforts of the U.S.-funded "opposition" and mainstream media to foment regime change in Cuba.

Choosing Political Parties and Leaders

The Blinken Statement also highlights one of the goals of Obama's visit to Cuba: to emphasize "that people [should be] free to choose their political parties and their leaders." The U.S. is blinded by the U.S.-centric notion of political parties and elections. The U.S. has its "multi-party" political system and the Cubans have an altogether different system.

The Cuban political process resulted from the Revolution. An essential feature of this Revolution stems from the tradition emerging out of the second half of the nineteenth-century revolutionary Wars of Independence against the Spanish colonizers. An essential ingredient was — and is — the need for one unifying political force to lead the Revolution.

The Communist Party of Cuba was born out of the combined political forces that were sacrificing their lives to defeat the bloody, U.S.-backed Batista dictatorship in the 1950s. The Cubans chose their leading political force and indeed their leaders during the 1950s until the Triumph of the Revolution in 1959. Furthermore, in that period and since, millions of Cubans have chosen to be part of that Revolution, rather than to stand on the sidelines "choosing leaders" according to some U.S. notion of democracy. The role of this unifying political force is entrenched in the Cuban Constitution, which people at the grassroots contributed to drafting. In 1976, in a referendum on the Constitution, 98 percent of the electorate voted and, of those voters, 97.7 percent approved the Constitution.

The Cuban political system also affords other formal legal channels so that Cubans can vote for their leaders. Once again, it does not conform to the U.S.-centric notion. Cuba is not based on the presidential system as it exists in the U.S. and other countries.

Let us take the example of Raúl Castro based on a quick summary of some of the steps leading to his election as president of the Councils of State and Ministers. In the last general elections in 2013, he was elected as deputy to the Cuban National Assembly of People's Power (Parliament) from a municipality in his home province of Santiago de Cuba. While there is only one candidate per seat, a candidate needs at least 50 percent of the popular vote. In the 2013 general elections, Raúl Castro garnered 98.04 percent of the vote. This was one of the highest among the 612 deputies who were elected.

Once the elections are over, in order to elect leaders, the deputies have their input on an individual basis and in private. Resulting from this consultation, a list of candidates to the Council of State, including the president of this body, is drawn up. The newly elected legislature meets, as it did, for example, on February 24, 2013. It chooses among the deputies in a secret ballot vote. It is beyond the scope of this article to cover more of the details and analysis of how this and the general elections occur. However, this is how Raúl Castro was elected as president of the Council of State (and therefore also of the Council of Ministers). This role is carried out as a function of being a member of these collegial and collective Councils. These bodies are in turn accountable to Parliament.

Furthermore, being a country that has forged itself in Revolution, Cuba has its own standards on leaders. Let us take another example. Fidel Castro is known as the leader of the Cuban Revolution. In the Preamble to the Constitution approved by the population, the Magna Carta recognizes the "leadership of Fidel Castro." Whether it is in the Constitution or not, the fact is that he is the leader of the Cuban Revolution and is recognized as such by the overwhelming majority of Cuban people. These facts regarding Cuba's leaders do not seem to be of interest to the U.S. ruling circles.

"Presidential Systems" of Venezuela, Bolivia and Ecuador

Washington's ideological/political pressure for people choosing their leaders is arbitrary. For example, from a superficial standpoint, one can say that Venezuela, Bolivia and Ecuador all have "presidential systems." Nevertheless, the U.S. does not really recognize as presidents directly elected leaders Nicolás Maduro, Evo Morales and Rafael Correa. Rather, the U.S. is continuously attempting regime change in Venezuela, Bolivia and Ecuador to overthrow these elected leaders and everything they stand for. Thus, with regard to leaders, the U.S. has an erratic stand that is manipulated to serve its own purposes.

Cuban "Civil Society"

In Geneva, the U.S. also rolled out its requirement for Cuba that "civil society needs to be independent." The U.S., according to its own formula and in the context of Obama's upcoming visit to Cuba, recognizes the "members of civil society, including those who certainly oppose the Cuban government's policies" (August 2016g). One could ask the U.S., if it succeeds in further winning over those individuals to U.S. policy, which is a foregone conclusion, whether it is not a fact that they will no longer be independent. On the contrary, they will be even more dependent on the U.S. than they were before Obama's visit. According to the U.S., if Cuban civil society works in harmony with the Cuban political process, then it is not independent. However, if it acts in accordance with the U.S., it receives bona fide credentials as being independent.

Improving the Cuban Political System

Despite the themes considered above, there remains room for improvement within the Cuban political system. However, the Cubans who debate this issue do not need advice from the U.S. It is up to Cubans to bring about change. For example, on August 14, 2015, during the joint press conference in Havana given by Secretary of State John Kerry and Cuban Minister of Foreign Affairs of Cuba Bruno Rodríguez Parrilla, a reporter asked Bruno Rodríguez a question about democracy in Cuba. He responded: "I feel very comfortable with Cuban democracy, and at the same time there are things that could be further perfected, as we are actively working on today with the processes related to the updating of our socialist economic and social model" (*Granma International News* 2015).

The necessity to ideologically and politically revamp the political system is part of their life-and-death struggle to bring about transformation in Cuba's socio-economic system despite the crippling U.S. blockade and other factors that are domestic in nature. This is, and will be, Cuba's own path.

OBAMA IN CUBA: WILL THE VISIT ADVANCE
THE U.S. CULTURAL WAR AGAINST CUBANS?[11]

With only several days until Obama's arrival in Cuba, the new Cuba–U.S. relationship is entering into a crucial and difficult stage. Historian Dr. Elier Ramírez, one of Cuba's most outstanding experts on the attempts toward "normalization" between the two countries, wrote an astute observation in reference to a remark Obama made on December 19, 2014 (two days after the announcement by both governments to re-establish diplomatic relations on December 17, 2014, or 17D). In the context of the U.S.'s desire to bring about change in Cuba, the president said, "How societies change is country-specific, it's culturally specific" (Obama 2014a). Ramírez Cañedo (2016) deduced:

> In the face of this open declaration of cultural war, understanding culture in its broadest sense, beyond the artistic and literary meaning, it would be naive to think that history will not be — indeed it already is — one of the fundamental targets of those who seek to undermine from within the socialist culture in Cuba.... But if some in Cuba or outside, especially in the revolutionary ranks, make the mistake of forgetting or neglecting the importance of study and deep knowledge of the past in the present circumstances, it would play into the hands of those who now with new clothes persist in their goals of destroying the Cuban Revolution at its very roots.

The Massive U.S. Media and Political War

There are several aspects to this cultural war that is presently being waged against Cuban socialist culture.[12] One of these themes is the massive U.S. media hostility and political disinformation campaign on the issue of civil rights in Cuba as part of human rights. The Obama narrative is that indirectly or directly — and grudgingly — it acknowledges Cuba's accomplishments in the realm of social rights, as a subset of human rights, with regard to health services, education, culture and sports. However, it accuses Cuba of violating individual civil rights and political rights. The U.S. discourse highlights, for example, the often-cited U.S.-centric double standard of the "right to free speech, free press and protest." According to this anecdotal explanation, Cuba is not a democracy, since it violates civil/political rights and, by extension, human rights.

However, civil rights, such as political rights, comprise an important part of the very foundation that safeguards and promotes the full spectrum of human rights. The most significant civil right afforded to Cubans — and demanded by Cubans — is to participate in their own political system. This tradition, while not perfect and always evolving, stems back to the collective mass revolutionary struggle leading to the victory of the Cuban Revolution and thus to the people's political power in January 1959. We cannot forget this history.

Civil Rights

This legacy has continued through many forms while seeking to improve participatory democracy. If Cubans had not had — and did not now have — the capacity to exercise their own political power, how could other human rights have been won and guaranteed? For example, if Cubans had not exercised their individual political rights in the 1950s to win political power, how would the securing of social rights — such as the right to health, education, culture and sports — have been accomplished in the first place?

Since 1959, the Cuban Revolutionary Government has strived to involve the participation of the people to improve these social rights. The citizens, for their part, endeavour to strengthen their own real political power to safeguard and upgrade their socio-economic and cultural human rights. There is ample space within the Cuban socialist culture for this debate and action to flourish in order to move Cuban socialism from one stage to the next. However, this democracy in motion is ignored by the U.S. ruling circles.

Obama and most of the U.S. mainstream media recognize only those civil political rights as a component part of human rights defined and demanded by what they call Cuba's "civil society." This very marginal "opposition" is ideologically and/or financially dependent on the U.S., which has created it in the first place. Their goal is to act as a U.S. Trojan horse to destroy the Cuban Revolution from within.

Of course, this fringe is hardly sufficient to undermine the Cuban Revolution. Thus, in order to reinforce the Trojan horse, the U.S. also targets the more than 500,000 self-employed workers. This growing section of Cuban society is wrongly perceived by Cuba's neighbours to the north as natural fifth-column recruits for the U.S. "way of life and values" (capitalism and dependence on the U.S.) to undermine Cuban socialist culture. The U.S. may underestimate the patriotism of the vast majority of Cubans, including the growing number of self-employed, as though they are detached from Cuban society and its socialist culture, which is not the case.

Challenges on the Horizon

There are several elements complicating the current situation in Cuba since the "thaw" that was initiated by both countries on December 17, 2014. Within Cuba itself, Ramírez Cañedo is rightly concerned about some "in the revolutionary ranks" who fall victim to this U.S.-fuelled cultural war. In my view, this would come about by forgetting Cuba's past regarding civil/political and social human rights, among other hurdles. Thus, individuals would fall into the trap of referring to the false dichotomy between civil/political rights and other human rights, such as health, education, culture and sports.

Outside of Cuba, the situation has also become more complex. Before December 17, 2014, many commentators had been strongly opposed to the U.S. policy on Cuba. It was a just position against the official American antagonistic stance toward Cuba, the most important of which were the blockade and the refusal to re-establish diplomatic relations with Cuba.

However, since 17D, the situation has changed. The new Obama policy consists of the re-establishment of diplomatic relations with Cuba and the opening of embassies in both countries, as well as limited measures to reduce the effects of the blockade. In many cases these measures are highly exaggerated as to their positive effects on Cuba. Thus, a myth has been created by Obama that normalization is within reach or even that it is presently being attained.

In this context, a trend has been developing in North America, Europe and Cuba itself that no longer sees the new U.S. policy initiated by Obama as being hostile to Cuba. It has shifted its focus from contesting U.S. aggressive policy and the blockade to blending into the Obama policy. This mindset now sees its role as promoters of the idealized U.S. policy while of course "keeping a check" on the U.S., which they consider, nevertheless, to be on the right track. This position facilitates facilitates Obama's policy on Cuba but overlooks the fact that the U.S. has only changed tactics. Those who adopt this mindset have morphed into apologists for the new policy, which serves to achieve its strategic goal of undermining —from within — the Cuban Revolution.

One of the political/ideological foundations of this new vocation is to say, in effect, "We concede that Cuba has made many achievements on social rights, such as health and education as part of human rights, but civil and political rights are being violated in Cuba." Political civil rights are thus set in contrast to socio-economic and cultural rights. Alternatively, some may remain silent on Cuba's revolutionary style of political civil rights, thus, wittingly or not, also assist the U.S. in its cultural war against Cuba.

For its part, the Cuban official newspaper *Granma* correctly wrote, in a decisive and cutting editorial on March 8, 2016, that "Cuba defends the indivisibility, interdependence and universality of civil, political, economic, social and cultural human rights." The question is, will Obama's visit to Cuba provide Cubans the opportunity to make headway against the cultural war, or will it allow the U.S. to make inroads? Or are both these scenarios on the horizon?

OBAMA IN CUBA: HOW "POLITICAL PRISONERS" MADE THE MEDIA HEADLINES[13]

During President Obama's visit to Cuba, the issue of Cuban "political prisoners" took centre stage in Cuba–U.S. relations for at least twenty-four hours in much of the international mainstream media. I was in Havana at the time, commenting on the visit for TeleSUR television. Foreign television outlets were temporarily set up for the occasion at the emblematic Lonja del Comercio (the fully renovated former Stock Exchange from pre-revolutionary Cuba) overlooking Old Havana. A cacophony of sound bites about political prisoners emanated from the reporters on the sets. It seemed that "Obama in Cuba" had become equated with "political prisoners." The only exception appeared to be TeleSUR, based in Caracas, Venezuela.

How did this come about? In reference to the discussions with the Cuban government in the joint press conference that brought together Presidents Raúl Castro and Barack Obama on March 21, Obama stated: "As we do wherever we go around the world, I made it clear that the United States will continue to speak up on behalf of democracy, including the right of the Cuban people to decide their own future. We'll speak out on behalf of universal human rights, including freedom of speech, and assembly, and religion" (Obama 2016d). The tone of the U.S. president's remarks, couched in a diplomatic speech, was not overtly hostile and did not contain accusations as such against the Cuban government. There was no mention of political prisoners. One can say, as indeed Obama himself stated, that this is the basic narrative of the U.S. when dealing with some countries. However, the haughty White House lectures to Cuba on democracy and human rights, as many Cuban colleagues justifiably consider them to be, are based on the exclusive U.S. notions of democracy and human rights. They are often directed to Third World countries on an arbitrary basis with varying emphasis and priority depending on the affinity of these countries to U.S. foreign policy.

After the presentations by the two heads of state, the floor was opened to questions from the large number of international and Cuban journalists. Obama immediately recognized the source of the first query: Jim Acosta, the Senior White House Correspondent for CNN. As Acosta indicated in his introduction to his question directed to Raúl Castro, he is a Cuban-American whose parents left Cuba. Such a prelude may serve as credentials, in the eyes of a reporter, to ask any question. This would allow for the ensuing interrogation to be carried out despite the reporter's virtually non-existent knowledge about Cuba, which was also circumscribed by his deeply ingrained preconceived U.S. views of Cuba. Acosta addressed his first question to Barack

Obama, and then asked Raúl Castro: "And, President Castro, my father is Cuban. He left for the United States when he was young. Do you see a new and democratic direction for your country? And why [do] you have Cuban political prisoners? And why don't you release them?"

President Castro's response was as follows:

> Give me the list of political prisoners and I will release them imme-
> diately. Just mention a list. What political prisoners? Give me a
> name or names. After this meeting is over, you can give me a list
> of political prisoners. And if we have those political prisoners, they
> will be released before tonight ends.

This question and response then immediately travelled around the globe as headline "news" that centred mainly on the U.S. as the protagonist in Cuba.

Obama did not have to mention political prisoners. It would have been considered by both the White House and the Cuban government a breach of protocol and diplomatic behind-closed-doors negotiations and exchanges — which is a positive feature of the new Cuba–U.S. relations. Conveniently for the president, the CNN Senior White House Correspondent raised the question for him instead. Obama's body language and the look on his face seemed to indicate that he was pleased with the question. Does this mean that the White House and Acosta were in collusion? Obama and Acosta know each other well. The CNN correspondent's role brings him regularly not only to the White House but sometimes he accompanies the president to other countries. Based on this intimate relationship, there is no need for them to carry out any collaborative agreement.

Noam Chomsky analyzed this dynamic many years ago in his ground-breaking book *Manufacturing Consent*, based mainly on the study of the U.S. media. He pointed out that mainstream monopoly media are guided by "the selection of right-thinking personnel and by the editors' and working journalists' internalization of priorities and definitions of news-worthiness that conform to the institution's policy" (Chomsky and Herman 2002). These journalists know exactly what to ask in press conferences, what to write and what to broadcast in order to not only maintain their jobs as correspondents but also to climb the ladder toward ever more lucrative and prestigious positions. For example, had Acosta ever asked the U.S. president — in the multitude of news conferences at the White House touching on a wide variety of issues — about the hundreds of political prisoners in the U.S., would the journalist even have been chosen to travel to Havana with the president? If Acosta had possessed the gumption to question human rights as practised in the U.S., he would not even have been "selected" — in Chomsky's words — in the first place.

In my article "Cuba–U.S. Relations and Freedom of the Press" (August 2015c; reprinted above), I wrote about Secretary of State John Kerry's visit to Havana on August 14, 2015, to officially hoist the U.S. flag at the reopened U.S. Embassy. One of CNN's most prestigious anchors, Jake Tapper, was sent to Cuba to cover the event. The article exposes how almost all the television reports consisted of little more than a litany of buzzwords about Cuba being a "dictatorship" and the "Castro brothers' tyranny." This treatment of the event was, of course, amplified and repeated by other anchors in the U.S.-based CNN headquarters.

To be fair, not all CNN reporters deal with Cuba with such flagrant media disinformation that borders on hysteria. Chris Cuomo, a high-ranking CNN anchor, for example, is the brother of the current governor of New York, Andrew Cuomo. Governor Cuomo recently visited Cuba as the head of a high-ranking political and business delegation. He thus has respectful relations with the Cuban government. When CNN's Chris Cuomo covered Pope Francis's visit to Cuba in February 2016, there was no evidence of the rants by his CNN colleagues against the Cuba government and "the Castros." Cuomo was also part of the large delegation of CNN reporters covering the Obama visit. We can perhaps examine his reporting on another occasion. However, suffice it to state here that he wore a traditional Cuban *guayabera* shirt, given to his father, Mario Cuomo (governor of New York from 1983 to 1994) by Fidel Castro (Balan 2016).

In contrast, what can we conclude about Acosta's role in Havana in March 2016 and other similar situations that unfortunately seem to be a main feature of CNN? Primarily, the relationship between CNN and the White House can be thought of this way: CNN does not have a senior correspondent in the White House but, rather, the White House has a trusted correspondent at CNN. This is a very strange predicament for a country that lectures others about the need for "independent press and journalists."

With regard to political prisoners, there is no evidence to date to indicate that any journalist has taken up Raúl Castro's challenge to furnish facts to back up Acosta's accusations. Given that the media war being waged by the U.S. against the Cuban people is an ongoing news story, we can expect there will be more to say on the matter.[14]

THOUGHTS ON CUBAN RESISTANCE TO THE U.S. IDEOLOGICAL/POLITICAL WAR[15]

Before leaving Montreal for Havana in March 2016 to cover the Obama trip, I wrote an article on Cuba–U.S. relations titled "Obama in Cuba: Will the Visit Advance the U.S. Cultural War Against Cubans?" (August 2016c; and reprinted above). Referring to the cultural war as one that is ideologically and politically aggressive, I pondered whether the Cuban resistance to Obama's visit would make headway against the cultural war, or if it would allow the U.S. to make inroads, or possibly both. One feature became clear during my stay in Havana and immediately following it: the repercussions of the visit not only continued but were being ramped up, both within and outside of Cuba. In fact, at the time of writing, a month after the trip, the ideological and political controversies persist.[16] This situation was further being fostered by Raúl Castro's April 16, 2016, Central Report to the Seventh Congress of the Partido Comunista de Cuba (Communist Party of Cuba — PCC). He devoted important sections of the report to the issue of Cuba–U.S. relations (Castro Ruz [Raúl] 2016).

Disinformation from *Within* Cuba

The Obama visit and its accompanying international media entourage was meant for the U.S., Canada and much of the West. It was characterized to a large extent by pointing, explicitly or implicitly, to what the U.S. president calls the lack of democracy in Cuba. Consequently, the argument follows, there is a lack of respect for human rights, of which civil/political rights take centre stage. This is nothing new, except for one game-changing feature. For the first time since the 1959 Revolution, the U.S. has had the opportunity to carry out this disinformation not from *outside* Cuba but rather from *within*.

For people outside of Cuba, especially in the U.S. and Canada, there is no need to detail this misinformation, as it was everywhere (except for a few exceptions) on TV, on the Internet and in print media. However, there is another feature of this ideological/political aggression that is perhaps not noticeable to many, even though it plays a significant role in encouraging the negative features of the U.S. Cuba policy. In the article mentioned above, I analyzed a trend whereby an anti-blockade stance morphed into an Obama apologist stance once the latter renewed diplomatic relations with Cuba. This about-face largely occurred *without* taking into account its many dangers for Cuba.

During the visit to Havana, I was hoping that this position would be weakened as a result of what was — to me and to many of my Cuban colleagues and people on the street — Obama's overtly arrogant attitude of preaching to Cubans about democracy and human rights. Much to my surprise, the opposite took place. The U.S.-centric view on democracy and human rights became *emboldened* among some commentators and even further morphed into U.S.-centrism.

The Problem of U.S.-Centrism

U.S.-centrism (with regard to democracy and other issues) is firmly entrenched in the mindset of many, including intellectuals. This situation caught the attention of internationally respected thinker Samir Amin, who wrote what has become a classic, *Eurocentrism* (published in French in 1988 and in English in 2009). Amin perceptively highlights Eurocentrism, since its emergence in Europe to the now dominant U.S., as a major obstacle in appreciating other political/economic systems that do not coincide with the Western/U.S. approach. The ideological/political barrier erected over many centuries by Eurocentrism and its offspring, U.S.-centrism, is complex and ingrained. It operates, as Samir Amin warns, "without anyone noticing it. This is why many specialists, historians and intellectuals can reject particular expressions of the Eurocentric construct without being embarrassed by the incoherence of the overall vision that results" (cited in August 2013: 7–8).

For example, while some writers outside of Cuba distance themselves from a few of the more grotesque features of Eurocentrism and U.S.-centrism — such as its shallow claims to be the defenders of a superior political and economic model for the world — they may still fall prey to its main ideological/political underpinnings. It is not a question of individuals but rather of the ideological/political position that objectively exists in societies. The only manner to advance a serious resistance to a parochial view on the Cuban political/economic/social system is to take into account two factors.

The first factor is that Cuba has its *own* system, whose tradition dates from the mid-nineteenth century. It is up to the Cubans to improve it, just as they are now striving to do. The second factor, irrespective of one's opinion of the U.S. socio-economic/political system, is that it is *theirs*. Their system has developed out of its own historical conditions and thus has nothing to do with the Cuban path.

The dangers on the horizon result from U.S. aggression based on its centuries-old desire for world domination. It is up to the American people to take up the pursuit of fundamental change, not only for their own good but for the very future of the world. This is bound to take place, as the American people — especially African-Americans, youth and intellectuals, in whom I have full confidence — are waking up.

Outside of Cuba, the highly charged political atmosphere surrounding the Obama trip sparked widespread and heightened political consciousness. Many progressive people and those on the left are sharpening their anti-imperialist consciousness. They are creatively dissecting the Obama incursion into Cuba with sharp political knives while fully supporting the visit and the Cuban Revolution. This is extremely encouraging.

Cubans on the Counteroffensive

What is also inspiring is the number of Cubans who confronted the U.S. ideological/political war during Obama's visit and who continue to do so. This was expected, as this courageous resistance was initiated following the statements by Obama and Raúl Castro on December 17, 2014, on the re-establishment of diplomatic relations and the opening of embassies.

On that occasion, Obama confirmed once again that the U.S. is dispensing with openly *antagonistic tactics*, which did not work, in favour of diplomatic tactics, which he hopes will function to finally attain the goal, of more than five decades, of snuffing out the Cuban Revolution and undermining the island's sovereignty. As a byproduct of this rapprochement, the White House, through this new incursion, hopes to elevate itself to a better position to influence events in Latin America — read "regime change" — by conventional or "soft power" warfare.

The counteroffensive to this in Cuba is not that well known to many foreigners, who may be interested but do not read Spanish. This consistent and long-lasting ideological/political struggle is found especially in blogs and websites. Among the dozens of examples are the blogs of many well-known revolutionary Cuban writers and academics such as Iroel Sánchez, Elier Ramírez and Esteban Morales. These blogs comprise a full compendium of critical articles on Cuba–U.S. relations that have accumulated since December 17, 2014.

Another of these "word warriors" is Luis Toledo Sande, whose blog, while not fully devoted to Cuba–U.S. relations since December 17, 2014, has the merit of dealing with controversial issues in the realm of culture. One example is the appearance of American flags in public places in Havana over the last few years and as clothing apparel in a carnival-type fashion. In my article "Cuba–U.S. Relations and the Perspicacity of Fidel Castro's Thinking" (reprinted above), Toledo Sande's analysis of this manifestation of cultural incursion allowed me to expose the complexities of the current situation on the island in the face of the new U.S. policy. Jesús Arboleya is another such writer and academic. His articles on the Cuba–U.S. theme are reprinted in the above-mentioned blogs as well as on the influential website of the Union of Cuban Journalists (UPEC), *Cuba Periodistas* and on the popular website *Cubadebate.*

Cubadebate, for its part, has been carrying critical articles on the new chapter on Cuba–U.S. relations and — in keeping with its name — provoking *debate* among its readers. Typically, hundreds of comments from the public may be published in reaction to a single article. Since December 17, 2014, *Cubadebate* has featured a section fully devoted to the new Cuba–U.S. relations, which has been updated almost daily while dealing with other national and international themes. The same applies to Iroel Sánchez's *La pupila insomne,* a hotbed for controversial articles. *Cuba Periodistas* provides a feed of this content to its provincial online websites.

Confronting the U.S.-Centric Barrier

Aside from a few exceptions, what the previously mentioned writers all have in common is publishing articles that are clearly in opposition to U.S.-centric views on democracy and human rights, even though not all of the pieces deal with this directly. What is important, in my opinion, is the ideological outlook as the base from which views on specific political issues flow. I would venture to say that the intellectuals mentioned above and many others are immune to any U.S. influence on their thinking, action or outlook. There is no way that these writers and the revolutionaries at the grassroots can be affected by this cancer, a disease that would eat away at the Cuban political culture from within if it were allowed to flourish.

These intellectuals and many others who are lesser known, even in Cuba, are at the base of this resistance, and they are far from being alone. As the commentators themselves on the blogs often divulge, the comments from the public that are published in response to posts or articles reflect what is being discussed, as they say, "on the street."

Furthermore, Fidel Castro's article "Brother Obama," released on March 29, 2016, provides sustenance and encouragement to all those fighting in the same trench against U.S. unilateral views on democracy, human rights and its own selective and opportunist view of history. This piece instantly became notorious in the international sphere and, of course, in Cuba. It is thus analyzed in this book based on different evaluations from the five interviewees in Chapter 3. The same effect can now be seen as a result of Raúl Castro's April 16, 2016, Main Report to the Seventh PCC Congress. Raúl cautioned that Cuba is not naive about the goal to subvert the Cuban Revolution. To top it off, on April 19, Fidel Castro attended and addressed the closing session of the Congress. His presence further galvanized the militants and the people who later watched it on TV.

This opposition to being gullible is not only present among the leaders. On April 18, it was inspiring to watch some of the proceedings of the PCC Congress on Cuban TV. One of the features that characterized the many statements by the delegates and invited guests was a clear rejection of the Obama Administration's subversive policy toward Cuba. In fact, self-employed workers who were elected delegates also joined this opposition to being naive. If Obama had seen these proceedings, his perennial smile would have turned to a severe frown, as it was this very "private sector" that he had hoped to win over as a Trojan horse within Cuba.

It is clear that the PCC, from the top down and bottom up, is a bulwark against the U.S. ideological/political offensive. However, the Cubans' defiance against the U.S. assault in the realm of ideas is not over. For example, not all self-employed workers share the outlook expressed by the delegates in the Party Congress. The situation among sections of the youth also represents a challenge.

Cuban Opposition Is Gaining Ground Against the U.S. War on Socialist Culture

My tentative conclusion is that *both* scenarios referred to earlier — that is, the Cubans making headway against cultural war *and* the U.S. making inroads — are presently being played out, with Cuban indigenous thinking making the most headway against the U.S. conceptual encroachment. My conclusion is seemingly forever "tentative" due to the complex and ever-changing dynamic. This is dealt with further in Chapters 4, 5 and 6.

It would be naive to deny that Obama-mania succeeded in making some inroads. This is noticeable in some of the comments left on various posts and articles and from reactions on the street. On the other hand, Obama's narrative had a boomerang effect. The unexpected result is a vigorous political debate at the grassroots and among many intellectuals against U.S. preconceived notions that Obama tried to force onto the Cuban socialist political culture. The depth and breadth of this movement is stronger than anything I have witnessed since I began closely following the Cuban political system in the 1990s.

I firmly believe that the balance of forces is in favour of the outlook that is combating the infiltration of U.S. prejudices within Cuban society. As Cuba's national hero José Martí wrote in 1895, "The greater war being waged on us is a war of ideas: let us win it with our ideas."

Notes

1 August 2015e.
2 August 2015d.
3 August 2015c.
4 August 2015b.
5 August 2016g.
6 All the quotes in this section are from Obama's January 13, 2016, State of the Union Address (Obama 2016h).
7 August 2016f.
8 While this book was going through the final stages of preparation, the Cuban and American governments issued a joint declaration on January 12, 2017, which stipulated an upgrade of the immigration relations between the two countries. Thus, Obama and his advisor Rhodes had to do an about-face and eliminate the wet-foot, dry-foot policy.
9 August 2016e.
10 August 2016d.
11 August 2016c.
12 According to Ricardo Alarcón, the U.S. cultural war against Cuba started in 1959. This is discussed in Chapter 4, in the section titled "Who Is Going to Win the Cultural War?"
13 August 2016b.
14 On April 25, 2016, a list of ninety-three supposed political prisoners was released by a Cuban "dissident." It was analyzed and does not name a single prisoner of conscience (Manzaneda 2016). See the section titled "Political Prisoners in Cuba: The List" in Chapter 4.
15 August 2016a.
16 In fact, at the time of preparing the manuscript for this book, in November 2016, the debate is still raging. It is dealt with further in Chapters 4, 5 and 6.

Chapter 3

INTERVIEWS WITH FIVE OF CUBA'S LEADING EXPERTS ON CUBA–U.S. RELATIONS

There were several reasons for my choice of the five Havana-based specialists I interviewed for this chapter. First, while there are many such authorities in Cuba, I already had working relationships with these five analysts, among others. Second, within the general scope of Cuba–U.S. relations, each of them contributes one or more specific perspectives, thus providing a broad spectrum of the subject matter. Third, they do not share the same opinions or place the same emphasis on the various aspects composing the two countries' liaison, nor do my perspectives necessarily align with theirs. Fourth, I deliberately opted for Cubans living in Cuba rather than in other countries such as the U.S., as the latter, unlike the vast majority of their peers in Cuba, enjoy mainstream media and their works already receive academic attention in the English language.

It must be noted that as part of the 17D fallout, the U.S. increasingly draws into its sphere of influence a small number of Cuban experts in Cuba who are promoted in Cuba and in the U.S. because of their apologetic stand on U.S. Cuba policy.

The interviews were carried out in Cuba in May 2016 with follow-ups by email communication the same month. The exchanges were in Spanish, translated into English and then sent to each interviewee for approval before publication.

JESÚS ARBOLEYA CERVERA

Jesús Arboleya Cervera (born in Cuba, 1947) holds a Ph.D. in history from the University of Havana. He is a full professor in the Faculty of Philosophy and History at the University of Havana and at the university Instituto Superior de Relaciones Internacionales "Raúl Roa García" (ISRI, Raúl Roa García Higher Institute of International Relations). His courses deal with, among others topics, U.S. hegemony, Cuba–U.S. relations and the history of Cuban emigration. He is a researcher on the U.S. in the Cuban Centre for Research of International Politics and a member of the National Jury of Scientific Degrees in Political Science. He was editorial coordinator of the Australian publisher Ocean Press as well as director of the information centre for the Cuban news agency Prensa Latina. His twenty years of experience representing Cuba in international diplomacy was served in the Cuban Mission at the United Nations in New York and in the Cuban Interests Section in Washington, D.C. (now the Cuban Embassy). As a journalist, he has penned numerous articles published in Cuba and in other countries. He is a regular contributor to Progreso Weekly, based in Miami. He has written more that fifteen books dealing mainly with Cuba and its international relations, some of which have been published in English.

ARNOLD AUGUST: In November 2015, I heard you give a talk in Cojímar, near Havana, on the tenth anniversary of the defeat of the FTAA [Free Trade Area of the Americas]. In analyzing the new Cuba–U.S. relations, you said that the U.S. does not have normal relations with anyone. I agree with you. Normalization is an important point, as it continuously comes up in the discussion and debate regarding the new Cuba–U.S. relations. Could you please elaborate on this? First, what did you mean by that statement? Second, based on December 17, 2014, and Obama's March 2016 visit, some commentators inside and outside Cuba (and especially in the U.S.) talk about normalization as if it has already occurred or is very close to becoming a reality. The concept of normalization seems at times to quietly slip into the debate as though it has been essentially accomplished. On the other hand, the Cuban government has repeatedly cautioned that normalization means a long and difficult road ahead. What is your evaluation of normalization at this time?

JESÚS ARBOLEYA CERVERA: In the relationship between the U.S. and the rest of the world, the hegemonic status of the U.S. is overpowering; the asymmetry, even with other world powers, is so marked that one cannot speak of a normalcy based on equality between parties. This is all the more so in the case of Cuba and the rest of the Third World countries, which lack the military and economic capability to impose their interests.

This does not mean that the U.S. can always get its way, for there are factors of a political nature that act to impose limits on its aspirations, and that is what is happening in the Cuban case. The Cuban people's resistance was the decisive factor in the failure of the "old politics," as President Obama himself has acknowledged the failure. This resistance is present as a factor in the ongoing negotiations, which are transpiring in a climate of equality and mutual respect, despite the existing power imbalance.

Neither does it mean that these negotiations are free to ignore the antagonistic contradictions between the two countries — some as old as the very existence of these nations — nor is there any guarantee that these contradictions will be resolved. The only thing that has really changed is that negotiation has gained ground on confrontation — no small accomplishment given the state of bilateral relations and of Cuba's relations with the rest of the world.

AA: Obama's visit was a success for both Cuba and the U.S. Aside from the statements he made, as well as the U.S.-led media hype promoting him, can we say that the actual content of Obama's statements urging Cubans to forget the past contributes to normalization? And what about his repeated attempts during the visit to appeal to sections of Cuban society in obvious opposition to the Cuban constitutional order? This is also backed by democracy promotion programs and other destabilization efforts. In one of your articles, you coined the phrase "co-existence between opposites" (*convivencia entre contrarios*). Are the U.S. policies mentioned above part of this "co-existence between opposites"?

JAC: I don't care for the word "normalization" because it is a confusing term; I prefer to describe the current process as one of building a climate of "co-existence between opposites." However, to use this term is to acknowledge that what we have here are in fact "opposites" and that each party will try to push its respective agenda. Obama came to Cuba on that errand, and that is the essence of his policy toward Cuba. The problem is that policies can be evaluated not only in terms of their intent but also in terms of their capacity to be brought to fruition, and that is where the Cuba variable enters the equation. In short, there is a will to continuously impose the U.S. agenda, but there may not necessarily be a way.

AA: Fine, we can substitute "co-existence between opposites" for "normalization." I prefer that, too. Can we, however, say that Obama's exhortations to the Cuban people to forget history also contribute to this "co-existence between opposites"? Which potential policies of his can help Cuba? And, when you say that "the Cuba variable enters the equation," can you give a specific example to expand on this idea?

JAC: This "change of methods" entails a change of image and, standing in the way of these changes, is an inconvenient history, which people will now necessarily have to relinquish. The goal here is also to defuse popular resistance, which is based very much on the historical legacy of past struggles. That is why Obama is proposing to wipe the slate clean. I stress that "co-existence between opposites" does not imply an end to the contradictions, nor does it erase the hegemonic agenda of the U.S. with respect to Cuba. It means only that this now needs to be done through the application of "smart power," which includes a change of rhetoric. The discussion as to whether or not there are "good intentions" in this policy misunderstands its basic aims and moves us further from our central objective, which is to analyze the objectives of U.S. policy regardless of what methods are used. Co-existence between opposites does not alter this reality; it is simply a new setting for the struggle.

The U.S. has no intention of "helping" Cuba in any sense of the word. Its goal is to help itself, to look after its own interests. The Cuba variable is decisive in this equation because it determines the limits of U.S. policy and the possible success of its agenda. The "old politics," based on hostility and aggression, failed thanks to the Cuban people's resistance and to international solidarity; now, it is necessary to update these resources in keeping with the dictates of the new conjuncture. In the long run, the decisive matters will be the country's political, economic and social stability and its capacity to influence the world's progressive forces, as well as the intelligence of its foreign policy, including vis-à-vis the U.S. If we are to successfully contend with the hegemonic aspirations of the U.S., we must also revamp the methods and discourse that we have used thus far.

AA: Revolutionary Cuba has been — and remains — proud to hold the banner of independence high, from the mid-nineteenth century to the triumph of the Revolution on January 1, 1959, and on to the present day. However, some people are now saying that under the present circumstances, "independence" is no longer a valid concept, and that we should be talking about "autonomy" instead — that Cuba's goal should be incorporation into the international community even as it maintains its autonomy. What do you think? Wasn't "autonomy" used by factions of the nineteenth-century struggle for freedom who demanded autonomy from Spain but favoured annexation to the U.S.?

JAC: The truth is that, at this point, I'm not aware of anybody in Cuba who is talking about autonomy as an alternative, at least in the sense that the term was used in the nineteenth century, when it referred to a political option under a colonial regime. The meaning of independence is so deeply rooted in Cuban political culture that the U.S. had to either bury the idea of annexation back in 1902 or try to turn the country back into a colony, as it did with other Spanish territories. It was driven instead to invent the neo-colonial model in order to establish its hegemony — a model in which, at least formally, independence is recognized.

AA: I was not suggesting that some observers are asserting that the term "autonomy" as it existed in the nineteenth century ought to replace the term "independence." They only use the word "autonomy" in its current sense. It is my opinion that this orientation could be dangerous because it makes me think of the nineteenth century's unfortunate outcome. And do you think that now, in the context of December 17, 2014, it is no longer valid to speak of cultural, political and ideological *war* against Cuba because the term "war" somehow became inapplicable when the Cold War ended?

JAC: I don't like using labels that do more to confuse matters than to clarify them. Cuban Autonomism was a specific movement that had its historic moment, and this explains its characteristics; nothing about what is happening now resembles that situation. Nor does it resemble "annexationism," frequently used in Cuban political rhetoric but without any grounding in contemporary realities. And the same is true of "Cold War," which defined a moment of conflict between two opposing superpowers that no longer exists. I prefer to describe what I believe is actually happening now, which is characterized by hegemonic and counter-hegemonic struggles in the sense of Gramsci, not only on the international stage but within individual countries, which no one can elude and which involve multiple actors and specific conditions.

Some of these struggles involve hot war; others take place on the terrain of politics. As always, the hegemonic power tries to establish the playing field and the ground rules. In the case of Cuba, we are forced to become "guerrillas" of a new kind and to exploit every chink in the hegemony's armour. The goal is to bolster a national conscience that can serve as a shield against the U.S. agenda and help us overcome our own deficiencies and distortions, through the development of socialist democracy. It is, in and of itself, an extraordinarily revolutionary and innovative endeavour.

What is novel about the changed historic moment is that revolutionaries can no longer count on the reassuring certainties of the past. We are up against a contradictory, unpredictable world in which we must begin by updating the Cuban revolutionary project. This gives rise to a wide-ranging debate, which is positive inasmuch as it helps to create new areas of consensus or to crystallize genuine areas of disagreement. The battle of ideas is a battle for people's minds, but utopias aren't good enough: we need concrete policies to back them up, and that is what will determine the success of the ongoing effort, which is not without its contradictions.

AA: In a March 25, 2016, article published right after the Obama visit, you had the courage to write what few in Cuba would admit:

> Desirous not to give the impression that the visit was "a honeymoon" with the U.S. president, Cuba's official treatment was respectful but distant. However, the population expressed itself in a warmer manner, especially when Obama strolled through the streets of Havana and imposed his undeniable charisma.
>
> It is not surprising that Obama awakened the sympathy of the Cuban people. It has happened everywhere else in the world, ever since he assumed his post. The reasons are not only attributable to his personality; the content of his ideas is also important. I believe that he is the most intelligent and articulate president the U.S. has had since Kennedy. Also influential is the natural identification of the majority of Cubans with his social origin — something that Obama knows how to exploit to stand as an example of "the American dream" — and his race symbolizes a transcendental change in the social history of the U.S., a process with which many people empathize.

Can you elaborate on "the sympathy of the Cuban people"? How deep was this? What proportion of the Cuban population sympathized with Obama? Did this positive attitude toward Obama change during and immediately after the visit as people took stock of the experience?

JAC: In the article you mention, this opinion is qualified by stating that Obama's popularity cannot be confused with support for U.S. aims. It is an expression of support for the virtues of the man and the symbolism of his presidency. Obama, moreover, did not arrive in Cuba with the stance of a conqueror, as U.S. presidents have been wont to do: he came with a respectful and elegant demeanour, even if that was betrayed by a few remarks typical of the vanity associated with so-called "American exceptionalism." A Cuban saying has it that "courtesy and valour are not mutually exclusive" (*Lo cortés no quita lo valiente*), and that was how Obama was received in Cuba. His personal merits were recognized by a majority of the population, if not by everyone.

AA: Did "Brother Obama" help set the record straight among the population?

JAC: As Fidel writes in that article, "We don't need the empire to give us anything." It might perhaps be added that Obama did not come with that intention; on the contrary, everything Cuba has obtained from the U.S. has cost our country dearly, and that will no doubt continue to be the case. I think that is the essence of what Fidel is trying to tell us.

AA: He begins the article as follows: "The kings of Spain brought us the conquistadores and masters, whose footprints remained in the circular land grants assigned to those searching for gold in the sands of rivers, an abusive and shameful form of exploitation, traces of which can be noted from the air in many places around the country." He does not come out and call Obama a "conquistador," but it is my impression that, using irony and history, he is issuing a warning to the Cuban people not to forget history and fall prey to naïveté. What do you think? Is that part of Fidel's core message?

JAC: I certainly agree with Fidel's sounding of the alarm on the history question. Remembering history strengthens us as we go head to head with the new "friendly" imperialism. It has been said that he who does not know history is condemned to repeat the same mistakes, and Fidel is the living history of the Cuban people.

ESTEBAN MORALES DOMÍNGUEZ

Esteban Morales Domínguez (born in Cuba, 1942) earned a Ph.D. in economic sciences from the University of Lomonosov, Moscow, and a Ph.D. in science from the University of Havana. At the University of Havana, he was director of the Political Science School, dean of the Faculty of the Humanities, research professor emeritus (1966–2010), director of the Department of Political Economy and a founding member and director of the Centre for Hemispheric and U.S. Studies. He was a member of the Academy of Sciences (2004–12). In 2009, he was honoured in recognition of his life's work. He was awarded the following prizes: three from the Academy of Sciences, fifteen for research at the University of Havana (four as author and eleven as co-author), four from the Ministry of Higher Education, three special distinctions from the Ministry of Higher Education and four from the National Economy and Critical Social Sciences. He is presently a member of the Scientific Council of the UNESCO Slave Route project, the Unión de Escritores y Artistas de Cuba (UNEAC) and its Aponte Commission against Racism and Racial Discrimination. He is the author, co-author or editor of fourteen books. Two of them, in English, won recognition in the U.S.: Race in Cuba: Essays on the Revolution and Inequality and Subject to Solution: Problems in Cuban–U.S. Relations. His blog is called Esteban Morales Dominguez.

ARNOLD AUGUST: You have been studying Cuba–U.S. relations for many decades and are recognized as one of Cuba's top experts on this issue. Did you see December 17, 2014, coming? In your September 3, 2013, article "Hypothesis on Barack Obama's Strategy Toward Cuba," it seems that you thought a change in the U.S. Cuba policy was going to occur but perhaps not as dramatic a change as the one that actually took place. Can you explain your thinking in that period of 2013–14?

ESTEBAN MORALES DOMÍNGUEZ: Obama paid attention to the topic of Cuba even when he was a senator [2008], and he came out against the policy being followed at that time. On the eve of his presidency, in his last campaign speech, he spoke of the need to talk to Cuba, although he did not say he would lift the blockade. That was the genesis of my hypothesis as to what Obama's new political strategy would be. I've been saying since early 2009 that Obama would divide the blockade into two parts: a blockade for civil society and a blockade against the government. This greatly resembles the theory of the carrot and the stick, but it was to be handled more intelligently — indeed more intelligently than by any other U.S. president of the last fifty years. My hypothesis is that Obama is engaging with civil society with a view to identifying the sectors that will come on board with the changes to Cuba policy that he wants to put in place. At the same time, he wields the blockade to prevent the political leadership of the Revolution from staying in control of the changes that Cuba must make, with or without Obama, if it is to continue to forge forward on its socialist agenda. I think this hypothesis has been borne out.

Obama may be the president who urged Congress in January 2015 to lift the blockade, but he is simultaneously the president who has imposed the harshest financial sanctions on Cuba: fines on transnational banking to keep our country from using the dollar. At the same time, he refrains from using all his executive prerogatives to relieve Cuba of some of the economic hardships caused by the blockade while it waits for Congress to lift it. U.S. and Cuban-American investment in Cuba is still banned. Obama is using the blockade in the same way as the carrot and the stick have hitherto been used: he has a carrot for civil society and a stick for the revolutionary government. This situation remains unchanged.

It is true that the talks between the two countries have gathered momentum and that Obama is already the president who has done the most to alter his country's Cuba policy, but the talks continue nonetheless to beat around the bush. The blockade, the Guantánamo naval base, the media aggression, the insistence on "democracy," the *Cuban Adjustment Act* [which encourages illegal Cuban immigration to the U.S.], compensation [for the effects of the blockade and other policies]: none of that has yet been addressed, yet there has been progress on a number of matters that help to lock in the change of policy. For these reasons, Cuba should not lose hope. It should move ahead with the talks, for progress in that context is the only guarantee that the clock will never be turned back. It is the only guarantee that any future president inclined to reverse course would have to make a conscious choice to do that and suffer the corresponding political consequences.

It can be assumed that when a man like Obama bravely and forthrightly admits, as he did on December 17, 2014, that fifty years of the U.S. Cuba policy have been a failure, with the result that the U.S. has isolated itself instead of isolating Cuba, he must already have an alternative policy waiting in the wings, based on a principle he himself stated: "We cannot keep doing the same thing and expect a different result." In other words, the strategy remains essentially the same: only the tactics and methods will change. When Cuba faces the U.S., it does not face just one political class or power structure but a whole political culture, one in which Cuba is still seen as forming a part of the continental U.S.

AA: What was your reaction to December 17, 2014? How did people at the grassroots see this announcement initially and in the weeks and months that followed?

EMD: I thought there would at least be a policy change toward Cuba. In an October 2014 interview with Fernando Ravsberg [a former BBC correspondent for Cuba], I explained that conditions were ripe for such a change; still, what actually occurred surpassed my expectations. Cubans as a whole reacted positively. There was some enthusiasm and even joy at the thought that the relationship between the two countries would change and that this would be positive for Cuba.

AA: During the period from around December 17, 2014, to Obama's visit in March 2016, you wrote four articles on the four packages of measures he proposed. I realize that it will be difficult to do, but could you briefly summarize and analyze each of them and the relationships among them?

EMD: The first article, in late December 2014, focused on Roberta Jacobson, head of the U.S. delegation [in the Cuba–U.S. negotiations to establish diplomatic relations]. From the outset, she was keen on the option of pressuring Cuba on democracy, human rights and civil liberties. We responded that it was too early to bring up such things when the negotiations hadn't even begun.

Since then, I have written three more articles about the packages of measures and the challenges the negotiations bring for Cuba vis-à-vis the U.S. The last article [April 2016] critiques the fourth package of measures, which holds out the possibility of allowing us to use the dollar but moves us no closer to that goal. The Cuban government is given nothing to facilitate its attempts to make use of that prerogative. I discuss how, after this fourth package was presented, Obama fined three more banks [for carrying out international financial transactions with Cuba], two of them American, and how he issued fourteen more financial measures designed to put pressure on Cuba and hinder it from doing business. In so doing, he kept a sword of Damocles hanging over our heads. He can hit at the banks whenever Cuba tries to work with them, to the point of imposing sanctions, even when the transactions are done in currencies other than the dollar.

The truth is that, while each package of measures contains its share of advances, it is impossible to work up great enthusiasm for them. The measures are insufficient, and there is no clarity as to how they will be brought to fruition. "Obama y el cuarto paquete de medidas" (Obama and the Fourth Package of Measures) cautions readers that we should not be optimistic about the prospect of one day actually being able to use the dollar. Even though Cuba is being assured that its use of the dollar is on the table, the promise is not being kept and the U.S. continues to use sanctions as a pressure tactic.

One of my fundamental objectives in dealing with the four packages was to alert Cuba to the need to prevent the U.S. from setting the pace and terms of the negotiations. After all, the negotiations are a key moment with regard to the balance and the equality of conditions mentioned by Raúl Castro as being essential to the maintenance of Cuban sovereignty within this process of establishing, and then later normalizing, Cuba–U.S. relations.

The twenty-three other articles I have written since December 17, 2014, have followed the course of the negotiations, characterizing, or rather critiquing, the executive measures put forward by Obama. Of particular importance here is the unilateral and limited nature of these measures, with no obvious benefits for the Cuban government. These measures are weighed down by the intent to benefit only those sectors of Cuban civil society that Obama identifies as having the potential to stand with him in his efforts to effect the policy change he wants to see implemented in Cuba. Finally, in one of my most recent articles [April 2016], I characterize the visit and ask President Obama rhetorically what, if anything, is to come next.

All things considered, I still believe that the negotiations represent progress and that some very positive things are continuing to happen, with high-level visits in both directions, new items constantly being added to the talks and both parties showing an interest in identifying opportunities for cooperation. Although some key issues are still on ice — the *Cuban Adjustment Act,* Guantánamo, compensation and so on — it is very important to keep moving ahead so that the process becomes irreversible.

I think the irreversibility of the process is a function of both countries' capacity to achieve the greatest possible levels of détente, to negotiate matters of mutual interest and to identify areas of cooperation that make possible the progressive removal of barriers. This is especially important in the context of the upcoming presidential election [November 2016], which will put the normalization process in the hands of a new U.S. president in 2017. The more progress we make now, the harder it will be for the new president to reverse course on the policy Obama is trying to put in place — a policy that, as we know, continues to have enemies among powerful interests in the U.S.

AA: I shared three memorable days with you and Cuban journalist Arleen Derivet on a special TeleSUR program from Havana, March 20–22, 2016, during the Obama visit. Therefore, I know your views as they were evolving during those three days. However, looking at those three days from the perspective of May 2016, what is your view of the visit now? What were the different reactions or opinions expressed on the street during those three days and afterwards? How many articles have you written since our appearance on that program? Do the articles reflect any changes in your views on the visit?

EMD: Not just the articles you mention but all the ones I have written since December 17, 2014, up to the most recent ones [April 2016], twenty-six in all — which can be found on my blog — devote close scrutiny to Obama's policy since he declared that a change was in the works.

AA: These articles were published online on many blogs and websites in addition to your own blog. However, none of them were published in the print editions of the dailies *Granma* and *Juventud Rebelde,* read by the majority, who do not have Internet access. Do you see any improvement on the horizon? Will these dailies start publishing pieces by you and other similar writers?

EMD: The dailies do not publish my articles, which appear only on my blog and on the Internet. There seems to be no interest in having them appear in the print media. They do circulate widely through what I would call the alternative media, by email and through certain outlets that reprint them.

Subsequent articles about the visit by other authors reflect all points of view, if somewhat unintelligently in some cases, with rather inelegant and ill-founded criticisms. Nevertheless, there are articles that have served very well — knowledgeably, eloquently, non-dogmatically — to pinpoint the true significance of the U.S. president's visit. It can be said that the reactions, both written and verbal, have contained a bit of everything, from smart and objective assessments of the significance of the visit to real provocations, such as the unprecedented, genuinely disrespectful, borderline racist article published in *Tribuna de La Habana* [the official newspaper of Havana Province] titled "Negro, ¿tú eres sueco?"[1]

In general, people's reactions to the measures adopted by the U.S. have been positive. However, there is also mistrust, which grows when people see the measures being manipulated, when they see that they are unilateral and that the Cuban government does not benefit, that is, the measures are solely aimed at promoting, strengthening and protecting the emerging private sector. Expectations are running high as to what will happen with the blockade, and some observers are already foreseeing that it will not be abolished before Obama's term ends.

In general, the president's visit was well-received and awakened interest, even though it was no secret or surprise to anybody that Obama was coming to Cuba, indeed just a few days before the Seventh Party Congress [held in April 2016 and focused on charting the course for Cuba's future]. Obama drew interest, and especially sympathy, for how he tried to build bridges to the people, to take part in informal activities that might bring him closer to the man or woman on the street. Some of these were rather surprising, such as his appearance on the highest-rated Cuban TV program *Vivir del cuento* [which deals with real day-to-day problems faced in Cuban society from a humorous perspective personified in Pánfilo].

The president handled himself with great aplomb and diplomatic skill, making smart use of his store of personal charisma. His speeches left many impressed, especially the one he gave to the civil society representatives. Still, among those who attended, many were educated, smart and experienced enough to perceive that Obama's mission was to sell us on the virtues of capitalism, to hold Miami up as a model worth emulating and to shrewdly exploit all the persisting inadequacies of our society. As time goes by, a more objective vision has developed to the effect that the president could hardly have been expected to behave differently than he did. Cuba gave him a platform and Obama took advantage of it to try selling his model of capitalism and beat us at the media game.

AA: What was your immediate reaction to Fidel's "Brother Obama" [an article written by Fidel Castro on March 28, 2016, just one week after the

Havana visit, ironically criticizing some remarks by the U.S. president]? How did it affect the various opinions heard from ordinary Cubans?

EMD: I think the article, with its carefully crafted irony, was effective in sounding the alarm. Obviously, there are some people who didn't like it. But Fidel has that rare ability to travel into the future and come back with a vision of what we can expect to happen. There were articles criticizing Obama, and I would say the immense majority were intelligent and well-focused. Many were objective pieces that assessed the visit without rancour or disapproval of what the president did. These were articles of political analysis with a strong empirical bent. For as I have said, the visit has to be reckoned as a step forward on Obama's part — and for Cuba as well — after more than fifty years of aggression. Coming to see Cuba up close and to meet with real Cubans is not the same as trying to get a sense of it from a distance. Fidel's article was not merely critical: it was also analytical, smart, encouraging and highly political.

All my articles, including the ones about the visit, despite their critical approach, have never ceased to highlight the fact that Obama is the president who has done the most to improve relations with Cuba. That is a legacy no one can take away from him.

AA: There have been many cultural visits from the U.S. to Cuba since December 17, 2014. What do these visits offer Cuba in terms of monetary benefits?

EMD: In monetary terms, we're talking about a certain type of tourist who rents rooms, spends money, buys gifts, pays to attend specialized conferences. There can be other spinoffs, too, if these visits lead to invitations for Cubans to go to the U.S. and if they expand Cuba's capacity for cultural and academic exchanges.

AA: You may be one of the few Cuban academics specializing in *both* Cuba–U.S. relations *and* the race issue in Cuba. So let me put it to you bluntly: during Obama's March visit, do you think that Obama and his advisors deliberately used the race card to win sympathy from the black and mulatto populations, and to drive a wedge between these populations and the Cuban government?

EMD: I don't think that this has happened only as a result of the visit. The race issue has long been used by the U.S. to provoke internal divisions, and it is being used in the context of the new relations. The idea is to evoke the public's sympathies toward Obama and to use this as part of the diplomatic offensive against Cuba. In the same way that a group of Cuban intellectuals to which I belong [UNEAC)] has been working on solutions to the race issue, there are others who find themselves unable to view it as anything but an instrument of internal destabilization. This is, after all, a very pressing issue in Cuban society, one that absolutely must be addressed so that it does not create internal divisions here. It is a highly sensitive issue that can easily divide us as a society. Unfortunately, it is one that languished unaddressed for many years, and it is thus ideally positioned to serve as a weapon of internal subversion. The issue is now receiving much attention on both the cultural and political planes, from civil society and government alike, but we have a lot of lost time to make up for: we must keep on working hard to eradicate racial inequality once and for all.

ELIER RAMÍREZ CAÑEDO

Elier Ramírez Cañedo (born in Cuba, 1982) earned a B.A. in history, with the title of most outstanding achievement and integral graduate at the University of Havana. He has a master's degree in contemporary history and international relations and a Ph.D. in history. He has authored or co-authored several books related to Cuba–U.S. relations, including the highly acclaimed De la confrontación a los intentos de normalización: La política de los Estados Unidos hacia Cuba (2014). He is a member of various professional associations, such as the Unión de Escritores y Artistas de Cuba and the U.S.-based Latin American Studies Association (LASA). He has important responsibilities in the Cuban Academy of History and the Cuban Institute of History. He serves as a member of the permanent national jury for Ph.D. programs in political science and works as an associate researcher at the Office of Historical Affairs of the Cuban State Council. As part of the national leadership of the Asociación Hermanos Saíz (dedicated to the promotion of culture among youth), he administers their blog, Dialogar, dialogar, which features articles from many sources on Cuba–U.S. relations.

ARNOLD AUGUST: What was your first personal (not professional) reaction to December 17, 2014? You have been studying Cuba–U.S. relations: did it come as a surprise to you? As a writer and journalist, how long did it take you to write your first article after December 17? How many articles did you write between December 17, 2014, and March 20–22, 2016, and then between March 20–22 and May 2016?

ELIER RAMÍREZ CAÑEDO: I confess that my initial reaction was one of surprise, mixed with excitement and rejoicing at the return of Antonio,

Gerardo and Ramón to Cuba [the three remaining members of the Cuban Five still in U.S. prisons until December 17, 2014], among other things. My analysis was that Obama would be certain to do something to relax U.S. policy toward Cuba. Never has a U.S. president had such a favourable internal and external context in which to try something different. Still, I never dreamed that it would go as far as the restoration of diplomatic relations, the announcement of the beginning of the normalization process and the decision to resolve the case of the Cuban anti-terrorists. That he spoke out against the blockade and even made a phone call to Raúl also surprised me. You have to hand it to Obama for the boldness with which he acted.

My first article was published within a week of the historic announcements of December 17, 2014. I published five more after that. During Obama's visit to Cuba, I wrote one article, followed by another after he left, analyzing his speech at the Alicia Alonso Theatre in Havana [the speech to the Cuban civil society in attendance and televised to the Cuban people].

AA: During Obama's March 20–22 visit to Cuba, how did people on the street react? You have written before and after March 20–22 on the U.S. cultural war in the broad sense, defining it to include ideological and political war as well. How do you think the resistance to this has evolved since March 20–22? Do people harbour many illusions about Obama and his visit? Have these illusions increased with the visit, or is it the opposite?

ERC: There were all sorts of reactions. For example, I was stunned, upon leaving the Ministry of Culture early on the morning of March 21 and walking up Avenida Paseo, to see the crowds waiting for "The Beast" — Obama's presidential limousine — to pass by on its way to the José Martí Memorial. But then it occurred to me that it was perfectly natural for so many people to be so excited to see the first U.S. president to visit Cuba in eighty-eight years; indeed, the first to come here specifically to focus on Cuba, not to participate in a Latin American event, as [President John Calvin] Coolidge did in 1928. The representative of the empire, right here in Havana — who would have imagined it?

There were people of all political persuasions in the crowd, from symbolic annexationists, who stake their hopes on Obama and the U.S. for material or spiritual betterment, to people simply wanting to see "The Beast," as well as many others who were curious for other reasons. That is, you cannot put all the Cubans who came out to greet Obama in one box. Most of the people in attendance were, of course, respectful, and this was to be expected from a people who have always given U.S. citizens a cordial reception.

When we say that the U.S. is now trying to make the cultural war central to the confrontation with Cuba, we are not referring to artistic or literary things but to the clash between capitalist culture and socialist culture in the field of daily life, ways of life, versions of happiness, and habits and customs. In the field of political and socio-economic thought, as well, since two societies whose structures are the polar opposite of one another are squaring off.

As during other historical stages, a culture of pure resistance has emerged from among a large part of the Cuban people, but there has also been a resurgence of some form of *anexionismo* [annexationist tendency] tempered by new circumstances. The war of symbols is now taking place at a higher pitch of intensity on the streets of Cuba, and especially in Havana. This independence–annexation pairing accompanies the historical evolution of Cuba to this day. I think we have great potential to withstand the new gusts of wind from the North; what we have to do is to wield and articulate this resistance with intentionality. A great strength of the Cuban culture is its universalism, as well as its capacity to metabolize external influences. The fact of having lived in close proximity to U.S. culture for over 200 years has enabled us to develop antibodies that may be lacking in other peoples. But we must not be blind and assume ourselves to be invulnerable; our optimism has to be active optimism. I think the enthusiasm for Obama's visit was situational and that its effects have faded away with the passing days. The majority of Cubans continue to expect something more than gestures from the U.S.

AA: Do you think that it is no longer correct to write about the cultural war, since the term "war" is often linked to the bygone Cold War?

ERC: Debate persists as to whether we can categorically state that the Cold War is over. While it's true that one pole disappeared, the U.S. is to a large extent continuing to use and expand the methods and characteristics that marked this stage of confrontation, directing them now toward new "enemies." The arms race persists, as do the threats and interference, especially toward anyone who would stand up to Washington's diktats. Above all, and at an even larger scale, the cultural war continues to be waged against those countries and projects who defy U.S. hegemony. For these reasons, imperialism and cultural war are more relevant and topical than ever.

AA: How did Fidel Castro's article "Brother Obama" affect you?

ERC: It had a profound impact on me. It was something we were expecting. Fidel's views on Obama's speech went on to be read around the world, showing that he is still a leader of universal stature. But it is wrong to think that just because he disagrees with many of the ideas expressed in that speech [to the Cuban people from the Alicia Alonso Theatre], Fidel is necessarily opposed to détente and a more civilized relationship between the two countries. For many years, I have studied the innumerable initiatives that he has put forward, from the beginnings of the Revolution to the 1990s, that show his openness to dialogue and to seeking at least a *modus vivendi* with the U.S. I think that if Obama and his advisors had scheduled a meeting [with Fidel Castro], he would not have said no. To claim otherwise is to ignore history.

AA: The term is often used to describe the current Cuba–U.S. relations as being based on mutual respect. However, when Obama asked the Cuban people to forget the past, can this be considered respect? Take a more recent example as expressed in the latest ANAP [National Association of Small Farmers] complaint about Obama's attempt to force the Cuban producers of coffee to deal directly on an individual basis with the U.S. and not through the usual channels. Can this be considered respect? And how about the ongoing democracy promotion programs that have even increased in 2015 and 2016? How do you evaluate the issue of mutual respect now and in the future?

ERC: I think there are considerable discrepancies between the discourse and what is actually happening in practice, and thus which affects something as important as mutual trust. It is not often that someone opens the doors of his house to a neighbour, especially one as powerful as the U.S., knowing that the neighbour in question is ultimately scheming to burn the house down. One of the most harshly criticized aspects of Obama's speech [at the Theatre] to the Cuban civil society representatives was when he said that we have to leave the past behind, which is very different from saying that we shouldn't be locked up in the past. He who forgets or ignores the past is condemned to repeat it. But even as he made such an ominous and incongruous statement — especially for somebody as educated as Obama, who ought to know that history is our guide through life, that it teaches us the lessons we need in order to face the present and the future with wisdom and confidence — the president of the U.S. offered a rather Manichean and incomplete version of what Cuba–U.S. relations have been. Moreover, although he said in so many words that there is no intent to impose regime change on Cuba, millions of dollars continue to be spent on subversion. There is, moreover, a political motivation in relaxing the blockade, wherein the U.S. keeps trying to push Cuba onto the road to capitalism through "empowerment" of the private sector and other sectors who could become "agents of change." There is constant discrimination against the Cuban state sector, as if seeking to sow division between the people and the government. Is it plausible to suppose that normal relations can be achieved in this way? What kind of normalization does the U.S. really want?

AA: Your blog *Dialogar, dialogar* has dozens of articles by you and other Cuban and non-Cuban specialists on the topic of Cuba–U.S. relations. What importance and role do you attribute to your blog with respect to other blogs and to *Cubadebate*?

ERC: Communication via the social networks and blogs has become a fundamental battleground on which to combat wide-ranging campaigns of lies and obfuscation that are always being levelled against alternatives to capitalism and especially to its neo-liberal variant. The topic of Cuba–U.S. relations today lends itself to all manner of confusion and manipulation; it is therefore an urgent task for those of us who are following this issue in Cuba to communicate the truth about what is happening and all the relevant analysis, especially since December 17, 2014.

AA: On human rights, some foreign Cuba–U.S. experts friendly to Cuba, especially in the U.S. and Canada, seem to have fallen into the trap set by Obama. They are now also claiming, like Obama, that political and civil rights are suppressed in Cuba, while, of course, praising other human rights such as health, education and culture. Do you see this trend as inadvertently helping to fuel the cultural war against Cuban socialist culture?

ERC: The campaign against alleged human rights violations is, of course, part of the overarching strategy of cultural war against socialism in Cuba but not only in Cuba: against the socialist ideal more broadly. The U.S. claims to be a human rights champion and we already know how much fallacy hides behind that image, which is marketed like just another product. Cuba, despite the U.S. blockade and siege, has much more to boast about, and much more prestige in this area than the U.S., and not just with regard to economic, social and cultural rights but also to civil and political rights. It should nonetheless be clear that the U.S. has never in fact been interested in human rights in Cuba. It was, after all, the Revolution that swept away a U.S.-supported dictatorship that was itself a human rights violator.

What really interests the U.S. in Cuba is hegemony: it wants to bring Cuba within its sphere of influence. This is why the U.S. keeps quiet and carries on "normal," indeed cordial, relations with countries that have a very weak human rights record; countries where journalists disappear, where political assassinations occur and where mass graves containing hundreds of corpses of the disappeared are uncovered. But the reason for such normal relations is that those countries submit to U.S. interests. If the U.S. were one day to stop politicizing the human rights issue, it would have an ideal partner, sitting just 145 kilometres (90 miles) off its coast, with whom to cooperate on the struggle to protect the human rights of millions of people around the world, starting with the most important of these rights — the right to life, which is more threatened than it has ever been.

IROEL SÁNCHEZ ESPINOSA

Iroel Sánchez Espinosa (born in Cuba, 1964) has an engineering degree in computer science. He was a director of Casa Editorial publishing house and president of the Cuban Book Institute, and a founder of the respected Cuban literary magazine La Jiribilla. He founded and developed EcuRed, an online encyclopedia that is known as the "Cuban version of Wikipedia." He has given lectures at many international events related to communication and technology at universities in Europe and Latin America. His blog La pupila insomne is one of the most active in Cuba. From December 17, 2014, through May 2016 [when the interview took place], it was one of the main sources in Cuba and internationally for daily articles on the most controversial issues related to Cuba–U.S. relations. Many of these pieces are his own, and they have been reprinted on websites such as Rebelión, Cubadebate and many others. On the basis of this work and on other issues, he regularly gives interviews to television stations such as TeleSUR and Mayadeen. His journalistic efforts have merited him the prestigious Félix Elmuza Award for outstanding journalism by the Union of Cuban Journalists (UPEC), of which he is a member. He is the author of the book Sospechas y disidencias: Una mirada cubana en la red.

ARNOLD AUGUST: How did you find out about the joint Raúl Castro/ Barack Obama simultaneous statements on December 17, 2014? What was your first personal reaction when you heard the news?

IROEL SÁNCHEZ ESPINOSA: I was excited, especially because it finalized the release of the Cuban Five and also because the president of the U.S. was acknowledging what Cuba had requested for over five decades: that we ought to sit down and discuss our differences on an equal footing. Like many at that time, I was thinking of Fidel, of his conviction that the Five would return and also, as recently published U.S. documents demonstrate, because he always sought to improve relations with the U.S.

AA: How were people on the street reacting?

ISE: Initially, there were expressions of joy and euphoria over our success in getting the Five released, a cause around which practically all Cubans had rallied. Gradually, the topic of conversation moved on to people's expectations with regard to renewed relations with the U.S. There was a general sense of optimism; however, there was some wariness toward those who immediately proclaimed that, although the strategy had changed, the goals remained the same.

AA: During Obama's March 20–22 visit to Havana, I know that you were very busy giving interviews and writing articles. Were you able to get any feedback from the grassroots? Did reactions change over the three days?

ISE: The reactions you get from the grassroots are always mediated through your circle of friends, relations, colleagues and neighbours. In this case, I was just emerging from a period of convalescence after a surgery and wasn't getting out much, but my sense is that people's reactions changed from great expectations for Obama's arrival to rejection of his paternalistic and at times outright interfering stance — take, for example, his meeting with the "entrepreneurs" and his speech at the Alicia Alonso Theatre in Havana.

AA: In this context of different and changing reactions over the period during and after Obama's visit, let's talk about Fidel Castro's article "Brother Obama." When it was published, what was your initial reaction? How did it affect other journalists and writers? How did it affect the grassroots? Did it, for example, result in people changing or modifying their respective positions one way or another with regard to Obama? It seemed to me that the article gave a boost to all those who share Fidel's ideas. So, my difficult question is, what if Fidel had not written it?

ISE: I think many people, both in Cuba and abroad, were waiting for this article by Fidel to clarify perceptions around Obama's visit. I think it rallied a majority of Cubans, with certain nuances, to his stance. My reaction was one of joy and, I won't lie, even satisfaction, because it confirmed what I had been expecting. Many intellectuals had already gravitated toward a certain reaction that was strengthened by Fidel's article: it consolidated and catalyzed a process that would, I think, have had the same outcome but over a long term. His intellectual and moral authority is commanding: not even the [foreign accredited] private media in Cuba, who were star-struck by the visit, dared to contradict what he had to say. Outside of Cuba, the mass media sought uneasily to deprecate what Fidel had written, publishing opinions ranging from White House spokesperson Josh Earnest to "centrists" such as Arturo López Levy [a Cuban-American academic living in the U.S.].

AA: I have a great deal of respect for your blog La pupila insomne. How many articles have you written and posted on your blog regarding Cuba–U.S. relations from December 17, 2014, to May 2016? What is the total number of articles you have posted in this period, including yours and all others?

I know that you are the only one who works on the blog. Yet, *La pupila insomne* seems to publish quality articles like machine-gun fire. In addition, there are many comments from readers, and you actively participate in these debates. What is your typical day like? How many hours of work does it take to accomplish this?

ISE: I haven't kept track, but for sure I have written a lot. I get up at 5 a.m. to read the news, or even earlier if I'm going to write, in order to be sure I'll have enough time. I read the comments on the blog and the social networks, then check my email, through which I am regularly offered articles for the blog. I edit them and then, along with the previous day's submissions, I try to finish updating the blog by 8:30 a.m. During the day, I may have some meetings at the Ministry of Communications, where I work, as well as administrative work related to EcuRed, which thankfully now has a strong team, leaving me more time for other things. There's the weekly TV program that I direct [*La pupila asombrada*] and also the coffeehouse we host once a month. In the evening, I read some more or I might work on a piece of writing. On days when I have a lecture to give, an event to attend, a student to meet or an interview to give, or when the TV taping goes past midnight, I don't get to this writing until late at night. Whenever I can, I try to go online and read more of the comments on the blog. On weekends, in addition to updating the blog and catching up on the news, I try to make progress on some books I've been reading and some writing on core issues that I'm doing, apart from spending time with my family and participating in cultural activities.

AA: One characteristic of the blog is that it seems to consistently post articles that, for example, on the issue of Cuba–U.S. relations, do not harbour illusions about the U.S. and Obama. For example, while you and *La pupila insomne* fully support the new Cuba–U.S. relationship, you also put up serious resistance to the ideological and political war waged by the U.S. How do you evaluate your contribution to this resistance? Would you say that *La pupila insomne* has an implicit editorial line?

ISE: I've never laid down a specific "editorial policy." I just try to get people thinking and writing on what I identify with: critical post-colonial thinking, contributing to a culture of anti-imperialism and anti-capitalism and denouncing media misrepresentation of Cuba. I think many people share this goal; having Internet access obligates me to help give a voice to those who lack access. I leave the evaluation to others; judging from attacks launched by partisans of this war on Cuba, something about my blog bothers them. It keeps me going to know that colleagues with a proven intellectual track record will be sending me their articles for publication.

AA: Another feature, which is unique among major blogs, is that it also exposes the role of what I would call the "left dissidents." In my latest book, I also deal with this, and I can identify with you because I think these so-called "leftists" are more dangerous than the right-wing ones, such as the Ladies in White and Y. Sánchez. The goal of these "leftists," many of whom are young and tutored by foreigners, is to recruit youth, intellectuals and artists to divert them from the revolutionary path. How do you see the role of these "leftists" and any success they may have had in recent months and years?

ISE: If you read the best study, *The Cultural Cold War* by Frances Stonor Saunders, you learn that the CIA prefers to wage its fight against the communists by working with the "non-communist left." Just like during the cultural Cold War, eventually we find out who is calling the tune and many people's reputations take a beating. The CIA knows that there is no political space in today's Cuban society for those who don't either identify as "left" or declare themselves to be on the side of sovereignty and social justice. Whereas Henrique Capriles [the pro-U.S. Venezuelan "opposition leader"] claimed to be fighting the Bolivarians "from the grassroots and the left," and whereas in Brazil groups of "socialists" and "social democrats" united against Dilma Rousseff, how does this approach play out in Cuba, where anti-imperialist, pro-social justice political culture is much purer? What's been shown is that, here, it's only a minority who are willing to play that game.

AA: What's your assessment of *La pupila insomne* as compared with other revolutionary blogs and the *Cubadebate* website?

ISE: I think the more forums for debate the better. *La pupila insomne* makes its contribution, others make theirs, not better or worse but differently, and I think it's great that this diversity exists within revolutionary ranks. It should be clear, as occurred with the reactions to Obama's speech at the Theatre, that *Cubadebate* plays a fundamental role in the ideological fight in the networks [Internet] and that a form of revolutionary, anti-imperialist thought is articulated through that site.

AA: I read the comments on the blogs, including yours and *Cubadebate*, regularly. When commentators consider certain posts related to U.S. Cuba policy to be exceptionally good and sharp, you frequently find them suggesting that the article ought to be published in *Granma* and *Juventud Rebelde*, given that only about 30 percent of Cubans have access to the Internet, hence to these blogs and *Cubadebate*. What do think about this problem? Even though Internet access is increasing, it still has a long way to go. Do you think that *Granma* and *Juventud Rebelde* will soon start publishing these controversial articles?

ISE: You should ask the editors of *Granma* and *Juventud Rebelde* that question.[2] I do think, and have written, that our press ought to be more involved in the ideological struggle and make more room for revolutionary intellectuals. Without that transformation, I don't think we can win in the increasingly intense cultural confrontation with the U.S.

LUIS TOLEDO SANDE

Luis Toledo Sande (born in Cuba, 1950) has a bachelor's degree in Cuban studies and a Ph.D. in philological sciences from the University of Havana. He was the editor at the Editorial Arte y Literatura publishing house, assistant director and then director of the prominent Centro de Estudios Martianos and professor at the Pedagogical University Enrique José Varona de La Habana. At the Ministry of Education, he carried out work with special attention to José Martí and was head of the editorial team and then assistant director of the illustrious journal Casa de las Américas. After working as the cultural councillor for the Cuban Embassy in Spain, he became a journalist for the highly esteemed and oldest Cuban magazine, Bohemia. He has received wide recognition as a writer. He has given presentations at numerous professional conferences in more than fifteen countries in the Americas, Europe and Asia. Author of a dozen books, he has also contributed chapters and forewords to many books. He was awarded Cuba's Ministry of Culture's prestigious Distinción por la Cultura Nacional. He administers his blog, Luis Toledo Sande, which carries a wide variety of pieces on cultural and political issues.

ARNOLD AUGUST: As you know, we connected on the issue of your articles before and after December 17, 2014, regarding the growing appearance of U.S. flags in Havana's public places and in a carnival-like manner on clothing and virtually all body parts. So, my first question is, has this trend increased since that period from 2014 to early 2016? Do you see this type of display as a political statement or is it just a fad like any other that appears from time to time? Or is it a combination of both? Do you see this as a danger that affects the Cuban socialist culture and its ongoing pursuit of Cubans' sovereignty and dignity?

LUIS TOLEDO SANDE: I don't have any statistics on this, and I'm not sure if any exist, but on the face of it, I would venture to assert that the phenomenon has grown and that this is due to a highly relevant fact: the commencement of the so-called "normalization process" between the U.S. and Cuba. I mention these countries in this order, not alphabetically, because the one with the greater responsibility in this process, if it really wants the process to be what it should be, is the U.S. Cuba wasn't the one that took the initiative to break diplomatic ties, to impose a blockade, to stage an invasion on a U.S. beach [Playa Girón, known as the Bay of Pigs] or via any other route; Cuba has not sponsored acts of terrorism against the U.S., funded that country's dissidents, set up radio and TV transmitters designed to subvert its system or occupied a square inch of its territory.

When the normalization process got going, Cuba appointed an ambassador to Washington, whereas — and this fact cannot be entirely separated from the latter country's imperial pride — the U.S. government has yet to appoint one to Havana. It is another sign of the asymmetry inseparable from the arrogance of a power whose president [Obama] unblushingly proclaims — has he no modesty? — that the job he does is the most important one on the planet. There is, in such affirmations, an element of a messianic attitude typical of the beyond-U.S. territorial economic extension and the apologies made for the systemic voracity of the empire.

But when it comes time to judge or analyze attitudes on the use of symbols of that power [such as the U.S. flag] in Cuba, it is not enough to consider the importance of normalization, which is also desired by Cuba, but to ascertain whether the island is indeed being relieved of the economic, financial and commercial persecution with which the empire has tried to strangle it for the last half century. What determines these attitudes has to do with how each person interprets normalization, and different readings surely have different causes; some people may indulge in rather tendentious interpretations of the situation, while others may lack the ability to interpret it in any other way. In a country that has been under attack and blockaded, how can people express their feelings by using the symbols of the aggressor nation? At this stage of the game, we can't be naive — foolish, maybe, but this is no time for foolery.

There are surely a number of motives. One is the enthusiasm associated with a belief that a process that begins is guaranteed to reach a satisfactory conclusion, and that a lifeline is, in this case, being tossed to the Cuban people. Another is the idea that the empire's announced change of position is an expression of generosity and not merely a change of tactics aimed at achieving the same ends as the blockade and the aggressions, as no less a personage than the imperial president himself has let on. While some might see generosity in this stance, others might well regard it, equally validly and perhaps more precisely, as an *affront*. Another motive for displaying the U.S. flag may involve the influence of a sham globalization that has nonetheless had ideological and cultural impacts associated with the preaching of a version of "postmodernity" in which flags are just rags, history and politics mere simulacra, pure fiction, masks.

This influence is a cousin to the multilateral and omnipotent media machinery of the empire, which shamelessly and successfully promotes the empire's benevolent image despite the crimes it commits every day around the world, meanwhile turning those crimes into a TV spectacle and even a sequence of "humanitarian" enterprises — a perversion of the language if ever there was one. And there is much more besides what I have enumerated so far. The flags may also be appearing out of irresponsible thoughtlessness or as a manifestation of the social indiscipline that has grown among us, probably further to a belief that was perhaps held for too long: that of supposing — an inexcusable mistake! — that the counter-revolution is strictly a matter of acts by the declared enemy, slogans explicitly targeting the Revolution and its principal leaders, whereas the theft, corruption and social disorder on which those and other social excrescences thrive are objectively and essentially counter-revolutionary facts, perhaps even more dangerous than others because they degrade and disarm people's consciences.

There are assuredly other causes to be considered, one of which it would be naive to ignore: some people's desire to disassociate themselves from a revolutionary process such as the Cuban one, even though, in doing so, they consciously or unconsciously — could it honestly be the latter? — pay tribute to the empire in the fields of ideology and culture, which can lead to other spheres. And there are some people who align themselves with *neoanexionismo* [neo-annexationist tendency)], an ideological orientation from which the "neo" could be deleted without error, for this is a century-old position whose core features have never changed. On the one hand, it is doomed to failure for having been rejected by both a majority of the Cuban people and the empire itself. The latter is not interested in annexing Cuba but rather in dominating it, exploiting its resources — as it does with Puerto Rico — and wiping out the example of its revolutionary history. On the other hand, *anexionismo* has always, in whatever form it appears, functioned as an anti-patriotic position designed to sap the people's revolutionary fervour.

While this ideological orientation may have been a factor, either consciously or unconsciously, in the use of the U.S. flag before December 17, 2014, the "fashion" has become more visible since then. We now see the imperial banner, alone or in conjunction with the Cuban flag, appearing on clothing and certain vehicles, some of them private but others owned by the state. This is what I was referring to in the articles you mention, which can be read, along with some others I will refer to in this interview, on my website, although they originally appeared in other publications. It is one of the arenas in which the ideological and cultural struggle is being — and must be — intelligently waged. For a country like Cuba (not remotely the only one), forged in a tradition of struggle in which national symbols have played and continue to play a primary role, a role with practical effects, it would be irresponsible or foolish not to consider this an important issue, even if ill-intentioned motives for displaying the flag are, as I believe, in the minority — which is not to suggest that they are insignificant.

AA: The Obama Administration appeals to Cuban youth as a possible ally in its attempt to attain the long-term goal of destroying the Cuban Revolution. Cuban youth are obviously not homogeneous. How do you see the different political and/or cultural trends among Cuban youth today?

LTS: If there is one question demanding that we devote serious examination to it in the hopes of finding equally serious answers, it is this one. Every young population — like every society, every culture, every country — is heterogeneous. We also know that children, in both their general and their more specific characteristics, are more of their era than that of their parents; that they tend to be more focused on personal pursuits — including class interests — than on the interests of their fellow citizens. However, these are not facts exclusive to one particular sector: they concern the whole society. At the base of it (though not in superficial or circumstantial things) and with the respective differences having been considered, a young Cuban revolutionary will bear a closer resemblance to an old French revolutionary than to a young Cuban counter-revolutionary. While it is not always said with the necessary clarity, youth is the hope *for all*: for the good and the bad, the best and the worst. Everybody was young once: George W. Bush and Angela Davis, Martin Luther King Jr. and a Ku Klux Klansman, Fulgencio Batista and, a quarter century later, Fidel Castro.

The empire is betting on creating or at least ensuring the existence in Cuba of a youthful population increasingly at odds with their country and not driven by their dissatisfaction to work for its betterment, to bring about a revolutionary transformation, as is incumbent upon people of all ages who are interested in saving Cuba and refining its ongoing political project. No, the youth targeted by the empire are those who would abandon Cuba, defame it, fight against it. By investing millions to make Cuba insolvent — as it has done in the cases of Chile, Venezuela and other countries, though there are those who would deny these facts — the U.S. strives to provoke dissatisfaction, instability and ultimately insurrection against the revolutionary government: it wants the whole population, not just the youth, to go over to the counter-revolution. The empire, its allies and its lackeys, with the help of some genuinely mistaken individuals, cast all the blame on the Cuban government not only for the bona fide hardships suffered by the people but also for fictitious ones, which they used to spread propaganda.

According to this view of things, the greatest disaffection with the socialist agenda may be found among young people because of their more immediate, physical familiarity with the hardships (and the social ills such as corruption stemming from them) that have been imposed on the country by the dismantlement of socialism in Europe [former U.S.S.R. and Eastern Europe] and especially by the U.S. blockade. Their elders have much more personal experience of how radically and comprehensively the Revolution has improved living conditions for the immense majority of Cubans since 1959, how it has restored their dignity. These gains have indeed been extraordinary, but younger people, particularly those not intelligently informed, might be inclined to take them for granted, or as gifts from heaven, rather than as the outcome of planning and effort.

The striving to make these gains is not a thing of the past, *nor must it become one.* When the country embarks on initiatives to achieve the economic efficiency necessary to make the project of building a socialist society prosperous and sustainable, this is envisioned and accomplished with the people's benefit in mind, and so it must continue to be. This aspiration must not stagnate into a slogan disconnected from reality. I use the word "project" so as to emphasize the unfinished nature of what is being attempted. Socialism is a work in progress, one that will require ever more daring and creativity to rise to a level as yet unachieved anywhere else, and to continue perfecting it.

The road to true socialism (which ought not to be confused with variants of state capitalism or with the legacies of the so-called Asiatic mode of production, as various permutations and combinations of these modes may exist) demands that the core function of the economy be that of serving politics and social justice. Politics and social justice must be guided by economic goals. In defending this agenda, it is indispensable to combat the *caciquism*, privilege, corruption and nepotism that may occur not only in the area of employment, but also in that of material perquisites and privileged lifestyles, as has occurred in so many places. It is truly complex and challenging. Every era has its vanguards and rearguards, and between them, human agglomerations — the so-called "masses" — with undeniably complex dynamics. This is not, of course, to imagine that vanguards and rearguards are ever simple realities, nor that vanguards are always perfectly angelic and infallible.

It is incumbent upon the most enlightened and conscious sectors of Cuban society — in difficult harmony with the rest of the population — to spearhead the struggle to make the empire's plans fall through once more, due to its hostility toward the Cuban nation. This hostility is to be maintained, according to the current office-holder [Obama], via the path of "normalization." Talk about carrots and sticks! Meanwhile, Cuba continues to be blockaded and the island continues to suffer under despicable imperial laws, such as the *Cuban Adjustment Act*, and to be illegally and immorally occupied at a site, Guantánamo, that the empire has converted into a monstrous prison even as its mouthpieces insist that the return of this land to its rightful owners is not up for discussion. What kind of normalization is that?

Obviously, Cuba needs the blockade to end, but even if that monstrosity and others should persist, it must ready itself to continue making progress. This imperative falls to society as a whole, although each sector has its own characteristics. Moreover, these characteristics are thrown into relief in a society in which the class structure, which is never as simple as some may claim, becomes even more complex. This is so with the increase in private property — termed, in an inauspicious euphemism, the "self-employed sector" (*cuentapropismo*). This is a subterfuge that, while it may derive from the best of intentions, overlooks the unavoidable fact that there are substantial differences between the bosses and their employees — between exploiter and exploited — that inevitably make themselves felt. Thankfully the euphemism has begun to lose ground, even in official discourse. Better late than never!

We must ponder, for example, whether it is reasonable to suppose that Cuba will continue to be a land free of strikes, a place where the very concept is practically demonized. This was possible when the tasks of administering property, directing production and enforcing the law were combined almost exclusively within the state, resulting in a rather paternalistic dynamic. And the admission that this paternalism existed should lead us to recall that its resemblance to authoritarianism can be stronger and more damaging than one might imagine. The "update" of the Cuban economic model would fail, or be very incomplete, if it did not organically and sincerely include an intensive effort to strengthen participatory democracy, with the concomitant development of a sense of citizenship with regard to rights and duties. Such a model is a far cry from the sham that is capitalist democracy.

This is challenging in conceptual terms, let alone in practice. The imperialist imposition of a neo-colonialist republic in Cuba led to the conscious or unconscious repudiation of the very idea of a republic, even though that idea was born in struggle here, intertwined with the thrust for independence. Later, in the unsatisfactory republic founded in 1902, the struggles against the interventionist power that led to the triumph of 1959 began to take shape.

The devaluation of the concept of republic runs counter, however, to the fact that Cuba is, as its constitution proclaims, a socialist republic, a republic of workers. You [Arnold August] have lived in this country and made an honourable study of its institutions and its social and political workings. You know that we have an imperfect democracy, but that it's one that rests on foundations and purposes that allow for, indeed demand, its improvement. This is a vital task, for which the U.S., ruled by powerful corporations and by an obsession with dominating the world, has not the slightest legal — let alone moral — authority to lecture anyone.

AA: Obama visited Cuba from March 20 to 22 with his whole family: his wife Michelle, their two daughters and his mother-in-law. Having lived in Cuba and, more recently, spoken with Cubans, I know how the family holds a place of supreme importance for Cubans. Of course, the family is important in all societies. However, it seems that the Cuban family holds more importance than in most other societies. Is this right? For example, what is the importance of the family in Spain compared with Cuba? The point is, Obama seems to have wanted to project an image of the young American family in order to win some sympathy from Cuban families. This way, it is hoped that Cubans would forget that Obama is at the forefront of U.S. imperialism. In other words, the effect is to "depoliticize" the U.S. presidency. What do you think?

LTS: Those quotation marks are very appropriate. "Depoliticization" and "deideologization" are smokescreens behind which one particular political concept, one ideology, attempts to supplant another. Where imperialist machinations are in play, this consists in invalidating anything smacking of revolution and anti-capitalism, and putting in its place the values, or value voids, characteristic of the empire. The man in the White House is the commander-in-chief of the empire and his chiefs of staff are headquartered in the Pentagon. The family is universally important, but how that importance is expressed will depend in each case on cultural and religious traditions, national and regional paths, and economic and political models of leadership — in short, on the paths each particular society has followed; Cuba resembles Spain in many respects but remains Cuba in others. While feudalism once reigned supreme in that nation [Spain] and fascist sedition later crushed its attempt at republican modernization, Cuba rebelled against the servitude that Spain sought to impose upon it. From that struggle emerged the revolutionary Cuba we have today. Nor is the miscegenation that occurred in the Spanish case identical to what happened in Cuba. Here, the people brought over from black Africa added complexity to the island's ethnic makeup and infused an emancipatory dimension associated with the fight against slavery into our politics. Let me now come to the case of Obama's visit to Cuba.

On March 8, 2010, an article I wrote about the growing enthusiasm around Obama was published on the *Cubarte* portal [Cuban cultural website]: "Sí, Obama es mejor que Bush" (Yes, Obama is better than Bush). It isn't on my site, which was launched in October of that year. I still contend, as I did in that article, that the current U.S. president was or is better than his coarse predecessor, whose monstrous behaviour would be difficult, though not impossible, to outdo. I likewise contended then, and still do, that the new president was "more dangerous" because he commits or promotes outrages just as Bush did, only he does it so "elegantly" and with the endorsement of an unmerited Nobel Peace Prize. In another essay, in seeking to stress the cinematic qualities of President Obama, I wrote that it is as if Denzel Washington were in the White House!

The actor-president Obama, whose name I use here and elsewhere as a synecdoche for his team of sharp advisors, is onstage every day at the White House and wherever else he may go. When he visited the island this year [2016], nothing that he did was unscripted. Various observers noted how his gracious and attractive image was beamed into masses of Cuban households, not over a radio or TV station that is private or an enemy of Cuba — such as those that have offended the nation by disrespectfully using the name of José Martí [the Washington-funded TV and radio broadcasting programs based in Miami] — but on Televisión Cubana [the entity responsible for all Cuban television channels, which in turn is administered by the state's Cuban Institute of Radio and Television]. This television entity, purportedly so tightly controlled, does not derive revenue from capitalist advertising but from the labour of the nation's people, the sugarcane workers, builders and miners; from those who uphold the country's prestige in the areas of medicine and other sciences; from the efforts of all those who contribute to the country's economy. And the president of the empire did not appear in just any slot but on a highly popular prime-time program [see "'La Revolución will be televised': Which 'Revolución,'" in Chapter 4]. He did not deserve such a gift.

Anyone who thinks this was an individual exploit by some artist or technician in the employ of Televisión Cubana is guilty, it seems to me, of utter naïveté. The actor who gained the most was the one in the White House, the same one who landed at José Martí International Airport with his wife, daughters and mother-in-law in tow. If he'd had sons-in-law and grandchildren, he might have brought them along as well. He knows that the image of the family man can be profitable in itself. It also has the capacity to draw attention, as if by contrast, to a country in which the political, labour and school dynamics, plus the dynamics of our necessary armed defence — of a true and profound Revolution — have at times provoked dramatic family ruptures.

Moreover, Obama, in exhibiting his own family — a far from reprehensible act if done with decency — wanted to set himself apart from the style of personal presentation prevalent in the Cuban Revolution. Following the example of its *máximo* leader [Fidel Castro], public figures in Cuba do not generally appear with their family members at events and ceremonies. This tradition could be criticized as something that does not strengthen the family institution, and might well turn out to be a deserving topic for the much-discussed imperative of changing mentalities in this country. It could also, however, be praised as a resource for these same officials, one they can use to protect their privacy and avert the kind of gossip on which public relations agencies around the world thrive. Most important, this tradition has helped with the sincere, resolute, effective, across-the-board fight against nepotism, an evil that has done much harm to revolutions the world over.

AA: Shortly after Obama's visit, some much-discussed events occurred in Cuba: the shooting of a *Fast and Furious* sequel [a Hollywood blockbuster action film series], the arrival of the first U.S. cruise ship in Havana, the Chanel fashion show. Even the daily *Granma* published an unfavourable opinion about these events regarding the cultural effects. What is your opinion about them?

LTS: I might begin by saying that none of these three events appealed to me, but it would be an insufficient answer, among other things, because a country is not as a rule designed to satisfy individual tastes. Perhaps I should insist on one fact: to the mainstream foreign media, the purveyors of (dis)information, Cuba is damned if it does and damned just as well if it doesn't. On the one hand, they criticize the country, demonize it, for being an international anomaly. However, I've always found it honourable and stimulating that Cuba has managed to remain an anomaly in a world dominated by imperial forces, a world shot through with the moral misery they generate or embody. On the other hand, they will not forgive Cuba even when it appears determined to "normalize," despite this being done in conjunction with a wide-ranging process to objectively establish diplomatic relations with the U.S. As it happens, the simultaneity of these dual normalizations is probably more or less a coincidence. Nevertheless, we are seeing how Cuba, which did not need this [normalization] to deserve the admiration of so many people around the world, has become "fashionable" since the announcement on December 17, 2014, of the process in question. This is so especially among certain people carried away by their own euphoria. Some visitors are undoubtedly just following fashion, but there are others who want to come to Cuba "before it changes," as well as people who take for granted that it will be swallowed up by the Yankee invasion.

But criticism of what Cuba does, or ceases to do, is not a recent phenomenon. To take one of many examples, when the massively attended Paz Sin Fronteras (Peace Without Borders) concert was held on the Plaza de la Revolución José Martí in 2009 [in Havana], the Revolution's enemies might have hoped it wouldn't happen at all, or that it would be wielded as a weapon against Cuba. But beyond any reasonable criticism or divergent view one might have heard at the time, the concert had a beneficial effect on the country's image abroad. Then someone purporting to be a revolutionary philosopher said that Cuba should be forgiven for having ceased to be socialist for the two hours that the concert lasted. This comment did not go unanswered, but it is an illustration of the premise that nothing about Cuba goes unnoticed, whether for the purposes of praising the country or attacking it.

If it does not receive cruise ships, if it does not play host to the sets of capitalist TV shows — some of them truly terrible — and does not offer its roads and public spaces for showy displays of what many consider utter banality, it is accused of being dictatorial, of isolating itself from the world, of being boring, leaden, behind the times. (But is every new trend worth imitating?) And if it opens itself up to these "cultural" manifestations (in many cases, "anti-cultural" would describe them better), not only do reactions come from those who reject these manifestations on revolutionary grounds but also from those who take advantage of them to discredit Cuba. Without money, you can't get anywhere in today's world, nor can you provide a decent life for people who deserve one. Cuba needs to swell its public coffers, which have been much diminished by a blockade that remains in effect — a fact that must be stated and restated for as long as it continues to exist.

So should Cuba condemn itself to inertia, to collapse? Recently, I was in Tenerife [the largest and most populous of the Spanish Canary Islands], where I heard railing on the part of ordinary people and local merchants against the cruise ships, which add little to the local economy: everything, or nearly everything, is already paid for onboard the ship. Yet cruise ships could give a boost to Cuban tourism and help counteract the image of an isolated country that some have tried to paint of us, at times by putting an unfriendly spin on the measures we have taken in our defence.

Let's say a person is seen on the Malecón [the seawall boardwalk in Havana] extending a U.S. flag to receive a cruise ship, or some genius — believing that in so doing he has pulled off a real coup — organizes a spectacle that compounds the sexist and commercial use of the female image with the misuse of the Cuban flag as material for rumba dress costumes. Could it be possible that no one notices that these acts might be considered a desecration of a zone of our cultural heritage as worthy as any other? All these are tangible facts that must be analyzed and confronted culturally, via persuasion and education, and also via any prohibitions that it may be necessary to apply.

If Cuba decides to augment the public treasury by allowing a foreign film crew to shoot a movie, or tries to improve its image overseas by hosting a fashion show staged by a company founded on a myth of twentieth-century fashion and fragrance (which is also said to have spied for the Nazis), it must take utmost care in doing so. Among other things, it must avoid annoying its citizens with street closings, a practice that has come to be applied too liberally. In addition, the public has a right to be annoyed — it has that right at least — if, besides being given no information (part of a deficit that the nation must do away with once and for all), it has to cope with street closings. This circumstance causes nuisances that may be exacerbated by our poor transportation systems.

I personally find it disrespectful to hold a fashion show with an admission price of $1,500 in a country that is the setting for a Revolution characterized as being "of the humble, by the humble, and for the humble," a country in which (as a result of both the blockade and our internal deficiencies) there is so much privation. Furthermore, while the country should not continue to be typified by overreliance on prohibitions, neither should it fear applying them when necessary. It should, in particular, have no qualms about doing so out of sincere respect for the citizenry, for the people whose resistance has allowed the nation to stay independent, sovereign and dignified. It is the citizens, after all, who have been decisive in persuading the empire that its policy of hostility and isolation against Cuba has not produced the expected results.

For the rest, dear Arnold, it suffices to direct our full attention to a concern that pervades your questions: to what extent does the Cuban nation run the risk of succumbing to the "new" interventionist schemes of the U.S.? One fact remains: nothing has succeeded in diverting Cuba, meaning the patriotic and worthy majority of its people, from the path of dignity, independence and social justice that has pitted it against the empire and made it a sovereign country. Nothing has succeeded: not the neo-colonial domination of Cuba by the U.S., initiated with the intervention of 1898 — which Martí had resolved to prevent with a war "as brief and direct as lightning," though the intervention lasted until the Cuban Revolution triumphed in the early days of 1959; nor the service provided to the imperial power by the "sensible patricians" and "great men" who have played or continue to play its game, and whom Martí denounced in his day; nor the half-century blockade and other forms of aggression, including armed aggression, imposed on Cuba to punish it for its will to sovereignty and to eradicate the example it has given the world by gaining its own sovereignty; nor the intense media and cultural campaign, before and after 1959, to sell the Cuban people on the "American way of life." Cuba's unique approach shines through in our culture, which has always been open to the world, from the moment it was forged and throughout its development. It is a culture unmistakably our own, one of resistance and triumph, the better to thwart the aggressors, the colonized and the servants of empire.

From now on, the struggle may be even more complex; it may require a more conscientiously emancipatory attitude and ideas on the part of the majority; but there are plenty of reasons to assert that Cuba will remain steadfast on its path and will continue to acquit itself with grace. What we have yet to achieve in this effort — starting with economic efficiency — we must now attend to more expediently than ever. And this naturally includes ensuring that the manoeuvres of the actor in the White House, and the confusions that they may create in some people's minds, do not cause more damage than the blockade and the aggression have already done.

Notes

1 This play on words literally translates as "Black man, are you Swedish?" but in colloquial terms, it means "Black man, are you dumb?" The journalist, who is black, refers to a line from Virulo, the well-known pro-Revolution leader of a humorous, musical comedy ensemble. This comment, which is widely known in Cuba, emerged in the 1980s: in a sketch, Virulo referred to a black man who attempted to pass himself off as a Swede to derive some benefit from associating with the burgeoning Cuban tourist trade.

2 I did not ask them, and do not intend to, as I firmly believe that it is up to the Cubans to deal with this issue. In fact, there seems to be a change developing in late summer 2016. The official press such as *Granma*, *Juventud Rebelde* and *Trabajadores* (the trade union printed newspaper) are reprinting a few blog entries from the "alternative" press, including Iroel Sánchez. See also Chapter 4.

Chapter 4

CHALLENGES FOR CUBA IN 2017 AND BEYOND

Luis Toledo Sande concludes, in the May 2016 interview, that "from now on, the struggle may be even more complex." This conclusion, similar to the conclusion reached in Chapter 2 that things will be "more difficult," resulted in both cases from an analysis of the period since December 17, 2014, compared with the context after January 1, 1959. While the evaluations were made before the Trump electoral victory in November 2016, they apply to the Trump presidency as well. As we analyze in this chapter, however, these assertions do not arise from any perceived new initiative that may be taken by Trump. Circumstances remain more complex and difficult for the same reason as they did under the Obama Administration. The U.S. Cuba policy consists in a change in tactics in order to achieve the goal of subverting the Cuban Revolution. It is likely that Trump will merge his rhetoric into the Obama policy, becoming its latest standard-bearer, albeit with the Trump trademark.

This chapter and Chapter 5 take us to November 2016 on the themes dealt with in Chapters 2 and 3, both written before the Trump electoral success. They show that the Trump Cuba policy will have to deal with these same subjects in one way or another. The Trump mandate also introduces new dilemmas for his administration and Cuba that are specific to Trump. The businessman/politician dichotomy is the most important of the Trump idiosyncrasies.

TRUMP AND CUBA

The first question to evaluate is which Trump will dominate Cuba–U.S. relations — will it be Trump the pragmatic businessman or Trump as influenced by the ideology of most of his entourage? At the time Obama visited Cuba in March 2016, CNN interviewed the main candidates for the Republican and Democratic nominations:

WOLF BLITZER: If you are elected president, would you continue to normalize economic and diplomatic relations with Cuba?

TRUMP: Probably so, but I'd want much better deals that I will make....

BLITZER: All right, so you say you're going to continue to try to normalize diplomatic and economic relations. Would you open a Trump hotel in Havana?

TRUMP: I would. I would. At the right time, when we're allowed to do it. Right now we're not. I wouldn't do it on the basis if you get a 49 percent interest, because right now you get 49 percent interest.[1] Nobody knows even what the economics are or what they're going to do. And maybe it won't work out.... But I will tell you, I think Cuba has certain potential, and I think it's OK to bring Cuba into the fold but you have to make a much better deal and you have to get all liabilities. You don't want to be sued in a year from now or two years from now for $4 trillion because they say we destroyed Cuba.[2] It has to be part of the deal.[3] (CNN 2016b)

In contrast to Trump the pragmatic businessman, on September 16, 2016, while campaigning as the Republican presidential nominee in Miami, Trump seemed to strike an ideological tone:

All the concessions that Barack Obama has granted the Castro regime were done through executive order, which means the next president can reverse them — and that I will do unless the Castro regime meets our demands. Not my demands. Our demands. Those demands are religious and political freedom for the Cuban people. And the freeing of political prisoners. (Caputo 2016)

Possibly egged on by his ideologically prone advisors, he was obviously catering to what he perceived as a pro-blockade vote among Cuban-Americans. However, the analyses from all political stripes agree that the majority of this section of the Floridian population *support the lifting of the blockade and increased travel and business.* In any case, it seems that Trump the businessman in March 2016 was more thorough, passionate and spontaneous in speaking about continuing the overture to Cuba compared with the few buzzwords learned by rote. This should not come as a surprise. In 1998, a company controlled by Trump secretly conducted business for potential golf courses and hotel construction in Cuba despite strict American trade bans that made such undertakings illegal (Eichenwald 2016).

Because of his unpredictability, it is very difficult to say which Trump will prevail: the pragmatic businessman or the politician affected by ideology. However, his most radical anti-Cuba positions were both presented in Miami. Therefore, one should perhaps not give too much weight to their significance, as a considerable amount is past history. One should also note that while he was echoing the violent anti-Castroite Cuban American National Foundation (CANF) narrative against Cuba, he could not hold back from speculating about the construction of a Trump hotel on the island.

Nevertheless, even if he decides to go the ideological route and pursue a hard stance on Cuba, it will be very complicated and difficult for him to roll back Obama's changes. Robert L. Muse is the leading American attorney in terms of expertise on U.S. legislation, executive orders and laws related to Cuba.[4] He is reported to have said:

> Mr. Trump seemed to believe that Washington had struck a single deal with Cuba, when in reality there are several agreements that range from direct mail to managing oil spills.
>
> Mr. Trump could pick through them one by one to eliminate the ones he dislikes and keep others. But … the American government could be financially liable if it pulled out the rug from under companies that had acted in good faith.
>
> Rescinding enhanced travel that Obama has introduced would be the most tragic thing Trump might do, but I don't think he will.… He has invested a lifetime in travel, resorts and hotel accommodations, and it's a global enterprise. It seems counterintuitive.

Because the companies struck deals in good faith based on existing U.S. regulations, they could be entitled to compensation or would need to be grandfathered-in to new policies, according to Muse. That interpretation is based on a provision of the Fifth Amendment of the U.S. Constitution, which says no one can be deprived of property "without due process of law; nor shall private property be taken for public use, without just compensation." Muse noted, "These companies have expended real time and money on these deals" (Whitefield 2016; Robles 2016).

There are many powerful forces in the U.S. that do *not* favour rolling back the Obama initiative. In fact, many of them want to go further and facilitate *increased* trade and travel. In fact during the transition period Trump nominated his Secretary of State who so far in words is *against* the "thaw," while his main negotiator on Cuban affairs is very much *in favour* of continuing the Obama policy. This is one more reason to believe that on balance, the evidence seems to suggest that while the Trump rhetoric and political posturing may differ from that of Obama, he will not substantially change the course put in place by Obama.

DOES PLURALISM EXIST IN CUBA?

In Chapter 2, I highlighted the role of the alternative media in contrast to the official media in Cuba as constituting one aspect of Cuba's version of pluralism. That pluralism actually exists in Cuba may come as a surprise to some, given that U.S. mainstream politicians and media continue to propagate the false notion that Cuba is the antithesis of a pluralist society — that is, it is monolithic or homogeneous. The fact is that Cuban society is heterogeneous, even if it does not mimic the U.S.-centric notion of pluralism, presented as the sole model for the world.[5] Nevertheless, the question remains, how should one evaluate pluralism in Cuba with the ongoing Cuba–U.S. debate as the backdrop? The short answer is that the Cuban situation is best analyzed in and of itself, not in comparison with the U.S.

Let us look back at one of my articles from 2016, "Cuba–U.S. Relations and Freedom of the Press" (August 2015c; reprinted in Chapter 2). In August 2015, U.S. Secretary of State John Kerry raised the flag in front of the U.S. Embassy in Havana. CNN seized on Kerry's relatively diplomatic statement at the time concerning the supposed lack of democracy in Cuba. The CNN reporter in Havana, Jake Tapper, editorialized about the "lack of freedom" in Cuba since it suffers under a "brutal dictatorship." This disinformation was, of course, amplified and repeated as sound bites by the most zealous, narrow-minded anchors at CNN's U.S. headquarters. Together, they painted a picture of a grey, monolithic, homogeneous Cuba devoid of debate, freedom of expression and a free press. However, during and since the Obama visit, Cuba is proving to be a hotbed of heterogeneity, a new experience of pluralism for a socialist society. However, one would not discover this by relying on the U.S. and other Western mainstream media.

The Alternative Media in Cuba and in the U.S.

The Cuban reality must be studied carefully without corporate media blinders in order to fully uncover the dynamic pluralism on the island. It manifests itself in many ways. One example of pluralism consists in the five Cuban experts interviewed in Chapter 3, who have their own respective critical views of the Obama visit and its aftermath, as is the case with many of their fellow academics, intellectuals and journalists. While all were fully supportive of the visit, their perspectives were generally far more critical, analytical and ideological than those found in the mainstream Cuban media. With a few exceptions in the short period surrounding the Obama 2016 visit, these views (and their authors) were not published in the official sources, such as the printed dailies *Granma* and *Juventud Rebelde* or the weekly *Trabajadores*. These periodicals are available to the entire population, whereas the alternative media is accessed only through the Internet and only by about 30 percent of the population.

The alternative media consists of the popular website *Cubadebate* and UPEC's *Cuba Periodistas,* which is less visited but influential in journalistic circles, as well as many blogs, including those administered by four of the interviewees. *Cubadebate* publishes most of the articles written by the five interviewees and other alternative writers. *Cuba Periodistas* likewise reprints most of them. The thinking of these five is but a sample of what Cuba has to offer. Their journalistic endeavours are not similar in either content or form to the main Cuban print media. In contrast, the alternative options respond to the decisive need to deal with the profound cultural conflict between Cuba and the U.S., rather than mere superficial reporting. In this chapter as in previous ones, culture is referred to in the broad sense to include the artistic, ideological and political spheres. Thus, the alternative articles are piercing. These intellectuals are not in any way swayed by diplomacy to the detriment of resisting the cultural aggression. Rather, they view diplomacy and the conflict over ideas and values as *complementary.* These writers are not lured into an overly conciliatory attitude toward Obama. Their work is an expression of Cuba's national dignity, thus inspiring many of their faithful readers. This journalistic endeavour educates readers daily to reflect upon the profound cultural differences emanating from both sides of the straits. This is what makes the writers so popular among Internet users; many of these readers invariably suggest (or even demand) in the comments on blog entries that these be published in the print media, to which the entire population has access.

Some journalists in the main print media, however, are now also dealing with the two countries' relations in a profound and incisive manner. For example, Sergio Gómez, the young director of *Granma*'s international section, has been writing critical articles. In addition, there has been a notable change in the print media since late summer 2016. The official media has started to more frequently reprint articles by notable alternative bloggers, such as Iroel Sánchez. It is noteworthy that this new and encouraging development does not result from these writers watering down their views or becoming more "moderate." On the contrary, their opinions and trenchant analyses have been maintained, even becoming more astute, prolific and mature. It seems, rather, that the *official media* is changing. It seems that the press *is* in fact responding to some degree to the burning needs of the time and grassroots input. The average person on the street is acutely aware of the dangers on the horizon accompanying the otherwise positive news of renewed diplomatic relations and negotiations. One cannot underestimate the political consciousness of the majority of Cubans.

A further evolution of this trend occurred in September when Cuban students' opposition to U.S. subversive programs impacted the daily periodical press. This episode is dealt with below in the section titled "U.S. Democracy Promotion in Cuba: As American as Apple Pie."

Despite what appears to be a timid new development in the official media, the growing community of online bloggers, writers, website editors and social media activists represents an alternative as they inspire the mainstream press to continue incorporating some of their articles. These reprints still comprise only a small portion of articles on Cuba–U.S. relations and on the U.S. itself. The latest developments, which began in late summer 2016, are a manifestation of the growing influence of this alternative, not only on the Cuban press but on the Cuban political scene. It is not a merger of the two. If this new evolution in *Granma*, *Juventud Rebelde* and *Trabajadores* does not develop further — or even stalls — the alternative remains fully alternative. Either way, the alternative to the mainstream press has already succeeded in establishing itself in Cuban media. This is one feature of Cuba's pluralism.[6]

The term "alternative" may seem to offer hope to those who favour a change in Cuba's political and social system toward a multi-party and capitalist system reliant on the U.S.; however, the concept of "alternative" — like "pluralism" itself — is manipulated by U.S.-centrism. "Alternative" translates differently — and even in contradictory ways — in Cuba and in the U.S. For example, in the U.S. (and in Canada, by extension), my articles are published by some *alternative* press who are opposed to the capitalist/ imperialist status quo on which the political system is based. However, "alternative" in the Cuban context, particularly in this era overshadowed by Cuba–U.S. relations, takes on another meaning. The divergent option, in contrast to much of the official media, highlights resistance to U.S. cultural aggression and defence of Cuba's system.

If there is concern among some that the alternative media in Cuba may be providing grist for the mill of the Cuban "dissidents" on and off the island, nothing could be further from the truth. Paradoxically, opposition to these "dissidents" — paid or unpaid by the U.S. to undermine the Revolution and Cuba's sovereignty — is mainly pursued *by the alternative* Cuban media, and *not* by the official press. In fact, the many blogs lining up to take on this role, such as Iroel Sánchez's *La pupila insomnia,* have self-imposed this vocation.

Unofficially, there are an estimated 1,000 to 1,500 such Cuban-based blogs and far more active Twitter accounts and Facebook pages. Some lead an almost daily, tit-for-tat ideological and political war against the "dissidents."

The Alternative in Cuban Television: Not from Miami but from Latin America

A second manifestation of Cuban pluralism is the most spectacular, considering that it affects all Cubans. It pertains to television, which is available in every Cuban household and avidly viewed. The state-run Televisión Cubana is responsible for the many national and provincial television channels. And then there is Telesur, a project of Hugo Chávez. It is a multi-state-funded, pan-Latin American terrestrial and satellite television network, headquartered in Caracas and sponsored by the governments of Venezuela, Cuba, Ecuador, Nicaragua, Uruguay and Bolivia. Argentina was also involved until the right-wing, pro-U.S. Macri government withdrew its support in March 2016.

Telesur is broadcast on one of the Cuban channels seven days a week, from early morning until well after midnight, interrupted only from about 4:30 p.m. to 9:30 p.m. for local prime-time shows and news. In terms of form and content, it is remarkably different from and superior to Cuban television. This is the view of most Cubans with whom I have spoken, even those who work for Cuban TV. Telesur's lively, no-holds-barred, well-presented and modern fully documented political and economic news analysis and reporting is exceptional. It also features special programs on sports, culture, health and gender diversity. However, Cuban TV and Telesur complement each other on news and special documentaries. One recent outstanding example was the coverage by both Cuban TV and Telesur of Fidel Castro's death and its aftermath. In general, Telesur is more radical and left-leaning than most current programming on Cuban TV, with notable exceptions, such as the *Mesa Redonda* program on CubaTV, anchored by Randy Alonso and Arleen Derivet. It is broadcast in prime time several days a week and retransmitted later in the evening. Telesur deals graphically with the U.S. domestic situation, covering items such as racial killings and Obama (at the time), as the leader of U.S. imperialism. It is staunchly and unapologetically against U.S. imperialism.[7]

A personal example comes to mind when zeroing in on Telesur as an alternative, and this is with regard to Cuba–U.S. relations. Telesur invited me to Havana to comment on the March 2016 Obama visit along with Cuban colleagues. Reference was made in some Cuban and international conglomerate press to the oft-repeated details surrounding the fact that the previous visit by a U.S. president was Calvin Coolidge in 1928 — he arrived on a military-escorted warship. This was often presented in comparison with Obama, who, of course, did not land that way. Consciously or not, this banal narrative served to paint a comparatively angelic picture of the nature of Obama's visit. In order to burst this bubble, the analogy I offered on TeleSUR TV was: "Obama's arrival was via a media warship armed with cultural aggression," followed by some examples of this U.S. cultural onslaught.

A Promising Future: Inadvertent Assistance from an Unexpected Source

How does the future of Cuban pluralism in the realm of the media look for 2017 and moving forward? With regard to the print media, it depends on whether it continues to be more inclusive of the alternative option. However, even if this does not take place, thanks to the increase in Internet access, more and more Cubans will be able to read and comment on the revolutionary alternative press on the Internet. As for Obama, he was dedicated, in collaboration with the Cuban government, to contributing toward increased Internet facilities on the island. This would translate into a positive, if unwelcome for the U.S., spinoff effect of U.S. Cuba policy, since it would accelerate Cuban access to the alternative media, which is strongly against U.S. imperialism.

The same paradox applies to TeleSUR. The future of the alternative TeleSUR in Cuba is secure, despite challenges such as the Argentine right-wing pro-U.S. state in shutting down TeleSUR in that country. In fact, Cubans will continue to become better informed, as TeleSUR has not rested on its laurels but, rather, continues to make improvements. In addition, the website version of TeleSUR is updated on a timely basis with high-quality reports and a variety of analyses and opinions supported by modern documentaries on a multimedia platform. Its Twitter feed and Facebook posts are perhaps the best in the progressive Spanish-speaking world. Thus, more and more, with increased Internet access in Cuba (perhaps assisted by the U.S.), people are consulting TeleSUR's website and interacting with its social media. TeleSUR boldly challenges the U.S.-led media war against Latin America by further developing its strong anti-capitalist and anti-imperialist orientation. The multi-state station constitutes a focal point to rally around for forces and countries in favour of a multi-polar world, which is so important for Cuba — nay, all of Latin America — in opposing the ongoing U.S. appetite for world domination.

FROM TROPICAL HELL TO TRENDY HOT SPOT FOR WESTERNERS

When I made the analogy on TeleSUR that Obama's arrival was "via a media warship armed with cultural aggression," I did not imagine how close to the truth that statement might be. As it happened, Cuba was about to be hit with a real onslaught of Western culture. It is a given that spring in Cuba is generally much hotter than in the North. The month of May 2016 proved to be particularly seething in terms of debate and controversy, as evidenced by the backlash against this encroachment by Cuban journalists and many other people at the grassroots level.

The "Cuban Spring"

Among the first to land in Havana at the end of April 2016 for ten days was the production crew for the Hollywood action film *Fast and Furious 8* (*Fast 8*), barely a month after the Obama visit. The elaborate installations, including vintage 1950s American cars along with many other vehicles, a helicopter and dozens of Hollywood filming trucks, occupied major sectors of Havana for the entire period.

The Malecón and some surrounding streets are the main thoroughfares of this city of two million people. Entire districts were turned into a Hollywood set and completely blocked off. I was in Havana at the time, and all the taxi drivers complained that the transportation system, already weak, was seriously hindered. The state normally provides traffic updates in all its media for major events, yet none were made available. People complained about the serious disruptions to their daily work schedules.

Fast 8 provided employment to 250 Cubans. When I asked some of them how they were paid, the usually conversational Cubans became tight-lipped. It later became common knowledge that they were paid between US$30 and $50 *per day*, directly by the Hollywood production company (Vargas 2016; Taggart and Batista 2016). This is in stark contrast to Cuban salaries, paid in local Cuban currency.

Many people, especially youth, lined the streets behind the barricades to get a look at the action and perhaps a glimpse or photos of the main actors. The film series, already very popular in Cuba, notably with young people, seemed to have peaked in esteem and even adoration.

The next invasion, in early May 2016, this time from France, was designer Chanel's Cruise Collection fashion show. Chanel imported to Havana not only forty-seven models (only two Cuban models were employed) but also 700 guests. They were ferried by 170 vintage 1950s American convertible cars from the Hotel Nacional to the classical and beautiful Prado Boulevard promenade, which was used as the catwalk. No Cubans were allowed to attend or view the fashion show. They were, in fact, kept back by barricades. The fashion show featured some clothing to apparently generate sentimentality for pre-revolutionary times. This was, of course, blended with some models sporting their version of Che Guevara's legendary starred beret. Lest anyone think that this was a nod to revolutionary Cuba, keep in mind that, in 2014, the same designer from Chanel mounted a fashion show in Europe mimicking the feminist movement. On that occasion, their models carried loudspeakers and uttered (ridiculous) slogans, mocking a women's rights demonstration. Likewise in Havana, Chanel's goal is to appear trendy, with that city serving as the backdrop. However, its only pursuit is profit, using the iconic scenery of the Prado and Old Havana to increase its gains. Was there any economic spinoff for Cuba? It is unlikely. Cuban journalists also questioned this, as outlined in the next section.

The CNN correspondent in Cuba did not miss the opportunity to report to the U.S. and an international audience that these types of fashion shows had been banned in Cuba during the early years of the Revolution. Thus, the disinformation flowed that the Cubans are now "free," liberated from Fidel's "oppression." One cannot underestimate the U.S. mainstream media continuously pointing a finger at Fidel Castro. It is not a personal issue, not of one man. The media are working to undermine the foundations of Fidel Castro and the Revolution — among other achievements, the dignity and sovereignty of the Cuban people. By denigrating his person, they hope to disparage the Cuban revolutionary project and create doubt and division. The U.S. cannot achieve its long-term stated goal of suffocating the Cuban Revolution while Cuba's pride in its independence and national socialist culture flourishes. These features of the Cuban Revolution act as a formidable shield to protect the socialist project despite its weaknesses, which the vast majority of Cubans are endeavouring to overcome. The name "Fidel Castro" is synonymous with the Cuban tradition of striving for equality, whereas "Chanel" implies the exact opposite of this ideal: unbridled and decadent opulence, consumerism and individualism, combined with well-calculated opportunism to make a fast buck.

The day before the Chanel show, the first cruise ship in over fifty years arrived in Havana's harbour. However, as some of the Cuban press astutely noted, none of the American passengers aboard the Carnival Cruise Line's *Adonia* were tourists. They had to travel as part of a licensed educational or humanitarian trip and thus were banned from enjoying tourist activities, such as visiting Cuban beaches, because in May 2016 this was still prohibited by the U.S. Furthermore, the travellers' expenses had already fully been paid directly to the cruise company as part of a package deal.

However, from the viewpoint of many Cubans, all of this was secondary. What erupted as a major controversy was not the monetary side as such. The ship was greeted with much fanfare — perhaps too much. It also was observed that the Americans were welcomed by two young Cuban women who were scantily dressed in rumba outfits made from the material of the Cuban flag. This scene was clearly organized by someone in the Cuban apparatus. Television viewers around the world witnessed the spectacle, as stereotypical-looking middle-aged American men posed with the flag-clad women. This is unheard of in Cuba, where the Cuban flag is a matter of pride and dignity for which so many have sacrificed their lives in opposing Spanish colonialism and then U.S. imperialism, not only before 1959 but since then as well. Therefore, this scene in Havana harbour very quickly contributed to the Cuban backlash. The Cuban response was hardly an exaggeration, given that, since this incident, the notorious use of the flag's image has been incorporated into the flashy publicity of Carnival Cruise Line seen regularly on American television.

The Cuban Response Was Fast and Furious

In response to this series of incursions, many acclaimed and well-known Cuban journalists and intellectuals responded immediately, one after the other. The reaction was outrage. Based on the comments to the blogs and websites, and speaking with people in Havana, this sentiment was manifested among many Cubans. I have never witnessed such a rapid and indignant backlash against U.S. cultural aggression since my investigation into Cuba began in the 1990s. Admittedly, there had never been such an ostentatious show of Western cultural penetration into Cuba. This was obviously one of the negative spinoff effects of the new Cuba–U.S. relationship and the resulting "opening" of Cuba to the West. However, the Cuban boomerang response solidified and further deepened Cubans' defence of their culture, national consciousness, dignity, socialist values and sovereignty.

Bloggers were, as usual, the first to respond, but they were not the only ones. The first salvo was fired by none other than the director of the international news section of the Communist Party daily *Granma,* twenty-eight-year-old Sergio Gómez. On May 4, 2016, when Chanel had just cleared the catwalk on the Prado, his blog post on the website Medium was a searing analysis of *Fast 8* and Chanel:

> It would be hard to overturn a revolution, much less Cuba's, by the
> filming of a Hollywood blockbuster, helicopter included, or by the

closing of the Prado Boulevard to show off a certain famous French brand's Cruise Collection. But the way these events are interpreted, in the context of a process of change that will define the destiny of 11 million people, could subvert the social consensus that the country has maintained for more than half a century....

There were many people on the Prado trying to see the show. But there were even more in the stores trying to find basic goods, such as chicken and cooking oil, with recently reduced prices. (2016b)

Graziella Pogolotti, the well-known and esteemed eighty-four-year-old Cuban cultural critic and journalist wrote a bristling editorial on May 7, 2016, for the Communist Youth League daily paper *Juventud Rebelde*. Her piece, which reflected what many Cubans were thinking at the time, provided a deep analysis of Cuban traditional culture in an original way:

> *Fast and Furious*, a commercial film of poor quality, erupted violently into the lives of the people of Havana. It disrupted transportation in key areas. It affected students and workers. It added tensions to the already difficult daily life. Something similar happened with the presence of the Chanel catwalk. Unacceptable prohibitions were imposed on the residents of some areas. The arrival of the first American cruise ship, according to our news media, was welcomed by a cabaret-style choreography: the young women wore scanty costumes made from the national flag. (2016a)

She went on to write that it is perfectly normal to open paths for commerce, investment and tourism. However, she asserted that Cuba has to "set the rules of the game."

What was astonishing — even refreshing and necessary — was that *Granma* reprinted Pogolotti's stinging article a few days later, with a notice on its front page that it was doing so "because of its importance" (2016b: 3). The daily newspaper generally reserves this prime spot for articles, with that qualification of "importance," by prominent Cuban leaders and political personalities.

On May 10, the Unión de Escritores y Artistas de Cuba released a statement focusing on the vulgar use of the Cuban flag: "Cuban writers and artists reacted with surprise, astonishment and indignation at the images of the reception of the *Adonia* cruise travellers, who arrived earlier this month of May, at the Port of Havana. Girls clad in swimsuits with the national flag as the print and moving to one of our traditional rhythms provided a deplorable sight for first-time visitors to Cuba."

Also on May 10, *Juventud Rebelde* carried an interview by journalist Onaisys Fonticoba Gener with Roberto Smith, president of the government film institute that acts as host for events such as the *Fast 8* filming. Her pointed questions revolved around the concerns of the people and her colleagues with regard to the "unique debate" — as she termed it — that had emerged. One question pertained to the disruption of traffic with no planning for the ten-day film shoot, but no direct response was given. On the touchy issue of economic spinoffs for Cuba, the answer was equally evasive, namely that they would "have no problem to offer the final tally of [their] income" (Fonticoba Gener 2016). It is no wonder that the lack transparency contributed to the rumour mill, which contained more than a grain of truth about *Fast 8* in Havana. One of the scenarios creeping along the grapevine was that the American *Fast 8* producers were handing out US$20 bills to Cubans. While it may not have been entirely true — though it seems something along those lines *did* happen — the rumour definitely made the rounds among people in some neighbourhoods. I cannot help but think of the return to Cuba of the "Ugly American."[8]

The "Cuban Spring" events were covered with much fanfare in the Cuban media. However, this attention seemed to be arbitrary. Iroel Sánchez, in his customarily outspoken and caustic way, posted a blog article on June 21, 2016, bringing to the attention of his readers that the legendary Chilean musical band Inti Illimani, with more than fifty years of history, including its links to the anti-imperialist social struggles in Latin America, was on tour in Cuba in June. The band recorded an album and gave a concert, but these appearances "did not make even one headline in the Cuban press," thus the ironic title of Sánchez's article "Inti Illimani clandestino en Cuba" (Inti Illimani Undercover in Cuba).

I fully sympathize with Sánchez, as I could not help but notice the attention afforded by much of the Cuban media to U.S. cultural personalities visiting Cuba. Sánchez and others are in good company, however. None other than world-renowned Cuban folksinger Silvio Rodríguez put Sánchez's post on his own popular blog. *Cubadebate,* too, contributed to bringing Inti Illimani out of the shadows, by reposting Sánchez's piece.

"La *Revolución* Will Be Televised." Which *"Revolución"*?

There is one other cultural issue, as part of the Western offensive in spring 2016, that does not seem to have been dealt with in Cuba, perhaps because it is not widely seen as negative. On June 16, 2016, starting with the sentence "La revolución will be televised," a U.S. media source announced:

Cuban programming is coming to U.S. airwaves thanks to DISH, the Colorado-based provider with 13.9 million TV subscribers. The company announced the launch of a new channel called CubaMax TV, which will carry entertainment programming created in Cuba featuring some of the island's most famous celebrities. The channel will not feature any political or news programming, but instead will focus on comedies, children's programming, music videos and telenovelas [soap operas].

The channel's operations will be in Miami, where producers will package shows from Cuba and distribute them to subscribers of DishLATINO. (Gomez [A.] 2016c)

The programming is officially determined by the Cuban side. However, a Miami-based media outlet considered to be against the Revolution reported the following, based on an interview with the Americans involved:

A message published in the Cuban media announced that the programming of CubaMax would be selected by RTV Comercial, the commercial arm of the Cuban Radio and Television Institute. Is that completely true?

"The decisions regarding content will be made jointly. All parts should be in agreement. Of course, it should always be for the sake of the best development of the channel." (Padrón Cueto 2016)

The mainstream media outlet *USAToday* reported:

"Connecting [Cuban-American] viewers with their [Cuban] heritage and culture is at the heart of the DishLATINO brand promise, and today marks an important milestone as we deliver movies and TV shows from Cuba that were previously unavailable," Alfredo Rodríguez, vice-president of DishLATINO, said in a statement. "With an estimated two million Cubans living in the U.S. *and many others* eager to learn about the island's rich culture, we're excited to provide a window into the arts and entertainment world of Cuba.".…

DISH's new channel will now expose American viewers to a slew of Cuban artists and characters.

The most well-known is Pánfilo, a bumbling old man played by actor Luis Silva, who played dominoes with Obama in a televised sketch during the president's historic visit to Havana in March. (Gomez [A.] 2016c, emphasis added)

Actor Luis Silva portrays Pánfilo on the most popular comedy show on Cuban TV. With unbridled parody, he skilfully deals with the daily problems of the Cuban people, especially retired folks. How did he get connected to Obama? The video, now (in November 2016) available on the White House's YouTube channel, tells the story. Produced with the aid of the Cuban state-run TV Cubavisión, it recounts how Obama's main advisor on Cuba, Ben Rhodes, was looking beyond regular diplomacy to connect with the Cuban people. This sought-after novelty was intended to be featured *in addition* to the first time a sitting U.S. president would be allowed to speak directly to the Cuban people on TV. The U.S. Embassy in Cuba was contacted and chargé d'affaires Jeffrey DeLaurentis suggested a sketch with Pánfilo. He said he had noticed right after arriving in Cuba that the show enjoyed a special place on Cuban TV and thus was a staple of the Cuban people's regular entertainment. Rhodes then asked DeLaurentis to contact Luis Silva, who immediately agreed and then worked out both sketches.

The first sketch consists of one half of the split screen featuring President Obama at the White House receiving a real phone call from Pánfilo. This montage included Pánfilo on the other side of the split screen on the set of the TV show in Havana depicting his house as an integral part of the TV set-up. The second sketch was carried out during Obama's visit in a specially constructed set that served as Pánfilo's TV "house," near where Obama had met earlier with entrepreneurs in Havana. The first episode was aired on Cuban TV a day before the Obama visit in March, and the second one during the last day of his visit. The U.S. Embassy documentary video correctly pointed out that the sketches would expose Obama as a regular person (White House 2016). This image contrasts with Obama as head of a state that many in Cuba consider to be the empire.

From a Cuban perspective, these two instalments are undeniably funny. However, it is important to consider them from the eyes of non-Cubans (i.e., Americans and others in the West), as the sketches are intended for both audiences, with English subtitles for Pánfilo and Obama when they spoke in Spanish, and Spanish subtitles when Pánfilo and Obama spoke in English. The sketches have had millions of online views. From the perspective of a viewer in the North, Pánfilo comes across as if Cubans are kowtowing to Obama. It is a cringe-worthy scene. It also serves very well, as is the Obama Administration's explicit goal, to "depoliticize" the president of the United States. The sketches feed into the colonialist and imperialist narrative of a helpless Cuba pleading with the U.S. for assistance. No less significant is the meaning of the word *pánfilo*: simple, gullible or stupid. The U.S. got to have the last laugh. If Obama's main foreign policy legacy is Cuba, then Pánfilo is one of his blue-ribbon conquests. Some international media even headlined that the two Pánfilo sketches have become the "symbol" of the new relations between the two neighbours.

Did Pánfilo have to act this way? In his regular Cuban TV sketches, Pánfilo pokes fun justifiably at everyday problems in the Cuban system. Why then did he not poke fun at Obama's allusions and suggestions to Cuba uttered since December 17, 2014, that, for example, there is no democracy in Cuba and that Cubans should forget their past? Had Pánfilo done so, one could assume that the Obama/Pánfilo sketches would never have materialized. So, who wrote the script? The White House or Pánfilo/Luis Silva?

Actor Luis Silva's deference to Obama is probably one of the reasons his Pánfilo character has been adopted for prime attention by the new TV channel based in the U.S. for American consumption. It was handed to the U.S. on a silver platter. While the U.S. mainstream media dealing with culture and television headlined victoriously that "La revolución will be televised," now that the real story of Pánfilo has been revealed, there are some serious issues to be confronted aside from how this dubious transaction took place.

The overall projection of the U.S. image of Cuba in this recent period is twofold. First, Obama concedes, as part of his diplomacy, that Cuba has accomplished much in health and education. But, second, even this limited recognition is eclipsed by a scene that casts Cuba as caught in the past of an outmoded economic and political system. The goal is to indelibly stamp in the American imagination the following: Cuba desperately needs American aid to the extent of giving up its gains and principles in order to extricate itself from a rut as it stumbles helplessly through a system inherited from a bygone era stymied by failures. Pánfilo is the bumbling fool who, with regard to the U.S., fawns over Obama. He has been chosen as a metaphor to play this out and bring it to the U.S. public. By striving to implant this convenient image of Cuba in the American mindset, it serves as a pretext for the current U.S. Cuba policy to rescue the Cuban people by undermining the Revolution, which supposedly keeps them enchained. The "revolución" that Luis Silva and his Pánfilo character depict in the U.S. is something that the U.S. can not only live with but can manipulate for its own purposes.

Discussing Culture in Havana: Obama, the Warm-Up Act

One cannot be naive about cultural aggression. There is an ongoing cultural war waged by the U.S. and the West against Cuba. With this in mind, during a visit to Havana in May 2016, I asked friends and colleagues about the Rolling Stones concert in the country's capital, curious to explore the reaction to what can be considered an example of this onslaught. The concert had taken place only a few days after Obama's departure from Havana in March 2016. It was somewhat surprising to discover that all the people I approached — members and non-members of the Party and the Communist Youth, youth and adults, mothers and fathers — had not only been to the concert but were unanimous in their praise for the Rolling Stones show. No one had a critical word to say about the event.

Some of the Cuban media highlighted that the concert had "repercussions" in the world and international media — and it did. But what spin did CNN and its Havana-based correspondent give the concert, a slant that was, of course, repeated by the always obliging U.S.-based anchors? The main sound bite from the concert that resounded in the U.S. was that this type of cultural activity was previously "banned" by Fidel Castro. As with the Chanel fashion show, the culprit was again Fidel Castro. Indeed, the Rolling Stones indicated during the performance that the concert was "not possible before," as if Cuba had been oppressed but was free at last because the Rolling Stones had finally performed in Cuba.

The desired political effect of such statements by the Rolling Stones and CNN is to drive a wedge within Cuba between the youth and the Revolution. The purpose, even if not explicitly stated, is to politically disarm the youth regarding the essence of Cuban history and its economic, social and cultural accomplishments, not the least of which is national dignity. Thus, it came as a shock to me to see in some Cuban media that a large image of Che Guevara was on display at the concert with (and I hesitate to write this repulsive note) the Rolling Stones logo as the mouth of Che. While this may have been the doing of a small group of apolitical youth, no one took it down.

During his review of the manuscript, my editor at Fernwood Publishing, Errol Sharpe, made some key observations and suggestions. Among the points he addressed was the role of Western — especially U.S. — culture and its resulting values (or lack thereof) as a major danger to the Cuban Revolution. As a worst-case scenario, he opined (tongue in cheek), Cuba may be able to get by with the blockade or Guantánamo Bay remaining in the hands of the U.S. To illustrate his point, he suggested that the blockade, though having created unspeakable havoc to the country's economic and social fabric, has had the "merit," ironically, of keeping U.S. and Western culture at bay — that is, *it was mainly doing so* up until 17D and its aftermath, including the notable turning point of Obama's Havana visit. One of Cuba's most prestigious intellectuals, Ambrosio Fornet, said in an interview on October 18, 2016, that the positive aspect of the blockade was that it "would allow us to put to the test our national project" (Cremata Ferrán 2016).

One cannot take the politics out of the concert nor out of its aftermath. Indeed, on March 21, 2016, in a joint press conference with President Raúl Castro, Obama said: "Even as Cubans prepare for the arrival of the Rolling Stones, we're moving ahead with more events and exchanges that bring Cubans and Americans together as well" (2016d). The president's mention of the Rolling Stones in his statement had the effect of rendering him relatable to Cuban youth while providing free PR and full endorsement for the Stones and similar concerts. The Stones did not miss the cue from Obama. Their special "Havana Moon" concert webpage proudly proclaims: "TV News reported that Obama was 'the warm up act' for the Rolling Stones and Obama paid tribute to the Stones in his first speech to the world's media in Havana."

The Rolling Stones as Featured Act

The Rolling Stones' website continued the superficial buzz by declaring that "the Stones took to the stage under a perfect 'Havana Moon' for a show that will forever go down in history books as a life changing moment for a country on the brink of change." But how is it "life-changing" for Cuba, and what do they mean by "on the brink of change," if not espousing the same delusion as Obama and the Western oligarchy?

The change that is desired by the West and especially the U.S. is, as indicated throughout this book, to undermine the Cuban Revolution and its sovereignty. This shared Obama–Rolling Stones objective was confirmed by Sir Mick Jagger himself, who received a knighthood from the Queen in 2012. Many fans were disappointed when he accepted the knighthood, since it seemed to contradict his "anti-establishment" stance, and it caused friction with band member Keith Richards, who was annoyed with Jagger for accepting the "paltry honour." In the course of this controversy, Jagger is reported to have said that, "apart from the Rolling Stones, the Queen is the best thing Britain has got" (*Wikipedia* n.d.). Compared with his euphoric evaluation of the British monarchical system, Jagger does not exude the same generosity toward Fidel Castro and the political system he represents.

Prior to the screening of their documentary *Havana Moon,* an interview was published in the September 16, 2016, U.K. edition of the *Sun* newspaper titled "The Rolling Stones in Cuba: Mick Jagger Talks Fidel Castro, Learning Spanish and Staying Match-Fit Aged 73." Regarding the international repercussions of the Rolling Stones concert, this is yet another one of the reverberations:

Recently, there was an amazing month for Cuba. You had the Pope, Obama, Major Lazer [an American musical band] and then the Stones, all there. But you'd have to ask Cuban people whether they're feeling anything or not. It's not a free place, you're still not allowed to say what you like, you're still not allowed to assemble and you're not allowed much internet access. It appears to the outside world that this is a liberated place but I don't know the answer to that. There was repression in a lot of Latin American countries because they were right-wing military dictatorships. It also happened in Franco's Spain where they banned rock 'n' roll and in the Soviet satellite countries and the Soviet Union. So Fidel Castro copied the Soviet Union's banning of bourgeois, decadent music. That didn't last forever.

There is more to the saga of the Rolling Stones in Cuba. While the concert was being staged in Havana in May 2016, it had unofficially become known that the Stones had prohibited professional filming of the concert by Cuba and its film/television industry. Thus, the British band enjoyed the exclusive rights. It soon became apparent why it was so important for them. On September 23, 2016, following the widely promoted sale of tickets online, a documentary film of the concert was screened in movie theatres around the world for one night only. The poster for the film features a list of credits and collaborators but *not one word* about Cuba. In other words, Cuba (and especially trendy Havana) as a "set" was appropriated by the British band as a freebie from Cuba; Havana was then rapidly swept under the rug as soon as the band flew out of the country the day after their concert. The film was shown almost everywhere, except in Cuba.

I viewed the film in a Montreal movie theatre as part of the international screening, critiquing it from the perspective of non-Cuban audiences, as was done with the Pánfilo character earlier in this chapter. A Cuban audience, most likely enthralled with the music and worldwide fame accorded to the Havana concert, may overlook the code words and red flags intended mainly for foreign audiences. Seen through the lens of audiences in the more than fifty countries in North America, Latin America, Europe and Asia where it was screened, there are some controversial themes, despite the common view that the Stones are an exceptional rock band.[9] The film begins with the "making of" the event, a behind-the-scenes look into how it was produced. Highlighted with dramatic images were the incredibly large number of containers and crates of supplies imported into Cuba to construct a mind-boggling, state-of-the-art stage for the performance. This was followed by an interview with the four band members wherein Jagger declared that before their show, the "Castro regime banned rock and roll." To his credit, Keith Richards did say that Cuba still attracts people as a result of Fidel and Cuba having stood up to the U.S. for such a long period. Jagger referred to Obama's visit to Cuba as "the opening act" leading to their concert, which presumably means that the Rolling Stones were the main feature. Jagger reckoned that the concert constituted "a liberation" for Cubans.

Nevertheless, the well-produced documentary, in the style of a Hollywood musical blockbuster, went beyond *musical* "liberation." Among the first scenes are several sequences filmed in Havana, perhaps from atop a multi-storey building. This type of projection appears on two different occasions. It scans the closely knit rooftops, scattered with a miscellany of household items, at heights and angles that create the impression the buildings are more congested than they are in reality. With the use of purposely blurred and dramatic images for the desired effect, the sequences portray Havana as though it were a shantytown. From the Montreal audience, one could hear gasps of dismay at the sight of these lodgings, ostensibly designed to evoke such pity.

Despite all the funds at the disposal of the film production company (not to mention the millions of dollars in profit deriving from its screening in hundreds of cities around the world), no other views of housing were presented. There was not a single sequence of Cuba's bustling countryside towns. For the Havana scenes, not one second was devoted to portraying a hospital, cultural centre, school or university. The film's opening behind-the-scenes footage featured young Cubans playing soccer on an improvised field but disregarded the relatively modern sport facilities that contribute to Cuba punching above its weight in international competition.

The ultra-modern set for the concert, with its fantastic surround sound and big screen fed by boom shots, enthralled Cubans. It was perhaps good enough reason for many just to witness it in person. It was as if a smaller, musical New York Times Square had been suddenly transplanted to Havana for a day. The show and the futuristic set moved many in the young audience to tears of joy, scenes that were captured by the film crew for the big screen in Havana and then featured in the documentary. One Stones member claimed, in the behind-the-scenes introductory segment, that half the city of Havana was in attendance; another claimed that *all* of Havana was there. The Rolling Stones website later claimed that there were "1.2 million adoring fans" on-site. With the portrayal of unbridled happiness, it was as if Havana and the Cuban musical/cultural scene had permanently fallen into the orbit of Western culture. Jagger at one point repeated onstage the familiar refrain that their type of music was not previously enjoyed in Cuba. This was followed with a shout that resembled a political slogan: "Finally the times are changing!" The obvious goal was to provoke a reaction from the audience, which it did.

This buzzword of "change" is not the goal of the Cuban Revolution but rather a reflection of the ideology and political aims of the British Empire regarding countries such as Cuba. This version of "change" applies even more so to Obama's strategy and today's U.S. Cuba policy. The film depicts some concertgoers waving the British flag — and others wearing it integrated into their apparel — and zooms in on the Cuban flag in a number of instances as well. The documentary was produced by Eagle Rock Entertainment, reputed to be the world's largest producer and distributor of music programming for TV, DVD, Blu-Ray and digital media. Its ultra-high-definition visuals and surround sound make it a spectacular music movie. In fact, during the course of viewing the film, audiences may have surmised that the event was not so much the *concert itself* in Havana but the *film of the concert*.

The documentary records the end of the concert when the superb Cuban choir Entrevoces, directed by National Music Award winner Digna Guerra, appeared onstage. They were the only Cuban group to accompany the British band. They sang a beautiful rendition of Jagger–Richards' "You Can't Always Get What You Want." Disappointingly, the choir received only a subdued response from the audience. When, at the end of the concert, as is the custom, Jagger introduced and thanked all the musicians, including the Cuban choir, the reaction was remarkably muted for the Cubans, especially when compared with the mention of the Rolling Stones band members and other associated musicians. It was almost as if Cuban music and cultural talent were acting as spoilers to the Western rock concert.

The very last scenes, however, appear to drive home the theme depicting the Stones as the "liberators" of Cuban youth who want "change." As the set is being cleared of all the performers and the spectators are dispersing from the huge outdoor concert grounds, the camera pans slowly and dramatically over the emptying area, giving the impression that concertgoers are grudgingly returning to the streets of Havana. The film audience perceives a procession of sadness and resignation as Cubans head to their supposedly dilapidated housing, still fresh in the viewers' minds, and back to the supposedly grey drudgery of their daily life in the Cuban Revolution, bereft of Western culture.

At the end of the documentary, which captivates its audience from the first to the last seconds, a long list of credits rapidly scrolls down the screen. These seemingly endless acknowledgements only incidentally mention the collaboration of the Cuban Institute of Music and make no reference to any other Cuban entity. The only Cuban musician listed is the well-known singer Isaac Delgado. While he returned to Havana in 2014 from an eight-year stay in Miami, he is an American citizen. He thus travels frequently to give concerts in Miami, where (unlike other patriotic Cuban performers), he is welcomed (Arias-Polo 2016). One can deduce that the Rolling Stones know which side their toast is buttered on, and so does Delgado. The realization that the Havana event was not the concert itself but the documentary film was immediately confirmed after the international screening on September 23. The Stones' *Havana Moon* webpage announced that the high-tech DVD version would be released about three weeks after the one-day screening in movie theatres.

Will the youth eventually realize that their idols had the last laugh at Cuba's expense? Will they catch on that the Stones' "philanthropic" objective in staging a "free" concert was mainly to exploit one of the most sought-after backdrops in the world for their next exclusive film and DVD, along with the worldwide free publicity it generated? This is where principles, values and national dignity can go down the drain. However, on July 8, 2016, the Minister of Culture, who was ultimately responsible for these activities, was removed from his post even though there was no official reason given. He was replaced by Abel Prieto, one of Cuba's outstanding defenders of its socialist culture against Western encroachments.

Hipster Colonialism?

In order to flesh out this analysis of the artistic features of cultural aggression, which constitute a major threat to Cuba's socialist project, I look at additional examples. Recall that several of the articles in Chapter 2 deal with cultural encroachment in the larger sense of the term "cultural." It is from the perspective of culture as including the ideological and political features of society that the section later in this chapter titled "Who Is Going to Win the Cultural War?" approaches challenges for Cuba in 2017 and beyond. The artistic sphere of culture often goes unnoticed as being "non-ideological" and "non-political."

Such a seemingly innocuous inroad arose with some of my companions in Havana in May 2016. In conversations with these friends, I shared some background information and thoughts regarding cultural visits that had been highly publicized within and outside of Cuba. Havana has become so trendy that it seems virtually every self-respecting American superstar (in particular, singers) wants to see — and be seen in — the Cuban capital city. But, I asked my friends, what is the outcome of these visits?

My acquaintances were dismayed by details relating to one such visit, by pop superstar Rihanna to Old Havana. She, of course, revelled in what is now the traditional walk through Old Havana among the swarming, obviously adoring, young Cuban fans. Aside from the photo opportunity this presented for her, Rihanna also posed for a *Vanity Fair* cover story in a series of carefully choreographed Old Havana shoots by a world-renowned photographer contracted by the famous celebrity magazine. This unique historical "set" does not exist anywhere else in the world and features what some Westerners consider — somewhat condescendingly — to be nostalgic symbols of the 1950s: old and relatively dilapidated walls of homes facing the street, the ubiquitous colourful vintage American cars, more cracked walls with murals featuring quotes from Fidel and the image of Cuban revolutionary hero Camilo Cienfuegos (as if the ideals and work of these leaders are now relegated to the past, much like the Chanel fashion show models wore their version of fanciful "Che berets"). The most lucrative of the shoots, perhaps, was the singer lying nude on a "typical" old bed in a "typical" bedroom with "typical" old walls in a "typical" old home (Robinson 2015).

When my friends learned about this story, they began to reflect upon whether the values of these superstars are those that the Cuban youth should uphold. There are many similar examples. Can these and other such visits — like the filming of *Fast 8*, the Chanel fashion show, the Rolling Stones concert and American music stars, with their inevitable aftermaths — be considered "hipster colonialism"?

Paradoxically, while investments by U.S. or other foreign firms in Cuba are the new normal as part of the U.S. imperial system under the new impetus arising from 17D, they do *not* represent the danger to Cuba that hipster colonialism does. For example, it was announced at the end of June 2016 that the huge U.S. Starwood Hotel chain signed three new hotel deals in Cuba, marking the first U.S.-based company to enter the vacation/travel market in nearly sixty years. This announcement followed the green light from the U.S. Treasury Department for Starwood to operate hotels in Cuba. This was a positive result of the visit by Obama, who was accompanied in March 2016 by the main executive of Sheraton (a Starwood brand). Keith Grossman, Senior Vice-President and Deputy General Counsel of Starwood, said: "Through our discussions and due diligence, it became clear that Starwood was the right choice for its unique approach to hospitality, sustainability and design that would enrich the local communities and enhance the guest experience. We plan to cultivate local talent, provide career enriching opportunities, and locally source art, décor, food, and materials to ensure we deliver authentic experiences" (Business Wire 2016). Developments like this do *not* pose a threat to the Cuban socialist project, including its cultural dimension. Indeed, according to the Cuba–U.S. agreement, Starwood will be promoting *Cuban* talent for the guests in their hotels. Likewise, the export of U.S. farm products to Cuba and even the construction of farm-tractor plants in Cuba represent progress. There are many other such trade and commerce examples that do not constitute a hazard to Cuba. Incongruous as it may seem, however, the Western "invasion" of Havana by the likes of *Fast 8,* Chanel, the Rolling Stones and American glamour superstars — who do not invest even one cent in Cuba — *does* represent a cultural danger, when compared with capitalist investors who invest millions. In contrast to these traditional investments and joint transactions, the cultural intrusions bring into Cuba American or Western values, such as extreme individualism, instant gratification and superficial, cultural expressions. The cultural flow into Cuba may subtly and covertly introduce some Cuban youth to the pursuit of the American Dream: the delusion of becoming rich and famous like the pop stars, a goal that is not only impossible for principled Cubans but also for virtually all Americans.

Perhaps the most devastating cultural challenge to Cuba, and especially to its youth, is the infiltration of individualism. The vast majority of these pop stars are almost entirely immersed in their own careers, wealth and notoriety. They do not show one ounce of collective or social concern regarding the fate of the peoples of their own countries nor of those oppressed and attacked by the West in the Third World. The few exceptions where there is an ostentatious show of "philanthropy" and taking up "causes" consist primarily of publicity stunts — sources of free PR to further the individuals' careers rather than a demonstration of any real social concern.

The promotion of individualism is caused, among other factors, by an eclectic vision of the Western musical stars: they are idolized but the values they represent and their motivations in visiting Cuba go unquestioned. Above all, this selective appreciation consists in detaching the dramatic Havana visits from the overarching Western artistic intrusion as part of cultural aggression since 17D. For example, Obama endorsed the Rolling Stones concert and the Stones picked up on it by declaring that Obama was the opening act. This should have been a red flag to Cubans that the artistic sphere of culture goes along with its ideological and political aspects. U.S. presidents are not essentially music impresarios but rather the political and ideological promoters of "American values" and policies. Musical icons represent the epitome of individual pursuit of fame and fortune, which ultimately contaminates the minds of youth. Hipster colonialism seeks to conquer the youth by suppressing social and collective values, a precondition for detaching youth from Cuba's Revolution and a key ingredient in subverting it.

The invasion by the foreign icons also presents a challenge to Cuban dignity. For example, on Cuban TV, American idols have been seen with hundreds of Cuban children and youth running after them. What does this say about Cuban self-worth, when we know that these stars are just using the "locals" as free "extras" for their own careers? The only result of these forays is the promotion of Western values to those who are impressionable. These beliefs are geared toward colonizing the minds of Cubans in order to undermine their collective dignity and adherence to sovereignty. This mindset is in blatant contradiction with those values of independence and social justice for which Cuba has fought from the time of José Martí and into the twenty-first century.

In conclusion, not only is there such a phenomenon as the artistic aspect of Western cultural aggression and hipster colonialism in all its manifestations, but it constitutes one of the most dangerous consequences of Cuba–U.S. relations since 17D. This is an important aspect of the Obama Cuba legacy. The outcome largely depends on the continuing influential role of the dynamic Minister of Culture Abel Prieto, revolutionary intellectuals and the most conscious Cubans at the grassroots.

CUBA-SILICON VALLEY-CUBA: THE MAKING OF A TROJAN HORSE?

From June 22 to 24, 2016, the U.S. hosted the seventh annual Global Entrepreneurship Summit (GES). According to its website:

> When we connect global entrepreneurs with the access and exchange needed to create and innovate, we unleash their power to change the world. A clear example of this is found in Silicon Valley where thousands of firms have achieved success. With that in mind, what better place to gather entrepreneurs at all stages of business development for the 2016 Global Entrepreneurship Summit. (2016a)

In his welcoming address in Silicon Valley on June 24, 2016, Obama announced:

> There are 11 Cubans who are here today — the first Cubans to join us at one of these summits. (Applause) Hola! Mucho gusto. (Applause) They're ready to help create new opportunities for the Cuban people. Where are they? (Applause) There they are. I want to thank Antonio

Gracias — a leader in private equity and one of our Presidential Ambassadors for Global Entrepreneurship — because his support was critical in bringing these young Cuban entrepreneurs here. So that's deserving of a hand. (Applause) (2016a)

Who is Antonio Gracias? There are no figures as to his wealth, but "this person is connected to 16 board members in 16 different organizations across 19 different industries" (Bloomberg n.d.). His credentials, according to the U.S. Department of Commerce (2015), which sponsors the GES along with the White House, includes his involvement with companies such as Uber, whose CEO, Travis Kalanick, was one of featured speakers at the GES (2016b).

Uber Technologies is an American developer and marketer of a mobile app that allows consumers with smartphones looking for a ride to connect with drivers who use their own cars. In addition to Uber being the epitome of a capitalist enterprise, the multinational corporation has notoriously under-mined the livelihood of traditional taxi drivers around the world, sparking demonstrations against Uber in the U.S. and in major cities across Canada, Europe, Brazil, Costa Rica, South Africa, Australia and elsewhere. In addi-tion, it became public knowledge that, since 2014, Uber has been involved in sabotaging competition from similar companies, threatening journalists who report unfavourably about Uber and much more (Lazzaro 2016).

The question is, how can U.S. capitalists such as Antonio Gracias, with his Uber pedigree, teach Cuban entrepreneurs anything other than capitalist values? Uber's "free market" law of the jungle contradicts the Cuban socialist culture, which applies to all, both in the private sector — composed of the self-employed — and in the state sector. In Cuba, the small enterprises of the self-employed and all their members, whether the owners or the employees, are considered by the system to be part of the socialist society. This social consensus is a feature of Cuban political culture based on the collective good, which is not in opposition to individual success and prosperity. For example, the majority of the people involved in this private sector are already unionized. Some were elected delegates to the Communist Party of Cuba Congress in April 2016, as indicated in my article titled "Thoughts on Cuban Resistance to the U.S. Ideological/Political War" in Chapter 2. Becoming delegates to the Party Congress and actively participating in its delibera-tions is in itself another indication of social and collective commitment. This value was also displayed by some small entrepreneurs who attended the meeting with Cuban private sector representatives hosted in Havana by Obama himself, as is seen below.

So, who were the eleven Cubans attending the Silicon Summit about

whom Obama triumphantly boasted? The Miami-based *OnCuba* magazine, an apologist for the outgoing president, interviewed one of the Cuban
participants:

> "What do you hope to achieve from this Summit and could it
> directly benefit your venture?" I ask Yondainer Gutiérrez, founder
> of AlaMesa, a directory of restaurants and "paladares" [private
> household restaurants] in Cuba.
>
> "This is a really good opportunity to learn, to make contacts.
> My intention is to absorb all the knowledge that I can and try to
> participate as much as possible in the collateral events, directly
> or indirectly related to AlaMesa. GES is an ideal space to meet
> people like us from all over the world who are trying to add value
> to the places where they live and the people that surround them.
> It is very important and beneficial to meet, exchange ideas with,
> and learn from them. It is really important to me to get to know
> and understand the ways in which an entrepreneurial venture
> can forge paths in cultures, economies and different societies."
> (Recio 2016)

The interviewee, Yondainer Gutiérrez, had participated in the Obama meeting with entrepreneurs during his March 2016 visit to Cuba. One cannot
speculate about motivation. However, it can only be taken as a bad omen
when learning from capitalism appears to be so enthralling.

Thus, while Cuba strives to maintain its hallmark collective spirit and
social consensus among its half million self-employed, one cannot idealize
the situation. It would be naive to think that almost all — or even a sizable
portion of individuals — in the private sector maintain this social commitment typical of Cuban society. For example, if the quote above is indicative
of the group of eleven entrepreneurs seeking guidance from monopoly
capitalists in the context of accepting the Obama Administration invitation
to Silicon Valley, they are easy prey for the U.S. plan to build a fifth column
in Cuba. When the White House invites Cubans to participate in one if its
events in the U.S., it chooses only those considered an American asset. This
encroachment through Trojan horse politics, by its very nature — and like
the encouragement of individualism discussed earlier — tears at the Cuban
social fabric and thus at Cuban sovereignty and dignity.

Let us be clear. The U.S. wants Cuba to become capitalist and U.S.-
dependent but not an outright colony. The initial invitation to the
Silicon Valley GES was made by Obama during the meeting with Cuban

entrepreneurs in Havana. In his address, he *subtly* introduced the notion that capitalism is best for Cuba:

> In many ways, the history of Cuba can be understood through the labor of the Cuban people. For centuries, under colonial rule, and then during decades of American involvement, the toil of the Cuban people was often used to enrich others as opposed to the people who were doing the work. And then, for much of the past half century, it was virtually impossible for Cubans to operate their own businesses. But in recent years, that's begun to change.... For the first time, we'll welcome Cubans to our annual Global Entrepreneurship Summit, which I'll host in Silicon Valley later this year. (Obama 2016e)

It is instructive to deconstruct Obama's analysis of Cuban history, thus exposing the preaching of capitalism and the subversion of national sovereignty and dignity as the ideological and political foundation of the Trojan horse. He said that "during decades of American involvement, the toil of the Cuban people was often used to enrich others." The "decades" in fact stretched from 1898 to 1958, more than half a century. Even "involvement" is a gross distortion. In reality, during that long period, the U.S. dominated Cuba through fraudulent elections and imposed bloody dictatorships by coups d'état when elections did not succeed in co-opting Cubans economically, politically and socially into the multi-party system of rule.

Obama was also employing his selective memory when he stated that Cuba was "under colonial rule, and then during decades of American involvement." He conveniently glosses over the fact that the U.S. confiscated Cuba's victory over Spanish colonialism in 1898 to convert Cuba into its own neo-colony until this was defeated on January 1, 1959. Let us also look at another understatement: this period was, according to Obama, "*often* used to enrich others." In fact, U.S. neo-colonial domination of Cuba had as its modus operandi to *always* enrich the U.S. and those Cuban capitalists and big landowners who were part of this domination.

However, the best (or worst) is yet to come. In his next statement, Obama proceeds to misrepresent the revolutionary change since 1959: "And then, for much of the past half century, it was virtually impossible for Cubans to operate their own businesses." He blatantly lures anyone in his Havana audience who worships unrestricted free enterprise (and there must have been some) to move surreptitiously from the U.S. domination era to post-1959 revolutionary Cuba, as if both eras were equally detrimental to small businesses/owners. This is simply false. The most grotesque form of unbridled monopoly ownership before 1959 existed in the countryside. The peasants were exploited to the bone by wealthy owners of huge areas of land. Soon after the Revolution, however, under the *Agrarian Reform Law*, these colossal tracts of private land were parcelled up and given to 200,000 peasant families who had tilled them. Thus, they became the new owners of modest-sized plots of land.

In the cities, the Revolution has tried, with differing degrees of success, to combine the collectivity with individual private ownership, often resulting in problems. Among these issues, some entrepreneurs defy the law while continuing to run their businesses. Although some are quick to accuse the Cuban government of being harsh, the fact remains that it is no easy task to combine small-scale private enterprises with socialist values. One only has to look at an October 2016 move by the Havana municipal government to try and curb illicit business practices. A report published by Reuters on October 18, 2016, speaks for itself:

> Havana's city government has temporarily suspended issuing licenses for new private restaurants [*paladares*] in the city and warned existing ones to obey tough regulations, according to several owners of the businesses popular with foreign tourists.
>
> The list of violations that officials read out included paladares not paying taxes, buying supplies on the black market, labor code violations and having more than 50 seats [these restaurants are limited to a maximum of 50 seats] according to two restaurant owners who attended meetings.
>
> Other alleged violations were running bars masquerading as restaurants and contracting entertainment outside official channels, staying open after 3 a.m., disturbing neighbors, dubious sources of capital and illegal purchases of buildings. (Frank 2016)

It is instructive to note that some of these illegalities contributed to the government closing down many of these private businesses way back in 1968. In these cases, then and now, government precautions do not limit individual rights; rather, it is some of these small owners who violate, by disturbing neighbours for example, the rights of individuals. Some of these local businesses also harm the collectivity in general by violating social property and tax regulations designed to spread some of their increased income throughout society.

Other efforts to promote individuals' rights took place right after 1959. For example, based on the *Urban Reform Law*, in the cities huge and medium-sized housing properties were confiscated, divided up where possible and then given to the poor virtually rent-free. During my fieldwork in 1997–98, I stayed in a medium-sized apartment block in Havana. Before the Revolution, the building's owner, a wealthy Cuban sugar plantation magnate, arbitrarily set the rental rates; after 1959, it was confiscated. The family that had been living there and paying rent for a relatively long time before 1959 was given the largest apartment in the building rent-free. They have not paid one cent in rent since that time. Other apartments, occupied by families for a relatively short time, were turned over to those families at extremely low rates that were essentially symbolic. Huge luxury apartment blocks in Havana built for the elite in the 1950s were confiscated to provide housing for students brought in from the countryside to pursue studies in the city. Single-owner mansions were expropriated and converted into social necessities, such as schools, in compliance with the priorities of the Revolution.

In his speech to the entrepreneurs in Havana, Obama asserted that individual opportunities and betterment never existed in Revolutionary Cuba, yet these examples from the countryside and cities provide sharp contrast to his statement. In referring to the alleged impossibility for Cuban individual initiative and opportunity, Obama then conceded, "but in recent years, that's begun to change." His hope that the Cuban government and people are opening up to capitalism ignores the real course of development. This folksy remark about "things changing" is not innocent. It amounts to infusing these entrepreneurs with the false hope — and an elusive objective — that they should work for capitalism and thus become decoys for the U.S. in Cuba.

It is true with regard to the self-employed sector that it is not necessary that formerly state-run small enterprises — such as restaurants, cafeterias, lodging, even barber shops and beauty salons — remain entirely under state control. This outdated system burdens the state, which should concentrate on the principal means of production. Any analysis about the macro- and micro-economic implications of the *cuentapropistas* (the self-employed) is beyond the scope of this book. Nonetheless, suffice it to assert that, for this sector of the economy (encouraged to expand by the government), Cuba needs assistance from the U.S. A good example is the U.S.-based Airbnb, which is now established in Cuba. This service allows not only Americans but also Europeans to reserve vacation home rentals/homestays (*casas particulares*) online. This is a big boon, not only for the *casas particulares* throughout Cuba but also for the entire tourist industry in Cuba. The state-run hotel facilities cannot currently meet the demand (as of November 2016), nor are they likely to do so anytime in the near future. Given that the number of U.S. tourists heading to Cuba is on the rise, some within this tourist sector of Cuban society, such as *casas particulares* and *paladares*, could function as a back door for capitalism and its values. Thus, Cuba is between a rock and a hard place.

The video of Obama meeting in Havana with Cuban and American entrepreneurs (broadcast live on Cuban TV) shows the punctuated applause by *both* Cuban entrepreneurs *and* their U.S. (millionaire) counterparts in favour of Obama's remarks and, indeed, of his very presence. In fact, this trend is dealt with in Chapter 5, in the section titled "The Blockade, Cigars and Rum: The Loopholes," under the heading "Feeding the Trojan Horse."

This level of enthusiasm, as exhibited in the meeting with Obama, was repeated to a certain extent at other events during his visit, including the one involving the Pánfilo sketches. In fact, this anomaly is part of the overall U.S. cultural aggression that includes artistic, ideological and political dimensions. The question is, how successful can such aberrations of the U.S.-led cultural war be in the future despite Cuban resistance? This challenge is evaluated below, in the section titled "Who Is Going to Win the Cultural War?"

"GUANTÁNAMO IS NOT ON THE TABLE": U.S. ARROGANCE

U.S. Cuba policy is interested in the private sector, attempting to assimilate sections of the society into the American sphere of influence. This policy of seduction is in stark contrast to the U.S.'s refusal to return to Cuba territory it expropriated in 1903. In order to return Guantánamo Bay to Cuba, the U.S. must first shut down its prison on that territory. However, on June 13, 2016, Reuters reported that the "Obama Administration is not pursuing the use of an executive order to shutter the Guantánamo Bay military prison after officials concluded that it would not be a viable strategy" (Mason 2016).

A special panel was featured at the annual meeting of the Latin American Studies Association (LASA), this one held in New York on May 28, 2016. The title of the panel was "U.S.–Cuban Relations after December 17." The panel consisted of the organizer William LeoGrande, speakers Soraya M. Castro Mariño (Investigaciones de Política Internacional affiliated with the university Instituto Superior de Relaciones Internacionales "Raúl Roa García,"or ISRI), Jeffrey DeLaurentis (chargé d'affaires at the time, the equivalent of ambassador, U.S. Embassy, Havana), José Ramón Cabañas (Ambassador of the Republic of Cuba to the U.S.) and Josefina Vidal (Director General for the United States, Ministry of Foreign Affairs, Republic of Cuba). It was unusual that the de facto U.S. ambassador to Havana would be required to face questions from a progressive and informed audience, as was the case at that panel. One professor asked DeLaurentis if the U.S. is discussing the return of Guantánamo Bay to Cuba with the Cuban side. The answer from DeLaurentis was simply that it was "not on the table, not on the agenda." For all the talk from Obama and negotiators about "normalizing relations" with Cuba, the answer reflects the arrogance of a superpower that is not even willing to negotiate the return of Guantánamo Bay, despite its being a part of Cuba. The issue is not that the prisoners are still being held at the military prison on the base, as the exchanges between the audience and DeLaurentis illustrated; it is that the U.S. will not concede Guantánamo Bay to Cuba, even if the military prison is eventually shut down.

There is a link missing on the Gitmo issue. Many well-intentioned Americans, such as business people, Congressional representatives, and politicians at the state and municipal levels, work intensely for an end to the blockade. The commercial advantage for them is evident. However, there are no financial gains for them if Gitmo is returned to Cuba. Thus, they do not yet include it as part of what is supposed to be a normalization process. The Cuban side, however, has reiterated on many occasions — and will continue to do so — that there can be no normalization while Guantánamo Bay remains under the control of the U.S.

There is a movement under way in the U.S. among academics and social activists to demand the return of Gitmo to Cuba. But is this stirring among non-business and non-politicians sufficient to turn the tide in favour of returning the contested territory to Cuba? If the business and political sectors of the U.S. ruling circles come to the just conclusion that their interests could be better served by full normalization with Cuba, and yet Guantánamo Bay remains a roadblock, then a future move on Guantánamo Bay might be in the offing. All the same, the Trump presidency will make this goal even more difficult to achieve.

U.S. DEMOCRACY PROMOTION IN CUBA: AS AMERICAN AS APPLE PIE

During the same LASA special panel mentioned above, I asked DeLaurentis the following questions:

> My question is regarding the annual U.S. democracy promotion programs for Cuba. Is the Obama Administration obliged to organize and fund the yearly programs because it is codified in law, such as the *Helms-Burton Act,* as part of the U.S. blockade against Cuba? If Obama is not obliged, why does he do it? If he is obliged, does he have leeway to reduce the funds substantially to make it far less effective?

DeLaurentis avoided the question by saying that these yearly programs are part of what the U.S. does elsewhere in the world. This is similar to what Obama stated in Havana in 2016 regarding Cuba:

> But as is true with countries around the world where we have normalized relations, we will continue to stand up for basic principles that we believe in. America believes in democracy. We believe that freedom of speech and freedom of assembly and freedom of religion are not just American values, but are universal values. They may not express themselves exactly in the same way in every country, they may not be enshrined in the founding documents or constitutions of every country the same way, or protected legally in exactly the same ways, but the impulse — the human impulse towards freedom, the freedom that José Martí talked about, we think is a universal longing. (Obama 2016d)

Aside from the anomaly of invoking José Martí's name to sow the seeds of doubt among some Cubans about their right to choose their own destiny, the U.S. appears to reserve the privilege for itself to preach democracy to other countries, even those with which they have *normalized* relations. It is on this basis that the White House website document on Cuba policy states:

> The U.S. Congress funds democracy programming in Cuba to provide humanitarian assistance, promote human rights and fundamental freedoms, and support the free flow of information in places where it is restricted and censored. The Administration will continue to implement U.S. programs aimed at promoting positive change in Cuba, and we will encourage reforms in our high level engagement with Cuban officials. (White House n.d.-a, accessed November 2016)

U.S. democracy promotion is based on a truism that claims, "We are the judges of democracy." The U.S. must, according to this premise, go to the rescue of other countries that are not up to its standards. Exceptions to this aphorism abound when it comes to other countries, such as Saudi Arabia, that are staunch U.S. allies but blatantly anti-democratic and extreme violators of human rights. They are let off the hook and even provided with billions of dollars in military and other aid. Thus, the title of "judges of democracy" is akin to an edict in U.S. international foreign policy.

This dictum is rooted in the seventeenth- and eighteenth-century origins of the U.S. The Pilgrims, from whom modern U.S. foreign policy finds its source, considered themselves to be the biblical "light of the world," "a city on a hill," to be revered and beheld by all. According to this rather twisted interpretation, the "chosen people" (the U.S.) are ordained by God to bring light to the world. All U.S. presidents fully support and follow this notion even though the face of this ingrained Bible-thumping mission may be camouflaged from time to time. The most glaring example of this convenient mask is the Obama phenomenon. This is why Cuba–U.S. relations in the Obama era is also fraught with dangers.

The U.S.-sponsored World Learning initiative for Cuba is the latest democracy promotion program. In September 2016 information surfaced about its program targeting Cuban youth. It perhaps exemplifies the most significant of the perils, as it reveals the subtle nature of Obama's new tactics, that is, a move from aggression to seduction. However, the reaction to this latest program in Cuba contributed to changing an aspect of the Cuban political landscape for the better. It also served to further improve the Cuban media. According to its website: "World Learning is a nonprofit organization advancing leadership in more than 60 countries. We envision a just world, driven by engaged citizens and thriving communities. Our mission is to empower people and strengthen institutions through education, sustainable development, and exchange programs" (n.d.-b). The website also claims: "World Learning has helped civil society organizations (CSOs) around the world advocate for effective democratic processes, more efficiently deliver services, and foster policies that support basic human rights" (n.d.-a). While it has no physical presence in Cuba, it offers summer programs online for students between the ages of sixteen and eighteen (n.d.-d). It seeks to bring successful applicants to the U.S. for the summer, with expenses fully paid through a scholarship. The ultimate objective is to send them back to Cuba in order to act as "leaders."

World Learning's goals are sugar-coated and designed to be accepted in Cuba, but many Cubans consider this approach highly deceptive. This U.S. approach is now possible as a result of the re-establishment of diplomatic relations, a game-changer in attempts at rapprochement. However, World Learning's website does not tell the whole story.

First, the outreach to Cuban students does not reveal that USAID is directly involved in World Learning. On the contrary, its documentation gives the impression that it is an NGO. USAID's website's initial premise is: "USAID is the lead *U.S. Government* agency that works to end extreme global poverty and enable resilient, democratic societies to realize their potential" (USAID n.d., emphasis added). USAID is perceived throughout Latin America, as well as in much of the West, as a CIA front, fomenting subversion in countries in the name of democracy. The World Learning/USAID connection is affirmed in a conveniently secondary location on its own website. A World Learning executive, in his own words, reveals that he was a "Deputy Administrator in 2010 of USAID" and is "proud now that my current organization, World Learning, has been a partner of USAID" (n.d.-f). Furthermore, World Learning published remarks by its CEO Donald Steinberg that show the close ties between USAID and World Learning:

> I am pleased to have this opportunity to address the distinguished alumni of USAID. When my good friend and World Learning trustee Tom Fox raised this idea with me, it seemed only natural that I use this opportunity to reflect on my experience as deputy administrator at USAID under the first term of the Obama Administration and on my subsequent contact with USAID as CEO of World Learning, *a non-governmental organization* committed to capacity building and youth empowerment through exchange, education and development. (n.d.-e, emphasis added)

As for Steinberg, according to the World Learning website,

> Prior to World Learning, [he] served as deputy administrator at the United States Agency for International Development (USAID)... In his previous work with the United States government, Steinberg served as director of the U.S. Department of State's Joint Policy Council, White House deputy press secretary, ... [and earned] the State Department and USAID Distinguished Service Awards, and six State Department Superior Honor Awards. (n.d.-c)

The second caveat to the NGO/diplomatic veneer relates to the *inside story* about how this program *actually operates* with Cuban students. It is as revealing as the USAID ties. This exposé was presented on the September 29, 2016, broadcast of the TV program *Mesa Redonda*, hosted by Randy Alonso and accompanied by Iroel Sánchez. Also present at the roundtable were students, student association leaders and the director of *Juventud Rebelde,* Yailín Orta. She informed the public that the U.S. Embassy in Havana is promoting this program. One of the students at the roundtable was Alejandro Sánchez, a former scholarship recipient who had recently returned from the U.S. after a one-month stay. He testified how, far from being the neutral, apolitical program that it was presented to be, the activities in the U.S. were highly political. The program dealt with subjects such as the difference between democracy in the U.S. and dictatorship, the U.S. presidential elections under way at the time, public speaking and other related training. Alejandro Sánchez concluded that the education program, the filming of whose activities in the U.S. was prohibited, has the goal of creating a platform outside of Cuba's institutions with these young students as the leaders.[10]

To provide context, this timely and informative TV program coincided with demonstrations across Cuba by high-school and university students, who held meetings in September to expose and denounce this latest U.S. incursion. They labelled the World Learning program a "regime change initiative." Cuban TV showed the students in action, and the mainstream press featured front-page reports with photos. Some of these scenes included wall murals on which students signed their opinions against the U.S. "subversive program." For perhaps one of the first times since 17D, the word "Yanqui" was publicly used to describe the U.S.

Granma and *Juventud Rebelde* also featured articles by student leaders and Yailín Orta, as well as alternative bloggers and writers. For example, *Granma* published a post by Enrique Ubieta titled "Being a Revolutionary Today" (Ubieta Gómez 2016). In addition, *Granma* featured its well-known journalist Oscar Sánchez Serra, who wrote a prominent opinion piece in relation to World Learning titled "What Normalization of Relations Are We Talking About?" Thus, the Obama Administration's regime change plan as part of democracy promotion seems to have momentarily backfired. The students' outrage contributed to the movement already under way in the Cuban mainstream media to place at least as much importance on Cuban resistance to the U.S. offensive in Cuba as on the necessary diplomacy and discussions. The youth started the process of simultaneously taking up two challenges.

The first challenge consisted in the youth contributing to making improvements to the Cuban mainstream media, as indicated above; the second was the challenge to the subversive U.S. democracy promotion programs, as indicated now. Since 17D, this opposition by Cuba had remained mainly within the confines of Cuba–U.S. negotiations, bolstered by resistance among alternative bloggers and writers. Despite the resistance, there was an *increase* in funds by the Obama Administration to the regime change programs. Beginning in September 2016, however, resistance led by the youth started to take on a grassroots quality. One cannot underestimate the political consciousness of the majority of Cuban youth. Obama did not exhibit any appreciation of the Cuban youth as a revolutionary force during or after his visit but identified them, rather, as a potential group to be lured away from the Revolution and its leaders. This miscalculation is bound to provoke further backlash and thus impact the Cuban political landscape.[11]

There is yet another crucial spinoff effect from the youths' September 2016 resistance. Immediately following 17D, an outlook was developing in the U.S. and also in some Cuban political thinking that promoted diplomacy and negotiation to the detriment of the imperative of Cuban resistance to the U.S. cultural war. This viewpoint was emphasizing diplomacy and negotiations — so necessary to the Cuban government and its Ministry of Foreign Affairs. However, this indispensable diplomatic government orientation is assumed to be applicable to the entire Cuban political scene, even though it harms the all-important resistance to the U.S. cultural war. In the initial stage after 17D, resistance was mainly the work of the alternative bloggers and writers, who bore the burden of intransigence. Yet, the negative tendency of diplomacy to the detriment of resistance was festering. It did not show its true features of being in alignment with U.S. Cuba policy. It was chameleon-like — at times appearing to oppose U.S. pressures and at others exclusively promoting diplomacy.

However, the winds changed in September due to the grassroots actions of youth. With the marginal outlook based on a one-sided and speculative emphasis on diplomacy put to the wall, the nature of this option seemed to reveal itself. We can take one example as a point of reference, even though the importance is not on the individuals but rather on an existing ideological frame of mind. One archetype is Carlos Alzugaray, a Havana resident who describes himself as a retired diplomat and professor, essayist and independent political analyst (2016a). It is not a question of individuals but trends of thought as exemplified by Alzugaray. The goal of this analysis is to deepen awareness with regard to certain ideological and political anomalies. It is my hope that this analysis will result in a fertile and frank mutual exchange through our respective social media. He wrote in relation to the student resistance: "In my opinion it would be counterproductive to stir up a tempest in a teapot, which may *complicate diplomatic work*. The scholarships of World Learning are not that out of this world. I visited their website. I read some of the materials and I see *nothing subversive* per se" (2016b, emphasis added). This mindset appears to be an apologist for Obama. However, thanks to the student movement, the reality is now out in the open. Alzugaray criticizes *Cubadebate* for the emphasis it placed on resistance to World Learning in his article titled "Different Treatment of the World Learning Theme by MINREX [the Cuban Ministry of Foreign Relations], *Granma* and *Cubadebate*" (2016b). As the title suggests, it contributes toward creating divisions within the ranks of the Revolution. This approach, far from assisting MINREX, places additional pressures on the diplomats who are already working under difficult conditions.

At a time when the Cuban Revolution is waging a vitally important struggle to defend its dignity, sovereignty and socialist culture against U.S. pressures, it is imperative for Cubans to identify the *mindset* that assists the U.S. in subtly introducing its new tactics to achieve its same goal of regime change. This ethos distorts Cuba–U.S. relations by tipping the scales in favour of the U.S., and thus will be increasingly promoted by the establishment within Western nations in 2017 and going forward.

Subversion and democracy promotion will undoubtedly carry on and gain momentum through the Trump presidency because U.S. policy is perhaps now encouraged by the illusions, based on the blind worship of diplomacy, that have taken root to a certain extent in Cuba. Democracy promotion is now set in stone as a key block in the foundation of U.S. Cuba policy, irrespective of any other mitigating factor, such as the changing of the guard in the White House. The conciliatory tendency in Cuba, as the "tempest in a teapot" reference above indicates, goes so far as to oppose Cuban youth who are combatting regime change and the ongoing cultural war. The students and other important components of the Cuban political system, such as revolutionary bloggers and writers, are increasingly being denigrated as "spoilers" by pro-Obama policy adherents within and outside of Cuba. This option has taken the eclectic view on diplomacy and resistance to a new level, hitherto unimaginable to some, even though many of my Cuban colleagues and I saw it coming. The example above is, unfortunately for Cuba, not an isolated case.

There are some youth in Cuba who have a tendency to think only of themselves; consequently, they become detached from the Cuban collectivity, culture and traditional social consensus. Such individualism is actively promoted by U.S. cultural incursions into the island. The outlook is fostered by the U.S. because its proliferation and consolidation are indispensable to the American program of luring students to the North for training as future leaders for Cuba. This leadership is expected to be inspired by U.S. values in opposition to Cuba's socialist and patriotic culture. This dilemma brings to mind a group photo of Cuban students in the U.S. on the World Learning recruiting publicity. One cannot, of course, read the minds of these students. However, the looks on their faces — and how they seemingly pose as part of an American trophy earned by the USAID program — suggest a sense of "me, myself and I." How the struggle between the collectivity versus individualism plays out among youth will be a factor in determining the future of the Cuban system and the country's sovereignty. Cuban youth are thus faced with an important challenge. In order for programs such as World Learning to succeed, Washington counts on the spread of individualism among students. While it already exists on a small scale, it is being actively promoted by the U.S. as part of its cultural aggression, especially in the artistic sphere.

In September 2016, the situation had perhaps begun to change. Will the Cuban student activists and young journalists be able to continue expressing their indignation at being used as a resource to build a fifth column? Will they be able to create awareness among all students about U.S. plans? And will they be able to capture the political space necessary to continue demanding the end of the USAID World Learning program and similar democracy promotion initiatives? Given the U.S. offensive against Cuba on democracy and human rights, as analyzed in Chapter 5, in the section titled "The Blockade, Cigars and Rum: The Loopholes," the question of resistance by Cubans from all walks of life takes on even more weight. There is much at stake.

U.S. IMMIGRATION POLICY: AS AMERICAN AS THE AMERICAN DREAM

The American *Cuban Adjustment Act* is the foundation of its Cuba immigration policy. On August 19, 1994, President Bill Clinton announced his "wet-foot, dry-foot" policy: Cubans who landed on U.S. soil ("dry-foot") could remain in the U.S., even if they did not enter the country through the standard legal immigration channels, but migrants who were intercepted by the U.S. Coast Guard at sea ("wet-foot") would be returned to Cuba. The "dry-foot" migrants could then profit from the *Cuban Adjustment Act* of November 2, 1966. It applies to any native or citizen of Cuba who has been inspected and admitted into the U.S. after January 1, 1959, and has been physically present for at least one year and who is admissible to the U.S. as a permanent resident. This policy applies only to Cubans. It is clearly intended to encourage illegal emigration and to create a pool of people to be used as a political tool against the Cuban social, economic and political system. And just as President Bill Clinton initiated this Cuba policy, the Executive Branch has the power to abolish it.

A Washington press conference took place on February 18, 2016, with Obama's national security advisor, Ben Rhodes, just before the Obama visit. One journalist cut to the chase and asked whether the wet-foot, dry-foot policy was "something that the president [was] going to address" while in Cuba. Rhodes's response was disappointing but clear: "We are not planning to institute change with respect to wet-foot, dry-foot.... Our focus is on how conditions can improve in Cuba so that over time there's more economic opportunity and less of a need, frankly, for Cubans to have to pursue opportunity elsewhere" (Obama 2016g). This statement reveals that the U.S. exploits even a humanitarian immigration issue to pursue its policy of forcing Cuba "to change." America is lecturing Cuba on "improving conditions," presumably by following the standard U.S. recipe based on capitalism. The logic follows that, if Cuba does not heed the U.S. call to "change," it has only itself to blame for emigration problems.

During Obama's visit to Havana, the White House repeatedly declared that its policies are for the "well-being of the Cuban people." Despite this, Obama did not announce a reversal in the U.S. immigration policy. Such a move would have been a welcome gesture for the "well-being of the Cuban people," rather than leaving them to risk their lives at sea, lured by the "wet-foot, dry-foot policy." Later, in the July 2016 round of negotiations on bilateral immigration policies held in Havana, there was once again a stand-off with Cuban negotiators, who valiantly insisted that renunciation of the policy was a precondition for normalizing relations.

It is clear that the immigration policy is a U.S. instrument whose goal is to "prove" to Americans, some Cubans and the world that the American Dream is the only option for Cubans who try to "flee communism" with or without the "wet-foot, dry-foot" policy based on the *Cuban Adjustment Act*. It is set in stone and transgresses White House administrations. There is a new factor regarding the "wet-foot, dry-foot" policy. On August 29, 2016, nine South and Central American countries (Colombia, Costa Rica, Ecuador, El Salvador, Guatemala, Mexico, Nicaragua, Panama and Peru) signed a joint letter to Secretary of State John Kerry. These countries have been receiving large numbers of Cuban immigrants, mostly for economic reasons, as their stepping stone to emigrate illegally to the U.S. The letter calls on the U.S. to review its immigration policy which places people in vulnerable situations in these countries as transit points to the U.S. The letter goes on to say:

> The 1966 U.S. Public Law 89-732, known as the "Cuban Adjustment Act," and the policy commonly known as "wet foot, dry foot" have encouraged a disorderly, irregular and unsafe flow of Cubans who, risking their lives, pass through our countries in order to reach the U.S.… This situation has generated a migratory crisis that is affecting our countries. (Gobierno Nacional de la República del Ecuador 2016)

What has changed? Until 2016, the U.S. immigration policy was basically an issue between the U.S. and Cuba. However, the new Cuba–U.S. relationship stirred apprehension among some Cubans who wanted to emigrate to the U.S. and who erroneously thought that their preferred status may be immediately pushed aside by Obama in favour of normalization. The immigration issue was then rapidly converted into a problem involving many countries in the region. Among those who signed the request to the U.S. were countries that are relatively reliable allies of the U.S. on some international issues: Colombia, Mexico, Guatemala, Panama and Peru. These pressures may result in the U.S. modifying this immigration policy in Cuba's favour. However, even if there is some adjustment resulting from Latin American and domestic pressures as well as give-and-take negotiations with Cuba, the U.S. is still armed with its *Cuban Adjustment Act* and democracy promotion program as its bases for attracting people in search of the American Dream.[12]

CUBAN PARTICIPATORY DEMOCRACY IN 2016: WHERE WERE THE OBAMA ADMINISTRATION AND THE U.S. MEDIA?

From June 14 to September 20, 2016, millions of Cubans participated in a profoundly democratic event regarding Cuba's future. It took place after the Communist Party of Cuba held its Seventh Congress in April 2016. Prior to the congress, the 1,000 elected delegates in attendance debated two important documents: the "Draft Conceptualization of the Cuban Economic and Social Model" and the "National Economic and Social Development Plan Through 2030," outline the future of Cuba. These deliberations took place among the Party units at their places of work and education centres, where they had been elected as delegates to the Congress. They were then debated and amended during the April Congress.

Given their importance, and according to the Cuban tradition of democratic consultation, it was decided at the Congress that the documents were to be submitted for public discussion. These consultations took place from June 14 to September 20, at the grassroots level in the Party, the Young Communist League and among representatives of mass organizations as well as broad sectors of Cuban society. The documents were discussed at the grassroots level to also involve in the debate those who are *not* members of the Party and the Young Communist League as well as all their rank-and-file members. The Party was mandated to make the amendments and additions resulting from these deliberations among citizens. The final amended document will be sent to a special meeting of the Central Committee, after which it will be sent to the National Assembly of People's Power — the Cuban parliament — for discussion and approval. The final versions will serve as the basis for any new laws and constitutional amendments.

The documents are long and complex. The goal of this section is to illustrate how this type of discussion takes place in Cuba and allows for the input of the population at important junctures in Cuban history. It is Cuba's own unique form of participatory democracy. Let us take an example of how a debate took place among journalists, since the media and work of writers is a theme of this book. The following article, refreshingly from *Juventud Rebelde,* reports on the journalists' deliberations and provides an excellent insider's view as to how this democracy works. This particular debate took place among journalists at the national level. However, it was similar to the grassroots deliberations that were carried out at local places of work, such as factories and hospitals. Here are some excerpts from the report on the journalists' discussion, translated from the original Spanish-language report of July 1, 2016.[13]

> Communication [journalism] is a platform that brings together all the actors in society, so that political priorities can be converted into priorities for all. It is, at the same time, a strategic resource for the state and its various processes.
>
> The special session of the 6th Extended Plenum of the Union of Cuban Journalists (UPEC) analyzed the documents of the 7th Party Congress. This effort came about as part of a wide-ranging national consultation aimed at enriching and refining these documents that commenced on June 15.
>
> [One journalist] suggested that a paragraph be added addressing the need for a modern, efficient, public communication system. "The document ["Draft Conceptualization of the Cuban Economic and Social Model"] does not explicitly acknowledge the importance of a public communication system to the political, economic and social agenda of the Revolution, which might not succeed if there is no public information system to support and bolster its existence," he argued.
>
> In the same spirit, journalist Rosa Miriam Elizalde indicated that the document should clarify which are the basic means of production [of goods and services], and that a paragraph should be included declaring the means of communication to be a part of them, for they must not belong to a private entity or individual.
>
> On another note, Darío Machado, a professor at the José Martí International Institute of Journalism, opined that it is necessary to take stock of the history of what has occurred in Cuban society from the beginning of the Revolution to the present day. "We are discussing the future but no one has written a critical historical

assessment of the successes and mistakes, the advances and retreats, taking place within the revolutionary process. This is essential, especially for the new generations who did not personally experience this whole process," he said.

Heriberto Rosabal, a journalist with *Bohemia,* argued for the importance of including the organizations of socialist civil society in the paragraph of the document on the principles of socialism that sustain the model — in particular, with regard to socialist democracy, since the People's Power assemblies [National parliament, state and municipality] and other organs of the state are not the only entities making up our democracy.

Rosa Miriam Elizalde suggested that following paragraph 47, which emphasizes the primary role of the socialist relations of production in the model, it should be clarified that "political power must be preserved" in this process, and that this is to be achieved "with the participation of the workers and their control of the mass media, as the voice of organized society, and as a function of citizens' participation in political decisions and control by society."

After emphasizing that the text [of the Party document], despite its formal problems, deals with important concepts and evinces a realistic vision of the crossroads at which Cuban society finds itself, José Alejandro Rodríguez, a journalist with *Juventud Rebelde,* turned his attention to paragraph 80. This refers to one condition necessary for the smooth functioning of production: the existence of a revolutionary working class capable of working efficiently and productively to implement the plans. He proposed adding "which also takes part in the leadership and control of economic and social management."

This addition, he said, would serve to underscore the concept of people's control, empower the people and codify the existence of a revolutionary working class that exercises control. He also suggested adding to paragraph 62, which emphasizes the impartial treatment of petitions to the government and the need for a proper response to citizens, that such a response must be "expeditious, profound and transparent," for there are many middle managers who do not respond as they should. It is necessary, Rodríguez continued, to show respect for the citizens.

Luis Sexto, president of UPEC's Ethics Commission, proposed that some aspects related to paragraph 80 be clarified: "How do we acknowledge the ownership role of the revolutionary working class? What is owned by all the people? What concept of 'people' is used in the document? Is it a demographic concept, a sociological one or a political one? What is the role of unions and how do they represent the working class?"

Randy Alonso, the director of *Mesa Redonda* and *Cubadebate,* noted that the right to housing cannot be separated from the other rights of citizens, as occurs in paragraphs 69 and 70 of the Draft Conceptualization. He also proposed that the right to food be acknowledged in the document.

Journalist Ricardo Ronquillo brought up the issue of how the concepts of single party [Communist Party of Cuba] and democracy are separate in the document. "We have to demonstrate that the single-party type of organization is a part of the Cuban democratic system," he said. He proposed combining paragraphs 59 and 60 of the Conceptualization Document into a single paragraph. "We must make it clear that the Party forms a part of the nation's democratic system and how much this has benefited us."

Finally, in reference to paragraph 155, which indicates that the state appoints and removes the principal directors of the production system, José Alejandro Rodríguez reminded participants not to forget the role of unions. "We must give consideration to what the workers think, and it is therefore advisable to add: 'taking into account the opinions of the mass organizations and the workers as a whole.'" (Labacena Romero 2016)

Do such concrete proposals for changes, amendments and additions find their way into the final documents? My detailed study of the proceedings leading up to the Party Congress, in April 2011 (previous to the April 2016 one), affirms that hundreds of suggestions were taken into account. The original draft document at that time was radically transformed, including points being added. All this resulted from input at the grassroots level (August 2013: 118–35).

"We Already Know What Ravsberg Is All About"

The UPEC Special Extended Plenum where journalists debated the Party documents served as a pretext for a new ideological and political offensive by dissidents of the "left."[14] What is at stake is the Cuban resistance to the outlook promoted by the U.S. that Cuba is an authoritarian regime lacking in democracy and human rights such as freedom of speech. This U.S.-centric view of the Cuban system was expressed, as will be recalled, by Obama in his exhortations to the Cuban people in Havana in 2016 to overcome the restraints and violation of human rights. The latest polemic takes place under the ideological and political — if not necessarily structural — umbrella of the Obama initiative, thus its bearing on one of the basic themes in this publication: the U.S.-led cultural war against the socialist culture of Cuba.

At the centre of this latest controversy is a Uruguayan journalist living in Cuba and a former BBC correspondent there, Fernando Ravsberg. An earlier article I published provides the background to this story.[15] In that article, I show how Ravsberg, who poses as a progressive, used his formal credentials as a journalist to interfere in the internal affairs of Cuba by actively supporting individuals who were seeking regime change and were inspired by U.S. democracy promotion programs. The article includes a brief summary of a revealing informal interview I had with him in Havana (August 2012a).

However, perhaps my most telling writing about Ravsberg dates back to June 2011 (August 2011d, in Spanish only), as it has since become somewhat of a "classic" for some Cuban bloggers regarding the ongoing saga of Ravsberg. Based on a thorough study of his blog posts as well as the online comments that they attract, the article analyzes and forecasts how Ravsberg and similar "leftist" dissidents operate. He posts an article on his blog that is positive with regard to the Cuban Revolution so as to gain the trust of pro-Revolution Cubans. This is invariably followed by a post that jumps on an issue in order to discredit the Cuban Revolution, especially its leadership, drawing the somewhat gullible among the revolutionaries into his orbit. The main content of his complaints is the so-called "authoritarian" nature of "the Castros," or the "regime." His audience is composed of especially the youth, artists, intellectuals and journalists. Ravsberg's goal is to prey on the vacillating elements among these sections of society in order to divert them from the road of Revolution or, at best from his perspective, to actually enrol them in his "leftist" dissidence sphere of influence. In both cases, Ravsberg acts as their guru. Ravsberg has been successful to a certain extent in his endeavour to bring into play his sympathizers (many of whom are not conscious of his chameleon tactics) in this latest 2016 offensive.

In today's context, this subterfuge is related to the cultural war being waged by the West against the Cuban socialist culture. In fact, the dissidents on the "left" see the opening in Cuba–U.S. relations as an opportunity to strike while the iron is hot, knowing full well that the "thaw" places Cuba in a difficult and complex situation. The issue Ravsberg jumped on relates to a report UPEC posted on its website documenting the exchanges at the journalists' UPEC special meeting. This report included comments by young journalist Karina Marrón, deputy director of *Granma*, who sharply criticized the bureaucratic situation often found in the Cuban media as the cause of the alienation of young, recently graduated journalists. They are disaffected, she opined, to the extent that they at times seek to exercise their profession in the private media (foreign-owned media accredited in Cuba and abroad). Marrón testified that this regrettable option was not necessarily pursued for monetary reasons but rather out of frustration resulting from the double-talk by the decision-makers overlooking the Cuban media (Gorgoy Crespo 2016).

However, that was not all Marrón said. Perhaps reflecting the youthful frustration regarding the situation in the Cuban media, she seemed to direct some comments about the country's leadership for the alleged lack of capacity to deal with problems on the horizon. This portion was not published in the UPEC article. A journalist who was a delegate to this UPEC session surreptitiously recorded Marrón's speech. After the UPEC meeting was over he noticed that the speech was not fully reported upon in the press. Without asking permission from UPEC or Marrón, he transcribed and posted her talk on a local blog. This action was privately challenged by UPEC according to its norms, which he knowingly violated. The journalist at fault apparently feared that he may be removed from his job. Even while the investigation was ongoing, he ran to the person who specializes in protecting and promoting "victims" of the Cuban "authoritarian regime": Fernando Ravsberg. The latter immediately obliged and posted an interview with the journalist whose activity was being evaluated by UPEC, headlining that they are "firing a Cuban journalist" (Ravsberg 2016). This sensationalist headline and disinformation, similar to U.S. and U.K. tabloid gossip, was immediately reprinted by the Miami-based anti-Castro media as well as their Spanish counterparts. They relish any story that targets the "authoritarian Castro regime."[16]

The first vice-president of UPEC, Aixa Hevia, posted a response to this on her Facebook page. It was later posted by Iroel Sánchez on his blog *La pupila insomne* in order to reach a wider audience. Hevia made two comments that go right to the heart of the matter. She noticed that the journalist who recorded Marrón's entire speech deleted the following comment in his post: "We Already Know What Ravsberg Is All About" ("Ya Sabemos Quién Es Ravsberg"). Marrón was referring pejoratively to the well-known opportunistic manner in which Ravsberg operates in Cuba. Hevia also rhetorically asked if the journalist who illicitly recorded and posted Marrón's presentation was "looking for a story that would allow him to cross over to the mass media in Miami? A pretty ugly machination, if indeed it was the cause." Toward the end of her post, she mentioned that Ravsberg is getting on the nerves of decent people. This, Hevia says, is reflected in entries on some blogs indicating that they should throw Ravsberg out of the country for being someone who is constantly changing colours like a chameleon (Hevia 2016).

This general comment served as a godsend for Ravsberg. He immediately misrepresented the remark as an actual call by Hevia for his expulsion, jumping on the martyr's podium as the latest victim of the regime. Some naive youth went into action to defend him from this red herring of expulsion. They were joined by veteran "leftist" dissidents who expressed their support for Ravsberg through the always obliging *Havana Times* dissident media outlet at the service of anyone in Cuba against the "authoritarian regime."

On the other side, bloggers such as Iroel Sánchez, other social media writers and journalists took a stand against what they see as the latest in a long line of provocations against the Cuban Revolution. They dissect the charlatan methods of Ravsberg, his "leftist" dissident acolytes in Cuba and the "anti-Castro" Miami-based press that acts as an echo for all of them.

Nevertheless, there is a positive spinoff. The public controversy allows for a sharpening and deepening of the Cuban socialist culture, ideology and politics as the defence against the U.S.-led cultural war. In addition, the new offensive against the Cuban socialist culture is forcing the "centrists" to come out of the woodwork. The "centrists" are intellectuals on the sidelines who were waiting for the appropriate moment to choose their ideological camp — which they are doing now as a result of the Ravsberg issue. This makes it easier for Cuban revolutionaries to know where the difficult-to-detect centrists stand during this crucial period.

To conclude, Marrón (whose comments at the UPEC meeting served as a pretext for the controversy) co-authored an excellent report for *Granma* on September 9, 2016. The subject was the debate among the *Granma* workers on the Communist Party documents. Among other topics of debate, there were no less than four suggestions to amend the draft document in the course of what she termed a "fertile exchange" (Marrón González and Jank Curbelo 2016). Thus, even the concerted opposition of the dissidents backed by the hostile foreign media did not succeed in causing divisions in the revolutionary ranks. Ravsberg, who acts as a knight in shining armour promoting transparency, did not acknowledge this lively report by the journalist. He himself, only a few weeks previously, had lauded Marrón as an example of courage for her journalistic endeavours in the hope that he would lure her into his realm of influence. Once she reaffirmed her commitment to bring about change in Cuba's press from *within* the system, she was no longer useful to Ravsberg. Compare this to the appreciation and valuable assistance offered by Ravsberg to the journalist who "broke the story" about the UPEC meeting and then sought refuge under the auspices of his political and ideological outlook. It is important for the dissident "left" to bequeath the impression to the world and Cuba that no change is possible within the Cuban system. Thus, it must be brought from outside the system through the active support of a pro-U.S. "opposition" in Cuba under the aegis of the increasingly aggressive "democracy promotion" programs. This mindset is inspired by the Obama thesis on change in Cuba, either directly or indirectly.

Striving to Improve the Cuban Media from Within

While the debates and grassroots input surrounding the Party documents on the future of Cuba were positive, there were also weaknesses. These concern the widespread awareness of what transpired at the base. Darío Machado Rodríguez, Ph.D., holds the chair of investigative journalism and is vice-dean of the Faculty of Communication and Society at the José Martí International Institute of Journalism. He dealt with this preoccupation of many in Cuba about the lack of full information regarding the local meetings. In an article published on July 9, 2016, in *Cubadebate,* at the start of the deliberations and in the context of proffering a positive evaluation of them, he nevertheless warned: "We must … recognize that the media are still insufficient and only slowly making available to the society what arises in one place or another on these documents. It is imperative to quickly find a vehicle that allows for the expression of the feelings that exist in Cuban society and that reflects the vitality and importance of such a national dialogue" (2016a). This analysis and recommendation is another indication that there is indeed ample space *within* the Cuban political system to work toward change in media. *Cubadebate* is read by virtually all Cuban journalists. Machado's piece was reprinted in *Cuba Periodistas,* which is dedicated to journalism, among other issues. Given the relatively good quality of the subsequent reports on the debates, can one conclude that Machado's recommendation had a positive effect on some of the Cuban media? Whether as a result of his article or of journalists reaching their own conclusions, there seems to be a move in the right direction. However, the actual conversion of these local debates to the level of a national social deliberation may not have been as widespread as Machado seems to prescribe. There were not many such articles or TV reports, given the historical importance of the debates.

A polemical reflection concerning the media took place on September 14, 2016, at a time when the local deliberations on the Party documents were ending. The National Council of the Unión de Escritores y Artistas de Cuba met to debate the Party texts. Their agenda also included concerns related to its field of responsibility, the role of writers. The session was presided over by UNEAC president Miguel Barnet, noted poet and writer. Also present was the minister of culture, Abel Prieto, known for his outspoken positions regarding improving culture and the press. Given that the writers' section of the association includes journalists and authors who write articles, the report on the UNEAC National Council meeting dealing with the media proved to be of particular interest. In fact, the debate was heated. One challenging — but essential — comment was made by Esteban Morales, one of the experts interviewed in Chapter 3:

> [He] urged the intellectual vanguard to adhere to the efforts under way by the Cuban press and the mass media in general, to improve and allow them to earn more respect from readers. Morales reiterated that there are complaints about the press and the media in general, and so it is vital the press has the necessary qualities to increase the interest of our people to consult it. He said UNEAC must establish strategic alliances with the mass media so that UNEAC's membership has a presence in the pages of newspapers and on other platforms, with texts that stimulate debate, enhance emancipation paradigms that are based on national identity and counteract policies against Cuba promoted from the United States. (Hernández 2016)

Of significance — and encouraging — this report was published in *Granma,* and a slightly abridged version was printed in *Cuba Periodistas.*

Participatory democracy at the base, as exemplified by the deliberations on the Party documents, is often used in Cuba to reach important decisions. This feature of Cuban-style democracy took place following a long U.S. media blitz (especially on CNN) reflecting the White House Cuba policy. This biased reporting began on December 17, 2014, and encompassed the August 2015 flag-raising ceremony at the U.S. Embassy in Havana and the March 2016 Obama visit. These media reports, or rather disinformation, not only reflected the U.S. doctrine on democracy but further amplified it. Thus, the dramatic question that emerges is: Where were the White House and the U.S. media (especially CNN, which kept the same correspondent in Havana throughout these events) when this Cuban experience in democracy took place in the summer and fall of 2016? We can only conclude that the term "democracy" is manipulated by the U.S. to serve its own interests. With respect to Cuba, as long as the Revolution maintains its sovereignty and socialist path, the double standard that is applied to Cuba in comparison with other countries will not change with the Trump presidency.

THE COMMUNIST PARTY AS LEADER VS. THE PEOPLE AS SOVEREIGN

The U.S. and its media asserts that the Communist Party of Cuba "dictates." This accusation is based on the false U.S.-centric presumption that "dictating" by leadership or government bodies is a characteristic that applies only to single-party political systems, such as in Cuba. However, other political systems are characterized by leadership that "dictates." Let us take the example of the U.S. only to illustrate a point, inasmuch as Cuba and U.S. have two different political systems. Does the U.S. not have an Executive Branch (president, vice-president, cabinet, etc.) that enjoys its own prerogatives and powers?

It is true that in the U.S., unlike Cuba, there is more than one party. However, the goal here is to conceptualize "leadership" in relation to the other branches of government and society as a universal phenomenon, albeit in different conditions. To take one more example, in the parliamentary system as exists in Canada and the U.K., there is a cabinet that exercises strong leadership. However, there is no deep-seated mainstream narrative that the Canadian and British peoples are the victims of dictates. Why is this double standard applied to Cuba?

It is incumbent upon us to examine these U.S. accusations against Cuba, which are not going to disappear from Cuba–U.S. relations. What is the actual role of the Party in Cuba and how does it relate to Cuban society, both formally and in real terms? The Cuban Constitution stipulates the following in Article 5:

> The Communist Party of Cuba, a follower of Martí's ideas and of Marxism-Leninism, and the organized vanguard of the Cuban nation, is the highest leading force of society and of the state, which *organizes and guides* the common effort toward the goals of the construction of socialism and the progress toward a communist society. (Ministry of Foreign Affairs of Cuba 2003, emphasis added)

The same Constitution also stipulates in Article 3:

> In the Republic of Cuba sovereignty lies in the people, from whom originates all the power of the state. That power is exercised directly or through the assemblies of People's Power and other state bodies

which derive their authority from these assemblies, in the form and according to the norms established in the Constitution and by law.

We are dealing with Cuba, *not* the former U.S.S.R., nor the former Eastern Bloc socialist countries. One cannot view the Communist Party in Cuba based on preconceived notions — merited or not — of these other experiences. For example, in Cuba, the concept of the Party as the leading force in society emerges first and foremost out of the nineteenth-century Cuban tradition, which predates early twentieth-century Lenin and his concept of the Communist Party. While the Cuban communists proudly proclaim Lenin as an inspirational factor, the decisive source is the indigenous Cuban tradition. In the second half of the nineteenth century, José Martí developed the notion, in terms of political thought and practice, of the need for one political force to lead the Revolution and the Cuban nation against Spanish colonialism. This goal was intended to favour both Cuban independence and a more just society, taking the form of the Partido Revolucionario Cubano (PRC). This is one of the most important legacies of José Martí.

The party that Martí founded and the people in arms succeeded in defeating the far superior force of Spain — a victory hijacked by the U.S. It is also remarkable that, during the last phase of the war against Spain in the liberated territories, the PRC led the task of applying new social programs, such as health and education for all, with the full participation of the people (August 2013: 86; Izquierdo Canosa 1998: 37–41, 153). Furthermore, in 1958, the July 26 movement, led by Fidel Castro in alliance with other revolutionary forces inspired by Martí's work and constituting the seed of the new Communist Party, carried out similar programs while the U.S.-backed Batista regime was still in power. For example, with the peasants as protagonists in the liberated area, locally led services such as health and education were established. In addition, formal legal programs were instituted, such as the *Agrarian Reform Law* in the Frank País Second Eastern Front, led by Raúl Castro (August 2013: 94). After January 1, 1959, the movement that emerged out of the late 1950s started to regroup all the revolutionary forces. This difficult effort later resulted in the founding of the Communist Party of Cuba in 1965.

The Party is based in the grassroots workplaces, in the social and educational institutions and in the neighbourhoods. These local units put forward nominations and proposals for new members, who must be approved by a two-thirds vote of the members and then ratified by the next immediate level, for example, the municipal Party branch. The Party Congress meets in principle every five years and is composed of elected delegates from the places of work. It elects from among the delegates the Central Committee, which is responsible for leading the work of the Party until the next Congress (Communist Party of Cuba n.d.).

There are several recent examples worth considering when evaluating the role of the Party. In 2007, the entire Cuban population was called upon to identify any problems in society and propose solutions. This input served as a base for a set of guidelines for what the Cubans call an update to the socialist system. This led to another significant democratic and transparent debate, which took place in the period leading up the Sixth Party Congress in 2011. The deliberations covered the full program for the economic changes being developed in Cuba at the time. Once again, the entire population was involved, providing input that included new proposals and amendments and thus a new version of the program.[17] It should be noted that this approach to democracy was led by the Communist Party, supposedly the antithesis of democracy.

In the period from June 15 to September 20, 2016, we have the examples outlined above in this section regarding the debates at the grassroots on Party documents. The Party, as "the highest leading force of society and of the state," typically works out proposals in the Party Congress. The most significant ones go to the population for discussion and input. The Central Committee of the Party adopts the suggestions, makes appropriate modifications and drafts a new version. This is then presented to the National Assembly of People's Power, the only organ qualified to legislate, for discussion and then adoption with amendments that may arise. This final version subsequently serves as the basis for future laws and measures. It needs to be emphasized that Assembly deputies and mass organizations also have the right to propose legislation. Thus, one may further appreciate Article 3 of the Cuban Constitution regarding sovereignty being vested in the people. It does not, as some might believe, contradict Article 5, wherein the Party is the leading superior force of the society. The Party in Cuba is not above the people, nor is people's sovereignty detached from the Party's actions, which also strive to reinforce the notion that "sovereignty lies in the people."

However, the relationship between the Party that leads and sovereignty residing in the people remains an ongoing challenge. Ricardo Alarcón, in the 2014 Spanish-language Cuban edition of my previous book (August 2014), titled his foreword "The Long Road Toward Utopia." He captured the very essence of "Democracy in Motion," which by its very nature is continuously unfolding. One cannot say at any one point in time, "This is it! Cuba has attained the 'Nirvana' of a true democratic society!" Given that the Party and the sovereign will are two living entities that influence each other daily, they are necessarily dependent on this uninterrupted interaction. The relationship between leadership and people's sovereignty is a continuous, compulsory and dynamic process.

POLITICAL PRISONERS IN CUBA: THE LIST

In May 2016, the list of political prisoners (see Chapter 2) that Raúl Castro challenged the journalist to produce became available. According to the international media, which uncritically referred to a list produced by the avowed "dissident" Elizardo Sánchez, there were ninety-three "political prisoners" in Cuba. Of these ninety-three people, eleven were not even prisoners. They had been released in 2010 following an agreement between Cuba, Spain and the Catholic Church, and were given conditional acquittals. They lived in their homes without constraint, and ten of the eleven had travelled abroad to participate in anti-Cuban government events and to lobby for sanctions against Cuba. From the remaining eighty-two people allegedly still in prison at the time, seven were convicted of common offences, such as theft, illegal sales or refusal to pay fines. Five more were convicted of espionage and revealing state secrets. Another sixty-one of these individuals are in prison for the use of violence in varying degrees, and some are responsible for numerous homicides. Among their crimes are hijacking of boats or planes, rebellion and armed infiltration from the U.S., sabotage, mutiny, attacks, threats, weapons possession and public disorder and damage. That leaves only nine people out of the ninety-three who were charged with "disobedience" (*desacato*). The majority of these have yet to be sentenced, and not enough reliable information is available to reach any conclusion about them (Manzaneda 2016).

On the issue of democracy, Washington-accredited mainstream news correspondents focus attention on "political prisoners" and "repression" in other countries — except if the country is an ally of the U.S., not to mention in the U.S. itself. Obsessed with the U.S. self-anointed right to preach democracy for Cuba and irrespective of non-existent political prisoners in Cuba, Obama and his allies in the news media — and now Trump — will point an accusing finger at Cuba when it is convenient.

In fact, it is linked to the U.S. democracy promotion program that distributes funds to those Cuban agents, who, among other duties, draw up these false lists of political prisoners. This will not stop as long as Cuba pursues its own sovereign path.

WHO IS GOING TO WIN THE CULTURAL WAR?

Ricardo Alarcón, writing in 2003, highlighted the importance of considering the historical context: "The cultural aggression against Cuba began in 1959 and did not cease with the end of the "cold war." Not only does it exist, but it continues to grow.... The Cuban case is, for these reasons, absolutely unique; it is exceptional." Not only has this U.S. aggression against Cuba been going on since 1959, and will likely continue, but no other country has been subjected to such persistent hostility. There is every reason to place the unending assault, including the blockade and other hostile policies, and Cuban resistance to it at the very centre of Cuba–U.S. relations. The point of view that refuses to recognize the reality of the cultural war and pretends that it somehow disappeared with the Cold War, or 17D, has now in effect merged into the cultural aggression against Cuba. The cultural war's long historical antecedents and dangerous wide-ranging shifts in appearances over time do not leave room for neutrality.

Not an Easy Call

Given the current complex situation, rooted in both the past and the post-17D situation, it is difficult to evaluate which side — Cuba or the U.S. — will win. I wrote two articles, one just prior to the Obama visit and one immediately afterwards (2016c and 2016a, reprinted in Chapter 2), in which it was difficult to reach a conclusion, even though my analysis foresaw a positive outcome for Cuba. At the time of writing this book (November 2016), however, it appears that it cannot be taken as a given that the Revolution is winning. Recall that whereas many commentators had been strongly and justly opposed to the U.S. policy on Cuba before December 17, 2014, they have since shifted their focus from contesting U.S. aggressive policy to blending into the Obama Cuba policy, which will continue under Trump with his own rhetoric.

In the two articles mentioned above, I dealt with this metamorphosis. However, the transmutation has become even bolder as we enter the Trump period. The danger is amplified because the defence of the Obama policy increasingly exists both on and off the island, and they rely heavily on each other. Any developments in the metamorphosis taking place in Cuba is immediately detected by U.S. official circles. Although some commentators are perhaps not fully informed, they nevertheless promote this inclination as acceptable and credible. As a result, they are invited to speak in the U.S., write for American press and give TV interviews. The goal, through this disinformation, is to create illusions about Obama's Cuba policy. While positive, this policy also harbours the treacherous aspects initiated by the outgoing president that challenge Cuba's socialist culture. How will Trump deal with this?

The Transmutation: Dealing with Cuba

Two extreme perspectives have evolved with regard to current progress in the relationship between Cuba and the U.S. At one end of the spectrum is the view that nothing was accomplished, not even the re-establishment of diplomatic relations, aside from providing alleged credibility to the "Castro regime." It asserts that the U.S. did not exact any concessions from Cuba as a pre-condition for diplomatic recognition. At the other end is the almost euphoric impression that relations are almost normalized — or have even been normalized — and that the Obama visit and his statements were uncritically supported by all Cubans.

One can argue that the latter conciliatory attitude is preferable to the other extreme, which denies any positive change and even turns back the clock on historic developments. However, that viewpoint is in fact a red herring within the U.S. Cuba policy discussion to the extent that even Trump does not fully challenge the re-establishment of diplomatic relations. In contrast, appeasement plays on the widespread delusion surrounding the Obama phenomenon. This view was planted, even if only marginally, in the Cuban political landscape on 17D. And subsequently, during Obama's Havana visit, it was skilfully watered and fertilized by the PR-savvy White House.

This outlook has now morphed into an even further apology for and defence of the Obama Cuba policy. The writings of Alzugaray exemplify this conciliatory trend. It is helpful to further bring this polemic to public scrutiny. Alzugaray opposes the "old and sterile dichotomy between socialism and capitalism," and criticizes that "the very concept of 'normalization' has been called into question by many academics, journalists and citizens." This same perception affirms that "we are already in the full process of normalization," and it challenges the "immense majority of the commentators" who reacted "surprised and 'fast and furious'" to Obama's notion that "we Cubans should forget our history," asserting to the contrary that "Obama never has said that one should forget history." Alzugaray's apologetic mindset holds that other Cubans involved in analyzing Cuba–U.S. relations should be "more balanced and profound in their opinions" and also disagrees with those who claim that the current U.S. policy represents a "cultural war" (2016c).

Both the nihilistic and euphoric standpoints are faulty. However, the latter point of view, as fleshed out in the previous paragraph, represents a trend that has gone from being against open U.S. hostility, exhibited before 17D, to becoming an Obama apologist. Proponents of this orientation are growing in number, particularly inside Cuba. It is the more dangerous of the two extremes, as it is fosters illusions about U.S. intentions toward Cuba. The perilous perspective glosses over — or even eliminates from its discourse — a most important feature: as publicly enunciated by the U.S., the overtly hostile tactics to subvert the Cuban Revolution did not work, and thus the policy has changed to foster diplomatic tactics, in order to achieve the same strategic goal. This is not a minor issue. The seduced, inside and outside Cuba, play the role of a "credible" front for the U.S. cultural war.

This perception also censors the *critical yet supportive* attitude toward the Obama visit and U.S. Cuba policy that is most reflective of the many Cubans who wrote and testified so incisively along such lines during and after the Obama visit — and who continue to do so. This approach is generally excluded from the American discourse since it is not known outside of Cuba. The gap is widened by the pro-Obama trend that adds further disinformation by promoting the *dissident* bloggers and websites in Cuba. Complementing this, the concealment or distortion of the perceptive and revolutionary view is essential to ideologically and politically disarm some Cubans so that they board the pro-Washington train.

Reality is also obscured by surreptitiously placing Cuba and the U.S. on the same footing with regard to the Cuba–U.S. rapprochement. For example, the same ex-diplomat in Havana who criticized the students as being spoilers in the evolving relationship between the two neighbours, also wrote: "Given *our old conflicts,* no one can be surprised that there are mutual misunderstandings and disagreements, but what is clear to me is the *will of both governments* to move forward and make irreversible the changes and convert them into a solid foundation for the future" (Alzugaray 2016b, emphasis added). This outlook converts over fifty years of U.S. aggression and interference and the genocidal blockade against Cuba into *"our old conflicts."* The obviously asymmetrical relationship between the aggressive Goliath and the defensive David is converted into a symmetrical one. This political and ideological contortion suggests that the asymmetrical rapport can, in turn, be transformed into a fully harmonious one, with this responsibility resting on the shoulders of both sides *on an equal basis.* To speak about the *"will of both governments"* is to obscure the fact that Cuba does not impose a blockade against the U.S., interfere in its internal affairs or hold even one inch of U.S. territory and has never participated in terrorist acts on U.S. soil.

In contrast, the Obama Administration, even since 17D, has not given up on these sources of conflict, except for putting an end to the destabilizing terrorist activities in Cuba. The policy based on open violence is being replaced by an increasingly aggressive "pacific" democracy promotion program to attain the same goal of regime change. If this chimera about an innate symmetrical relation were coming from the U.S., it would not come as a surprise. However — and this is a crucial point — this outlook comes from *Cuba* and, even more astonishingly, apparently from within the revolutionary ranks. Is this the trend that encouraged Obama to go on a new offensive of democracy promotion, by co-opting Cubans into administering Washington's own subversive programs against Cuba, now under the guise of "transparency"?

As more roadblocks in the "rapprochement" inevitably emerge, the point of view coming from Cuba and focused on merging the "will of both governments" gives some credibility to the outgoing Administration's policy, to the detriment of Cuba. This can occur when the U.S. blames Cuba for not "changing" enough to suit the U.S. It is also a vision that results in blaming the Cuban students for upsetting the apple cart in their opposition to the World Learning program, promoted by a supposedly benevolent U.S.

In this situation, troubling from the Cuban perspective, it was encouraging to read the writing of two outstanding Cuban intellectuals. The title of the exceptional analysis of Cuba's culture, identity and history by award-winning philosopher and author Fernando Martínez Heredia is "Either Cuba or Washington" ("O Cuba o Washington"). The interview granted by the prestigious award-winning publisher and writer Ambrosio Fornet is titled "The Problem Now Is Not Platt But the Plattists" ("El problema ahora no es Platt, sino los plattistas"). A short explanation is in order. On December 25, 1901, Cuba was pressured by the U.S. into amending its constitution to contain the text of the Platt Amendment (named after U.S. Senator Orville H. Platt), which allows the U.S. to intervene unilaterally in Cuban affairs. Thus, the titles of the pieces by Martínez Heredia and Fornet say it all, while providing readers with a vivid idea of how Cuba has been in the throes of a major debate since 17D.

One of the most ominous features of the White House-based perspective is U.S. manipulation of the concepts of "democracy" and "human rights." This outlook reached a fever pitch in the U.S. and other Western mass media after the passing of Fidel Castro, as analyzed in Chapter 6. The U.S.-centric view, which is the foundation of the morphed pro-Obama trend, claims that there are two types of human rights: individual and social. This viewpoint concedes that Cuba has made accomplishments on social human rights, such as health, education, culture and sport; however, the perception persists that Cuba violates individual human rights. The "superior" U.S. model passes the test because it is self-defined as being a multi-party democracy and capitalist, and thus by its very nature is a defender of individual rights. Given the paramount international significance accorded to this aspect of human rights, it is incumbent to explore the following: What is the source of this dichotomy between individual and social rights?

Kneeling at the Altar of Individualism

Let us take a passage from Obama's televised speech to the Cuban people during his March 2016 trip:

> But we cannot, and should not, ignore the very real differences that we have — about how we organize our governments, our economies, and our societies. Cuba has a one-party system; the United States is a multi-party democracy. Cuba has a socialist economic model; the United States is an open market. Cuba has emphasized the role and rights of the *state*; the United States is founded upon the rights of the *individual*. (Obama 2016c, emphasis added)

The pro-Obama disposition on and off the island is aligned with the view held by the outgoing president himself. In his speech to entrepreneurs in Havana, Obama praised Cuba for its achievements in health and education to such an extent that he seemed to fawn over Cuba. However, this professed admiration merely serves as the cover for preaching to the extreme in favour of individual rights and opportunities that are supposedly mainly absent for Cubans. The entrepreneurs are thus encouraged to view the U.S. from the American perspective of being natural promoters of their interests.

Obama is correct in claiming that the "United States is founded upon the rights of the *individual*." At the time of the U.S. Declaration of Independence in the eighteenth century, there were two main sources of political and ideological inspiration: the individualism of John Locke and the collectivism of Jean-Jacques Rousseau. The authors of the U.S. Declaration of Independence rejected the latter as a source of motivation, even though Rousseau was one of the most outstanding thinkers of his time. He favoured collective and fraternal relationships over the individual possessive nature of capitalism. While Rousseau envisioned a new moral and social order based on equality, the new arrangement "did not suppress individual creativity" (Lambie 2010: 85). Rousseau pointed to the source of so many misfortunes and horrors that society has faced emerging from "the first man, who after enclosing a piece of ground, took it into his head to say, 'This is mine,' and found people simple enough to believe him" (2004: 27). In Rousseau's classic work, *Discourse on the Origin of Inequality,* he developed his thesis: democracy cannot exist based on a society nurtured on individualism. He concluded: "The various forms of government owe their origin to the various degrees of inequality between members, at the time they first coalesced into a political body" (46). He championed the need for common interests and well-being over and above particular or individual interests, and gave this warning: "If there were not some point on which all interests agree, no society could exist … Now it is solely in terms of this common interest that society ought to be governed" (57). At the same time, Rousseau placed the flourishing of the individual on par with the collective well-being, writing that a legitimate civil order is "a form of association that will defend and protect the person and goods of each associate [citizen] with the full common force, and by means of which each, uniting with all, nevertheless obey[s] only himself and remain[s] as free as before" (2007: xiii). Rousseau stood out for constantly striving to link the collective and the individual.

Despite this, the American founding fathers remained faithful to Locke, but the penchant for placing the common good over and above private property and interests, led by Rousseau and others, inspired progressive thinking in Europe and in the South. It would thus be a mistake, blinded by U.S.-centric prejudices, to attach advanced Enlightenment thinking and values to the experience of democracy in the U.S. The extreme individualism characterized by the U.S. was achieved through the sacrifice of individual interests of the vast majority at the time, most of whom were not even considered as *individual human beings* — for example, Indigenous peoples, enslaved Africans and women. Many others had their individual rights denied to the profit of the ruling circles, the notorious one percent of today.

What Is Behind the Perceived Horror of "the State"?

Obama and his supporters speak of the "socialist economic model" as if "the state" were a horror in contradiction with the individual. It should be noted that "the state" very much exists in the U.S.: it is the "hidden fist" that assists the "invisible hand of the free market" when it is in danger of losing its profits, for example, the Wall Street and auto industry bailouts.

However, there is another concept of the state that is loathed by the U.S. and its exponents. This contempt is understandable because this alternative vision of the state contradicts the U.S.-centric notion of the individual as sacrosanct. The Cuban system is an example of a state based on the collectivity. Its many accomplishments, recognized even by the White House, are well-known. But what about individual rights in Cuba, as challenged by the White House perspective?

To respond, one must ask once again how the Cubans built their state, which has performed internationally recognized social and education miracles. Before 1959, the U.S.-supported Cuban state was based on individual property in the cities and towns. During the 1950s, individual Cubans courageously rebelled against this by unifying their forces to overthrow the neo-colonial diktat. They forcefully exercised their individual rights, even though, paradoxically, these were denied by the dictatorship that was backed by none other than the U.S., the "world beacon" for individual rights.

While, in 1959, for the first time in Cuban history, collective values became the dominant ideology, this did not — and does not — mean that individual rights were or are suppressed. Cubans, for example, participate in the effort to improve upon the socio-economic achievements and the overall orientation of the Cuban Revolution. The debate among the journalists in 2016 is but one example of this. The suggestions and proposals for amendments came from individuals exercising their individual rights. Moreover, the deliberations also touched on freedom of the press and freedom of expression being strengthened and assured within the Cuban media.

Another example is to be found in the five interviews in Chapter 3. These individuals are sharing their respective personal views with readers, opinions that are part of the flourishing debate among individuals going on in Cuban society today on the subject of Cuba–U.S. relations and its political and ideological consequences. This debate is not "controlled" by the state. On the contrary, these deliberations constitute a challenge to bureaucracy carried out by those who refuse to conform to the illusionary outlook regarding Washington.

I attended dozens of meetings at the grassroots level from 1997 to 2014, where individual citizens made proposals and put forward complaints to be solved by the collective state. Is there room for improvement in this process? Yes, definitely, but this Cuban freedom of expression exists as a tradition going back to 1959. This individual participation is completely ignored in the perspective based on complicity with the Obama Cuba policy. It is done to fortify their view that the state in Cuba exists to the detriment of the individual, who allegedly has no role in the collective society.

Transmutation: Dealing with Cuba in Relation to Latin America

The perspective that normalization has arrived or is on the verge of being realized is based on completely extricating Cuba from the rest of Latin America. The change of tactics by the U.S. is linked, as the outgoing administration openly stated many times, to the U.S. desire to isolate Cuba from Latin America. The U.S. policy of insulating Cuba instead disconnected the *U.S.* from the rest of the region, and the new tactic has the goal of correcting this, and thus increasing U.S. influence south of the Rio Grande. This adjustment has been in the works since the 2008 Obama mandate, as analyzed in Chapter 1. Moreover, the change took on greater prominence during his March 2016 visit to Havana.

Obama, as noted earlier, continued his Latin America tour by flying from Havana to Buenos Aires, Argentina. This allowed him to further forge links with the new pro-U.S. right-wing government under Mauricio Macri, who was elected in October 2015. The Argentine leg of the Obama tour showcased for the world what the U.S. hoped would be the image of a rejuvenated neighbour in the North justifiably taking its place once again in the South. While the U.S. *itself* always flashes this as a trademark, the new approach to Cuba completely removes the island from the regional equation. This is done in order to more easily — and surreptitiously — promote the illusion of imminent normalization.

The U.S. is attempting to recover its lost influence in the region and roll back the positive developments of the left-wing governments in Latin America, especially since the election of Hugo Chávez in December 1998. Of course, the U.S., playing the role of innocent bystander, tries to give the impression that only insipient local movements are behind the conservative pro-U.S. restoration since the Argentine elections, the Venezuela legislative election in December 2015 and the Brazilian coup in 2016.

Much to the contrary of those who cling to the fantasy of the benevolent White House with regard to Cuba policy by covering up its activities concerning the rest of Latin America, the U.S. has been *fully* involved in attempting to overthrow the Venezuelan Bolivarian Revolution since 2013 (August 2015a). And what about Brazil? Marc Weisbrot, co-director of the Center for Economic and Policy Research, Washington, D.C., unearthed an important instrument of the Obama Administration's foreign affairs operations. In his revealing article "Washington's Dog-Whistle Diplomacy Supports Attempted Coup in Brazil," he shows in detail how the U.S. government participated in Washington meetings between key Brazilian coup plotter Aloysio Nuñes and a number of U.S. officials, including Thomas Shannon at the State Department. Shannon's meeting with Nuñes is an example of what could be called "dog-whistle diplomacy." It barely shows up on the radar of the media reporting on the conflict and is therefore unlikely to generate backlash. But all the major actors know exactly what it means.[18] Shannon has plenty of experience with coups, such as the 2002 coup in Venezuela and the 2012 coup in Paraguay (Weisbrot 2016).

One can observe that the situation in Latin America is messy. Therefore, the pro-Obama approach to Cuba–U.S. relations finds comfort in the relatively "calm" waters of polite diplomacy between the two neighbours, conveniently not tuning in to the high-frequency whistle. By restricting its political discourse to only Cuba, while sweeping the rest of Latin America under the rug, it is far easier to promote the image of a well-intentioned diplomatic U.S. Cuba policy. This is in step with the White House, which works hard to keep its destabilizing involvements in Latin America under the radar.

The double standard of the U.S. concerning Venezuela and Brazil is an example that contradicts the fallacy that American foreign policy can be a consistent source of good motivations and honesty. To enlighten us, here is an excerpt from a daily press briefing by Mark C. Toner, U.S. State Department deputy spokesperson, in Washington on June 3, 2016, at the height of the simultaneous crises evolving in both these countries.

> QUESTION: Great. So recently the U.S. joined the OAS in expressing concerns about Venezuela's democracy, and yet we have yet to see any concerns displayed about what's happening in Brazil. This week it was reported that the new ruling government, which, again, was not elected — came to power in an unelected fashion — has been using the military to spy on the PT [Partido dos Trabalhadores in Portuguese, or Workers' Party, the left-wing party headed by Lula da Silva and Dilma Rousseff], which of course was the incumbent party before they took power. I mean, is that really consistent with democratic norms? And why is there sort of an inconsistency in that we're willing to criticize Venezuela sort of violating democratic norms, but we're — we haven't done the same for Brazil yet?
>
> MR TONER: I'm not aware of the particular allegations that you've raised, and what I've said about Brazil previously remains. We believe it is a strong democracy, that it has the kind of institutions that can weather the political crisis that it's undergoing. But in terms of your specific allegations, I just don't have any —
>
> QUESTION: Do strong democracies allow the military to spy on political opponents?

MR TONER: I just said I don't —

QUESTION: No, I mean in theory — in theory.

MR TONER: I just said I don't have any — I don't have any — I don't have any details of what you're alleging.

QUESTION: Mark, when you say that you have confidence in Brazil's democracy, I mean, you believe that the impeachment proceeding is legit and that — as an outside observer, recognizing that you're not wanting to interfere in an internal political dispute in another country, but as you look at it from the outside, do you believe that the impeachment proceeding is a valid one and that they are — the Brazilians are, in fact, handling this situation in a way that comports with their constitution and their broader commitment to democracy?

MR TONER: I'm going to leave it where I left it just now, which is that —

QUESTION: Or are you concerned that maybe no?

MR TONER: No, I think — look, I mean, there's no doubt that it's a time of political upheaval in Brazil, but we remain confident in their ability to —

QUESTION: So you remain confident in the ability of the Brazilian — of Brazil's institutions to weather this storm —

MR TONER: Correct.

QUESTION: — and return to a —

MR TONER: Correct.

QUESTION: All right. (U.S. Department of State 2016c)

By not considering these U.S. machinations into Latin America in conjunction with the analysis of U.S.–Cuba relations and U.S. foreign policy in general is to create a further smokescreen regarding U.S. Cuba policy. In the same vein, the U.S. also employs dog-whistle diplomacy as part of its tactics in Cuba. When, in Havana, Obama talked about Cubans "deciding their own future," it may have seemed positive to some who believe that this amounts to a recognition of the Cuban government as the exclusive expression of the Cuban sovereign will. Yet, it could also mean to others both within and outside of Cuba that this has to be carried out *independently* of the Cuban state and, it goes without saying, its "authoritarian regime." This slip into obscurity is facilitated because the White House at the time mentioned that the Cubans need "freedom" and "democracy." Thus, this perspective finds its orientation in the notion that the lack of "freedom" and "democracy" can be solved by Cubans "deciding their own future." To further the analogy, the high-frequency dog whistle about "deciding their own future" is heard only by a select few with a penchant for U.S. values, such as some entrepreneurs and a few intellectuals and academics. These individuals tend to understand this to mean taking a path independent of, or even in contradiction with, the Cuban state to satisfy their own individual interests. However, the deceptive message is "not audible" to the patriotic and socially conscious vast majority of Cubans, who feel that the Obama litany of "deciding their own future" is what Cubans have been doing since the Revolution began in the late 1950s to its triumph on January 1, 1959.

To recapitulate, the pro-Obama trend sugar-coats U.S. policy toward Cuba in two ways. First, it creates illusions about U.S. Cuba policy itself by concealing the U.S. change of tactics to achieve the long-term subversive goal of undermining the Cuban Revolution. Second, it consists in the refusal to place Cuba in the context of the overall contentious U.S. foreign policy toward Latin America, where its real aggressive nature is exposed.

Where There Is a Will, There Is a Way

Most in Cuba do not fall for U.S. policy. For example, on June 8, 2016, Cuba's foreign minister Bruno Rodríguez Parrilla, in a meeting of the Alianza Bolivariana para los Pueblos de Nuestra América (Bolivarian Alliance for the Peoples of Our America — ALBA-TCP) in Caracas, called on the region to strengthen strategies to confront imperialist intervention and coup plots in the region. He also said:

> Latin America and the Caribbean have changed, we are no longer, nor will we be, the backyard of the United States, we will not allow for the return of the carrot and the stick and I repeat that no one can beguile Cuba, which is still under blockade and whose territory in Guantánamo is still occupied, while attempts are made to isolate Venezuela.... .The history of Latin America and the Caribbean is being decided in this battle, here in Venezuela, we will all defend, whatever the price, the legacy of (Hugo) Chávez and Venezuela will continue to have in Cuba a sister nation ready to share the same fate. (AVN 2016)

The minister likewise expressed full support for Brazil against the parliamentary coup and media campaign under way at the time against the country's legitimate president, Dilma Rousseff (AVN 2016).

Darío Machado Rodríguez (cited earlier), one of Cuba's most outstanding journalists and authors, wrote on June 10, 2016, that "there is a process of a right-wing offensive going on against all the peoples' processes in Latin America, including *most importantly the Cuban revolution,* an offensive dictated by the centers of power of the American state" (Machado Rodríguez 2016b, emphasis added).

The change in tactics by Obama represents a *new offensive* against Cuba. However, Foreign Minister Bruno Rodríguez Parrilla's statement above is representative of the growing post-17D movement by Cuban revolutionaries to resist this aggression in the realm of ideas. Likewise, Culture Minister Abel Prieto is in the forefront of the cultural counter assault. This is all the more crucial as the blockade is still virtually fully in effect and thus has constituted an ongoing daily offensive against Cuba since 1961.

Notes

1   Trump is referring to the fact that while Cuban legislation allows foreign investors to participate in selective, carefully monitored enterprises, the government permits those companies to maintain only 49 percent ownership of their operations. The other 51 percent is controlled by state enterprises. Cuban legislation also allows for 100 percent foreign ownership, but in practice the government rarely if ever approves permits for wholly owned foreign groups. However, when it does, it denies those companies the same tax benefits afforded to joint ventures with the Cuban state (Business News 2014).

2   He is referring to the economic damages Cuba is demanding as compensation resulting from the U.S. blockade, an estimated one trillion, one-hundred-and-fifty-seven billion U.S. dollars ("Cuba's Report on Resolution 70/5" 2016).

3   I remember watching CNN in my room in Havana after a day of work with TelesUR and commenting on the Obama visit. In one of the programs, the CNN anchors and reporters, upon viewing the above-mentioned clip on Trump, collectively raised their hands in despair, saying that Trump did not even mention human rights and democracy. He is only interested in business!

4   Robert Muse is a lawyer in Washington, D.C., with substantial experience in U.S. laws relating to Cuba. Among his clients are major corporations engaged in international trade and foreign direct investment. He has testified on legal issues involving Cuba before the Foreign Relations Committee of the United States Senate; the Foreign Affairs and International Trade Standing Committee of the Canadian House of Commons; the Trade Subcommittee of the Ways and Means Committee of the U.S. House of Representatives; and the External Economic Relations Committee of the European Parliament (Brussels) as well as the Parliament's inter-party group on Cuba (Strasbourg). Muse has delivered papers on the *Helms-Burton Act* and other U.S. embargo laws pertaining to Cuba at conferences sponsored by the *Economist* and various legal and international relations foundations based in London, Miami, Washington, Brussels, Toronto, Ottawa, Havana, Madrid, Barcelona and Amsterdam (Muse n.d.).

5 "Heterogeneity," as employed in this chapter, is restricted to social and political options and does not refer to national identity, which most Cubans argue is indeed indivisible.

6 This ongoing development in the Cuban media is one of the many issues dealt with on my Facebook Cuba-U.S. Relations page.

7 TeleSUR can be viewed live online at telesurtv.net in Spanish. TeleSUR does not broadcast in English; however, its English-language website (telesurtv.net/english) is among the best progressive websites in that language in the world.

8 "'Ugly American' is a pejorative term used to refer to perceptions of loud, arrogant, demeaning, thoughtless, ignorant, and ethnocentric behavior of American citizens mainly abroad.... The term was used as the title of a 1948 photograph of an American tourist in Havana ... but seems to have entered popular culture as the title of a 1958 book by authors William Lederer and Eugene Burdick. In 1963, the book was made into a movie directed by George Englund and starring Marlon Brando" (*Wikipedia* n.d.).

9 Based on notes taken during the screening of the documentary in Montreal.

10 This information is based on the notes I took while viewing the TV program and later translated into English.

11 Readers will recall that, in the section "'La *Revolución* Will Be Televised.' Which '*Revolución*'?" in this chapter, the role Pánfilo played dovetailed perfectly with the U.S. perception of a fictitious Cuban character fawning over Obama. That was the televised "revolución." However, no U.S. media reported or televised the mass movement by Cuban youth against the U.S. regime change program. The U.S. would rather believe in a Pánfilo-type Cuba.

12 While this book was going through the final stages of preparation, the Cuban and American governments issued a joint declaration on January 12, 2017, which stipulated an upgrade of the immigration relations between the two countries. The ink was barely dry on the Cuba–U.S. January 12, 2017, immigration agreement when the *New York Times* (2017) kept the American Dream afloat by quoting a dissident: people "who had that dream" to emigrate to the U.S. were forced to abandon it. Not only did news start to circulate that Cubans on the U.S. border near Texas were asking for political asylum (not forbidden under the pact) but this also serves the American Dream chimera. In all likelihood, Trump will not change the U.S. position as it coincides with his own view against illegal immigration.

13 The excerpts are purposely quite lengthy because readers are best served by familiarizing themselves with the full context and the actual examples of input by the base, a Cuban participatory phenomenon that is not well known to English-speaking people. In addition, the content of this report erupted into a major debate in Cuba and even, to a certain extent, internationally.

14 Cuban dissidence, in general, and the "left" variety, in particular, are examined in this book in Chapter 2 in the sections titled "Cuba–U.S. Relations and Freedom of the Press" (August 2015c), "Cuba–U.S. Relations and the Perspicacity of Fidel Castro's Thinking" (August 2015b) and "The White House National Security Agenda for Obama's Visit to Cuba" (August 2016f). In my previous book, *Cuba*

and Its Neighbours (2013), pages 136–42 are dedicated to an analysis of Cuban dissidence and how both the "left" and openly right variety intermingle and indirectly support one another.

15 August 2012b.

16 When Ravsberg defends himself as not being a paid agent, he points to his main current income as a professor of journalism in a Spanish university. However, one has to ask, do not these types of stories constitute part of his cv to obtain and maintain his employment?

17 The participation was so extensive that I devoted a full chapter to this phenomenon in my previous book (August 2013: 118–45).

18 "Dog-whistle politics is political messaging that employs coded language that appears to mean one thing to the general population but has an additional, different or more specific resonance for a targeted subgroup. The phrase is often used as a pejorative because of the inherently deceptive nature of the practice and because the dog-whistle messages are frequently distasteful to the general populace" (*Wikipedia* n.d.). The pro-White House perspective idealistically takes Washington's words at face value by refusing to associate the government with falsification or subterfuge.

Chapter 5

THE BLOCKADE

From Obama to Trump

The U.S. economic, commercial and financial blockade against Cuba, along with the American-led cultural war and the refusal to return Guantánamo, are the most important roadblocks to the normalization of relations between the two neighbours. Following the January 1, 1959, Revolution, the Cuban government, supported by the overwhelming majority of people, began to nationalize major foreign enterprises as well as U.S. and local private estates with colossal land tracts. The goal was to completely overhaul the economy and society in the interests of Cubans. At that point, the U.S. began another round of hostile activities against Cuba. The objective is best summed up by Washington itself. Lester Mallory, the deputy assistant secretary of state for Inter-American Affairs in 1960, wrote in favour of "denying money and supplies to Cuba, to decrease monetary and real wages, to bring about hunger, desperation and overthrow of government" (U.S. Department of State 1960).

This policy, formally imposed in 1961, is the basis of the U.S. blockade. While the blockade is essentially economic, it is linked to the cultural war — and has been right from the beginning. As Mallory himself wrote, the goal is to break the Cubans' revolutionary and patriotic spirit. This battle of ideas is designed to entice Cubans to "change" to capitalism as a condition for lifting the blockade. At the heart of the matter is also the political system. This is evidenced by the fact that the two main pieces of Congressional legislation serving to codify the blockade in law are titled the Cuban Democracy Act (1992) and the Cuban Liberty and Democracy Solidarity Act (1996).

THE BLOCKADE: WHAT IS BREWING?

There are several features to note regarding how the U.S. Administration applies so-called flexibility in its blockade policy. Coffee is one such example. On April 22, 2016, the restriction on importing Cuban coffee into the U.S. was partially lifted:

> The U.S. Department of State updated its "Section 515.582 List," which sets forth the goods and services produced by independent Cuban entrepreneurs that are authorized to be imported into the United States pursuant to Section 515.582 of the Cuban Assets Control Regulations (CACR).
>
> As of April 22, persons subject to U.S. jurisdiction may also import coffee and additional textiles and textile articles produced by independent Cuban entrepreneurs, in addition to the items previously authorized. Also, imports of these items no longer need to be made directly from Cuba. These changes allow for more engagement with Cuba's private sector through new business opportunities. The State Department will continue to update this list periodically.
>
> Empowering the Cuban people and Cuban civil society is central to our approach to Cuba. Expanding commercial ties between *independent Cuban entrepreneurs* and the United States creates new opportunities for such empowerment. As President Obama stated during the March 21 entrepreneurship summit in Havana, Cuba's economic future partly depends on growth in the private sector, and the United States wants to be a partner as Cuba moves forward. (U.S. Department of State 2016d, emphasis added)

The most important transnational coffee monopoly to act on this opening has been the Swiss-owned Nestlé Nespresso, known for its single-cup coffee pods. After the U.S. announcement, the company issued a communiqué on June 20, 2016:

> Nestle SA's Nespresso says it will become the first company to import coffee from Cuba to the United States in more than 50 years.... The regulatory change cleared the way for Nespresso to begin U.S. sales of Cafecito de Cuba, a premium espresso roast for its home brewers, in the fall of 2016.... Nespresso sells brewing machines and single-use coffee capsules. (Reuters 2016)

However, Nespresso, which received the licence from the U.S., "will begin its Cuba experiment by buying coffee beans from European importers, roasting the beans, packaging the coffee in pods and selling them in the United States" (Gomez [A.] 2016b). Thus, importation is limited, mainly because the U.S. applies the restriction of importation to independent Cuban smallholder farmers. However, the Cuban state regulates and exports coffee produced by the small producers, whom the U.S. conveniently calls independent farmers, perhaps with the goal of driving a wedge between the coffee growers and Cuban society. Karell Acosta González, a professor at the Centre for Hemispheric and U.S. Studies at the University of Havana, confirms that "all exports must go through state-owned companies. It's in the Constitution" (Williams [E.] 2016). In the face of the Cuban reality that the U.S. must deal with the Cuban state and not directly with the small coffee farmers, the new policy in fact is mere window dressing. The refusal to grant unrestricted importation of coffee in collaboration with Cuban state institutions results in the extremely limited importation of coffee to the U.S.

In contrast, in Canada, for example, where there are no restrictions, importers can conveniently deal with the Cuban state. Cuban coffee has been found for many years on Canadian shelves of large supermarkets, convenience stores and pharmacies, and even in local produce stands during the summer. Canada's population is small compared with the U.S. One can imagine the huge revenues for Cuban small farmers, and thus the Cuban economy, if the prized Cuban coffee were to be allowed to freely inundate the vast U.S. market, as it does in Canada and other countries. The potential demand in the U.S. for Cuban coffee, in addition to the vast market, would be amplified by important sectors of the U.S. population falling in love with everything Cuban after visiting the island.

Nonetheless, some U.S. high-ranking legal authorities involved in international trade seem to blame Cuba, and not the U.S., for restricting coffee imports. Janet Kim, a lawyer at U.S.-based Baker and McKenzie, one of the world's premier international law firms, is reported to have said, "At the beginning the bogeyman used to be US law, then as that relaxed a little since the initial announcement from Obama, now it's the Cuban government saying thank you very much, we'll think about it" (Whipp 2016). However, Kim seems to contradict herself as she goes on to explain:

> "The criteria for Cuban independent entrepreneur status may be difficult to meet as a practical matter" ... as it would probably depend on factors such as whether the Cuban government had a right to any of the revenue from land being used to grow agricultural products and whether there were non-tax payments to be made to Havana.

Thus, according to this more balanced logic, the fault does indeed lie with the U.S., as it has imposed conditions that are practically impossible for Cuba to meet. Let us allow the small Cuban farmers themselves to have the last word in this controversy. The Asociación Nacional de Agriculturos Pequeños (National Association of Small Farmers — ANAP) issued a declaration on May 5, 2016, several days after the Obama Administration's announcement of the limited opening to Cuban coffee imports:

> On April 22, the State Department announced the decision to include coffee on the list of Cuban products produced by the non-state sector which could be imported into that country. This [is] a continuation of a measure adopted by the government of the United States in February 2015, authorizing very limited Cuban exports, which excluded all goods and services produced by state enterprises....
>
> No one should believe that a Cuban small farmer can directly export to the United States. For this to be possible, Cuban foreign trade enterprises [the State institutions] must participate and financial transactions need to be in U.S. dollars, issues which so far have not been settled....
>
> We are conscious that the objective of these measures is to influence Cuban farmers and separate them from our state....
>
> Cuban farmers are members of this socialist civil society and exist as part of the state, which represents the power of the people, and not in opposition to it. Together with the workers and all our people, we confront the imperialist policy objective of promoting the division and disintegration of Cuban society, which is intended with a measure such as that recently announced. (*Cubadebate* 2016)

We can easily see through the U.S. imposing the term "independent" on the coffee producers, an appellation rejected by the farmers themselves, and then blaming Cuba. The U.S. castigates the Cuban side since it must take into account the role of the state, legitimate from the Cuban perspective. The U.S. is clearly trying to use the blockade as leverage to bring about change in Cuba, in this case attempting to convert the social cooperation and consensus among coffee growers to values of capitalism. To put it bluntly, the U.S. tells the Cuban coffee farmers and the state: change your system of production and marketing, and only then can you massively export to the U.S. This may be the reason that the U.S. never publicly responded to the statement by the Cuban small farmers' association rejecting this American coffee policy.

THE BLOCKADE AS LEVERAGE

Despite allusions to the contrary, the use of the blockade as leverage is in fact the real U.S. Cuba policy. For example, Secretary of State John Kerry, during an October 2, 2015, interview, in response to a persistent journalist's question about lifting the embargo, said: "It really depends, to a large degree, *on the decisions and choices made by Cubans.*" Kerry's remarks reveal that the problem is *not* the Congress but Cuba. This was confirmed when Kerry responded in the same interview that "the Congress of the United States *appropriately* is very concerned about human rights, about democracy, about the ability of people to speak their mind, and to meet, and to do things" (emphasis added).[1] If the Obama Administration is so opposed to the Congress majority's Cuba policy, why provide it with credibility by saying their concern about Cuba is "appropriate"? Furthermore, when Kerry goes on to assert that "*we'd* like to see … Cuba moving in the right direction," the "we" seems to be referring to the Obama Administration *and* the Congress. The policies in the two wings of the U.S. government do not seem to be so much in contradiction with each other. Kerry is in effect telling Cuba: *You* change and *then* we will lift the blockade. Obama has made similar statements, thus blaming the victim, Cuba, for the U.S.-imposed blockade.

This leverage policy, either through Obama's diplomatic manner or Trump's crude and amateurish ideological approach, is exemplified through another measure taken by Obama. On March 15, 2016, just a few days before his visit to Havana, his administration made what looked on the surface to be a dramatic statement. For the first time, the U.S. dollar could be used by Cuba in international transactions, a long-time demand by Cuba. The U.S. Treasury Department announced:

> U.S. banking institutions will be authorized to process … transactions in which Cuba or a Cuban national has an interest. This provision will authorize funds transfers from a bank outside the United States that pass through one or more U.S. financial institutions before being transferred to a bank outside the United States, where neither the originator nor the beneficiary is a person subject to U.S. jurisdiction. (2016b)

The Cubans pragmatically responded that they would test transactions before commenting on the new policy. The transactions, it was revealed, did *not* go through. U.S. writer and academic William LeoGrande, a specialist in Cuba–U.S. relations, wrote in a May 24, 2016, article:

Although U.S. banks can now legally process Cuban transactions with non-U.S. parties, the banks are refusing to do it.

In the past, the United States has levied enormous fines on international banks for processing Cuban transactions in violation of U.S. sanctions. In 2004, UBS was fined $100 million; in 2009, Crédit Suisse was fined $536 million; in 2010, Royal Bank of Scotland paid $500 million in fines, and Barclay's paid $298 million; in 2012, ING Bank was fined $619 million, HBSC $1.9 billion and BNP Paribas a record $8.83 billion. Even after December 2014, France's Crédit Agricole was fined $787 million. At least half a dozen other banks were fined smaller amounts, and dozens more were under investigation....

"Banks are very nervous about any type of misstep ... because the fines, even if you only make a small mistake, are huge," explained a Miami lawyer involved in international banking. "You have to scrutinize everything coming in and out. The problem is, who wants to take that on? You just can't make money on these accounts."

So it should not come as a surprise that even though OFAC has now licensed international financial transactions involving Cuba, the banks are still not willing to handle them. "It turns out it's easier to impose sanctions than it is to dismantle them," admits a U.S. official....

But, there has been no comparable diplomatic effort to reassure the banks that sanctions have really been lifted. FAQs on the Treasury Department's website are simply not enough, but so far, senior administration officials have been silent.

Havana's frustration was evident on May 16 [2016] at the third meeting of the diplomatic commission charged with managing bilateral relations. "It has still not been possible to normalize banking relations," Cuban diplomat Gustavo Machin complained. Washington, he said, needed to do something "which assures banks that they are not going to be punished for dealing with Cuba."

As of November 2016, the Obama Administration had fined forty-nine U.S. and foreign entities, most of which are financial institutions, for violating the blockade ("Press Release by the Cuban Mission" 2016).

What the U.S. administration must do is address the banks directly by making a bold, public formal statement, accompanied by ample fanfare, that would essentially guarantee that there would be no negative repercussions, not be even one penny in fines. This course of action is entirely within the jurisdiction of the Executive Branch. If anyone is serious about lifting the blockade, this is the least that could be done. The only hindrance would be the White House wanting to continue using the blockade as leverage to force Cuba "to change." This is corroborated by the fact that the Obama Administration levied fines on institutions more than any previous U.S. president. It is doubtful that even Trump could beat Obama's record. Given Trump's unpredictability, he could follow his business instinct and actually *reduce* the frequency of fines.

There are multiple factors to consider with regard to the full negative impact of the U.S. blockade against Cuba. Readers interested in further pursuing this critical issue may want to read the accessible forty-two-page Cuban Report presented to the United Nations General Assembly in June 2016 ("Cuba's Report on Resolution 70/5"). A concise update released in September 2016 by investigators at two Cuban research centres with the telling title "The U.S. Blockade of Cuba Remains in Full Force" (Etcheverry Vázquez and Zaldívar Diéguez 2016) provides additional information with regard to the blockade.

On September 13, 2016, Obama once again signed, as has been the case annually for all presidents since 1962, the "Continuation of the Exercise of Certain Authorities Under the Trading with the Enemy Act," which serves to maintain the blockade at this time only against Cuba (Obama 2016b). The Obama Administration defended this action by asserting, paradoxically, that it allows Obama to continue using executive prerogatives to soften the U.S. blockade. Given the extremely complex nature of the blockade in U.S. legislation going back to 1917 and the hierarchy of powers in which these laws are entangled, there may be a certain amount of truth to this. However, it would enjoy credibility if Obama did actually *use* his prerogative powers to gut the blockade of its worst effects on the Cuban people, as indicated in Cuba's report to the UN cited above. In fact, Obama used his prerogative powers much more forcefully *to enforce* the blockade; for example, the many harsh fines against financial institutions, resulting in serious repercussions against Cuba's economic interest.

In addition to the complex web of political and legal considerations, there is the ideological one as well. When Obama visited Cuba in 2016, he said in the televised address to the entire Cuban population, "'Cultivo una rosa blanca.' (Applause) In his most famous poem, José Martí made this offering of *friendship* and peace to both his friend and his enemy" (Obama 2016c, emphasis added). When Secretary of State Kerry presided over the August 2015 raising of the U.S. flag in front of the U.S. Embassy in Havana in honour of the re-establishment of diplomatic relations broadcast live to the Cuban people, he proclaimed the "two peoples who are no longer enemies." And yet, once again, Obama signed the *Trading with the Enemy Act* in 2016. In contrast, Cuba has been open, forthcoming, transparent and consistent with its outlook toward the U.S. This is another lesson for the trend within and outside of the island that carries illusions about Obama; this option, based on the fantasy of Obama's good intentions, tends to place the U.S. and Cuba on the same footing, as though they were equally responsible for the betterment of relations between the two neighbours. The controversy over the *Trading with the Enemy Act* represents a clash between two opposing mindsets, two contrasting criteria of principles on which political policy is based. Signing this Act provides de facto sustenance to the use of leverage.

Given the virtual blackout by the U.S. media on Cuba's report to the UN on the blockade, and on other Cuban statements and documents, many misconceptions about the blockade persist in the U.S. An American reader of my articles shared her frustration with me through email correspondence in September 2016. She reported that as a result of the international media hype surrounding the first of multiple daily commercial flights from the U.S. to Cuba (secondary cities outside of Havana) in more than fifty years, many people in the U.S. are actually under the impression that the blockade no longer exists. This misconception is going to grow in 2017 and beyond as these regular flights increase. Interestingly, until November 2016, none of these flights were scheduled to land in Havana. Then, for the first time in fifty-five years, on November 28, 2016, three weeks after the Trump win, United Airlines inaugurated a daily regularly scheduled flight to Havana. Seven other airlines quickly initiated flights to Havana, ranging from three daily for some, to weekly for others. At the end of November 2016, there were 110 scheduled flights daily to Cuba from the U.S., twenty of them to Havana. This growth in commercial flights accounts for part of the hike in American visitors, already up 80 percent in the first half of 2016. In reviewing some of the Florida press immediately after the Trump win, there are many examples of articles that favour (directly or indirectly) not only maintaining these liaisons but increasing them. For example, one Florida paper proudly points out that, of the ten cities authorized by the American government for commercial flights, four are located in Florida (Williams [J.] 2016).

At odds with Florida's reputation of supposedly being so much in favour of maintaining the blockade and opting for a rollback of Obama's policy compared with other states, Florida's population is demonstrating just the opposite. The Sunshine State is increasingly in the vanguard of the forces agitating for protecting the outgoing president's tactical policy in the short term. It is also favours expanding executive actions to gut the blockade of trade and travel restrictions, which Obama refused to do. Florida is even a base for lifting the blockade in the long term for commercial and family-related visiting.

Any attempt by the Trump Administration to roll back the Obama-initiated "thaw" would be so costly politically — and legally/commercially complicated — that he would probably not do it. It is difficult to imagine the new U.S. president attempting to stop these flights. Equally unlikely is his announcing to the U.S. public that they can no longer visit the island when so many have already tasted the forbidden fruit. However, he is unpredictable.

There is another factor to take into account. While the increase in flights and accompanying tourism is expanding as Trump's transition begins, travel-related business is going to grow further in the first year of his mandate. There is much speculation concerning what he will accomplish in the much-touted "First 100 Days." On November 21, 2016, he finally revealed several executive actions planned for that time — Cuba was not one of them (LoBianco 2016). He has many international issues and controversies of major importance to attend to. Therefore, why would the Trump presidency tamper with the Cuba theme so quickly, since it is comparatively uncontroversial, and even popular, among the vast majority of Americans, including Cuban-Americans?

THE BLOCKADE, CIGARS AND RUM: THE LOOPHOLES

The importance of not only retaining a space in Cuba's political landscape for resistance to subversion and democracy promotion but of vastly expanding it came to the fore once again on October 14, 2016. However, this latest round is far more damaging than any previous action since the so-called warming of relations. Obama announced new measures titled "Presidential Policy Directive — United States–Cuba Normalization." The scope and the importance given by his administration to this directive, which affects virtually all U.S. government departments and agencies, indicates that Obama's U.S. Cuba policy is indeed his signature foreign policy legacy. Through this unprecedented administrative involvement from all areas of government, the directive is designed to guide the U.S. in the future. While it can technically be revoked by the Trump presidency, this eventuality would be difficult because, among other reasons, for the first time the entire American government structure is publicly involved. The mainstream media in North America and the West headlined in tandem that, according to the October 14, 2016, document issued by the Treasury, American travellers to Cuba could now import Cuban cigars and rum without restriction for personal use, whereas this was previously limited to a maximum value of $100. Other amendments to the blockade sanctions include allowing

> the importation into the United States, and the marketing, sale, or other distribution in the United States, of FDA [U.S. Food and Drug Administration]-approved Cuban-origin pharmaceuticals ... [and the waiving of] the restriction prohibiting foreign vessels from entering a U.S. port for purposes of loading or unloading freight for 180 days after calling on a Cuban port for trade purposes. (U.S. Department of Treasury 2016a)

Aside from the extremely superficial and overstated amendment on rum and cigars, and other secondary concessions, even some of the more sophisticated North American analysts missed the main point of the directive. They pounced on the following statements by Obama as a major breakthrough in favour of Cuba: "We recognize Cuba's sovereignty and self-determination and acknowledge areas of difference" and "We will not pursue regime change in Cuba" (Obama 2016a). This is not the first time Obama has said this. On April 11, 2015, at the Summit of the Americas in Panama, he stated: "On Cuba, we are not in the business of regime change" (Obama 2015b). During his joint press conference in Havana with Raúl Castro in March 2016, he reported that he had affirmed to Castro "that Cuba's destiny will not be decided by the United States or any other nation. Cuba is sovereign and, rightly, has great pride" (Obama 2016d). During his speech to the Cuban people, he proclaimed, "We will not impose our political or economic system on you. We recognize that every country, every people, must chart its own course and shape its own model" (Obama 2016c). This is not to say that there is no development in terminology, especially with regard to the October 14 version explicitly recognizing "Cuba's sovereignty and self-determination" (Obama 2016a). Nevertheless, didn't the mutual extension of diplomatic recognition with Cuba on December 17, 2014, itself amount to a de jure recognition of the Cuban government? That is what it was. Thus, the October 14, 2016, announcement was not as earth-shattering as it was made out to be.

However, from 17D to Panama in 2015 to Havana in March 2016 and since then, the Obama Administration stepped up funding for and activities relating to democracy promotion programs, analyzed above in the section titled "U.S. Democracy Promotion in Cuba: As American as Apple Pie." These measures not only interfere in the internal affairs of Cuba but also represent a direct violation of sovereignty, with the goal of regime change.

In fact, standard international American democracy promotion programs *are* based on regime change, especially when it comes to Cuba.

Thus, given the long-lasting U.S. subversive policy intended for Cuba, one must wonder what major loopholes the Obama plan contains that sharply contradict the supposedly well-intentioned amendments regarding the blockade restriction, such as rum, cigars, the purchase of Cuban biotechnology products and the pledges to respect Cuba's sovereignty and to reject regime change. The escape clauses that are submerged beneath the supposedly good intentions and other similar examples are of the utmost importance. Yet, in much of the English-speaking world, the fine print on the full presidential directive is not as well-known nor has it been analyzed as much as it should be. Closely examining the full Obama directive, as well his national security advisor Susan E. Rice's statement (also issued on October 14, 2016), reveals two themes. One concerns the Cuban private sector; the second, democracy promotion and human rights.

Feeding the Trojan Horse

The section in Chapter 4 on the Cuban private sector titled "Cuba–Silicon Valley–Cuba: The Making of a Trojan Horse?" was based on events during and after Obama's visit to Havana. Only eight months later, on October 14, 2016, the Obama Administration unwittingly justified why the question was raised in the first place. In the directive, it dug in its heels, doubled down and considerably expanded its intentions toward the Cuban private sector, as discovered in what can be considered saving clauses.

Interspersed from beginning to end in his statement (Obama 2016a), Obama enunciates numerous intentions toward the private sector, tackling it from different angles. He declares that the U.S. is in favour of the "development of a private sector that provides greater economic opportunities for the Cuban people. Efforts by the Cuban authorities to liberalize economic policy would aid these goals and further enable broader engagement with different sectors of the Cuban economy." He goes on to say that the U.S. will "provide opportunities for Cuban entrepreneurs, scientists, farmers, and other professionals" and "promote social equality and independent economic activity." Further on, he reiterates:

> With an estimated 1 in 4 working Cubans engaged in entrepreneurship, a dynamic, independent private sector is emerging. Expansion of the private sector has increased resources for individual Cubans and created nascent openings for Cuban entrepreneurs to engage

with U.S. firms and nongovernmental organizations. We take note of the Cuban government's limited, but meaningful steps to expand legal protections and opportunities for small- and medium-sized businesses, which, if expanded and sustained, will improve the investment climate....

While the embargo remains in place, our role will be to pursue policies that enable authorized U.S. private sector engagement with Cuba's emerging private sector and with state-owned enterprises that provide goods and services to the Cuban people.

Yet again, he promises that the U.S. "will utilize our expanded cooperation to support further economic reforms by the Cuban government." Bringing into play virtually all the numerous U.S. departments, institutions and agencies, he says, for example, that the "Department of Commerce will continue to support the development of the Cuban private sector [and] entrepreneurship" and the "Small Business Administration (sba) will continue to engage with the Cuban government, entrepreneurs, small businesses, and cooperative enterprises."

Rice reveals important aspects regarding the private sector that have to an extent escaped public scrutiny in the West. In her speech titled "A New Day Between the United States and Cuba," prepared for delivery on October 14, 2016, at the Wilson Center in Washington, she says: "These changes [in the U.S.'s Cuba policy] are fueling Cuba's nascent private sector. The young people at the entrepreneurship event President Obama attended in Cuba would have felt right at home in Silicon Valley. There was a young graphic designer, who's now getting training from the Columbia Business School." Further on in her speech, she divulges that there were eight Cubans who had "arrived in the United States as part of the inaugural class of 250 Young Leaders of the Americas Initiative Fellows, who are making our hemisphere more interconnected, prosperous, and secure. That's in addition to the ten Cuban entrepreneurs who joined President Obama at this year's Global Entrepreneurship Summit." As an African-American, she also uses the race card, as did Obama in Havana: "Every Cuban should be able to share in his country's growth, especially members of marginalized communities like Afro-Cubans."

In an entry that Rice posted on the Department of State Official Blog (2016a), she included a video interview with the young designer she referred to above. Idania Del Rio, who heads the small design enterprise Clandestino in Havana, says in English, that "entrepreneurship in Cuba is the future." (The video post itself is titled with this quote.) Del Rio was also one of

Obama's featured guests at his March 21, 2016, meeting with Cuban entrepreneurs. Obama said on that occasion, "The bottom line is this. We believe in the Cuban people. We believe in artists like Idania Del Rio who designs and illustrates her own goods — '99 percent Cuban design,' she calls it." Del Rio then addressed Obama and the audience as follows: "And thanks to some things that have been happening — we have been invited to participate in WEAmericas, which is a State Department project. And because of those things of life, we entered the Columbia Business School. So we've been having business training, and that's essential for us" (Obama 2016e).

She is right: WEAmericas is indeed a State Department project (U.S. Department of State 2012). In addition to Rice's "250 Young Leaders of the Americas Initiative Fellows" cited above, the State Department program announced another program on August 30, 2016, the "Inaugural Class of Fellows for the Young Leaders of the Americas Initiative Exchange Program" (U.S. Department of State 2016b).

Making Subversion and Democracy Promotion Irreversible

Democracy promotion programs, under different terminology, constitute a key to grasping the essence of the U.S. Cuba policy going back to 1959, as indicated throughout the book. Nevertheless, few detailed interpretations of the October 14 provisions regarding democracy promotion and human rights have surfaced in the English-speaking world. Given their importance for the future of Cuba, critical analysis of democracy promotion programs is vital. Guidelines dedicated to this cornerstone of U.S. policy are uncovered throughout Obama's policy directive under different themes and government agencies' jurisdictions. In the document, Obama states that the U.S. seeks

> increased respect for individual rights in Cuba. Even as we pursue normalization, we recognize we will continue to have differences with the Cuban government. We will continue to speak out in support of human rights, including the rights to freedoms of expression, religion, association, and peaceful assembly as we do around the world. Our policy is designed to support Cubans' ability to exercise their universal human rights and fundamental freedoms. (Obama 2016a)

In the same document, he states: "U.S. engagement with the Cuban government will also be constrained by Cuba's continued repression of civil and political liberties." Further on, he seems to introduce human rights as leverage: "We seek greater Cuban government respect for universal human rights and fundamental freedoms for every individual. *Progress in this area will have a positive impact on the other objectives.* We will encourage the Cuban government to respect human rights" (emphasis added). And, supposedly through the U.S. Embassy in Havana, the U.S. "will utilize engagement to urge Cuba to make demonstrable progress on human rights and religious freedom." Perhaps basing himself in part on his March 2016 meeting with dissidents in Havana, Obama makes the point even clearer by also insinuating dissidence into internal dialogue: "While remaining committed to supporting democratic activists as we do around the world, we will also engage community leaders, bloggers, activists, and other social issue leaders who can contribute to Cuba's *internal dialogue* on civic participation" (emphasis added).

Paradoxically, the following pledge for transparency by Obama — mentioned three times, in reference to the White House, the State Department and USAID — is not as positive as some may think. Calling for the State Department and USAID to work together, Obama promises that the "State [Department] will continue to co-lead efforts with the U.S. Agency for International Development [USAID] to ensure democracy programming is *transparent....* The USAID will co-lead efforts with State to ensure that democracy programming is *transparent and consistent* with programming in other similarly situated societies" (2016a, emphasis added).

Rice fleshes out this policy with some colourful language: "Perhaps most importantly, this [Obama] directive is being made public. We used to have secret plans for Cuba. Now, our policy is out in the open — and online — for everyone to read. No more conspiracy theories for critics on the left or right to spin. What you see is what you get" (2016a). This statement by Rice is not, as some suggest, more arrogant than Obama's. Obama's directive was a formal written statement in his name. In contrast, given that Rice was only guided by a statement intended for delivery, she had reflected its full nature. She appeared to have assimilated the directive and did not contradict it. Thus, on behalf of the Obama policy, she ad-libbed this barely veiled warning against anyone who tries to challenge the democracy programs. (We will see below that in fact some are being intimidated.)

Rather than seeing this transparency angle as positive, it may be worthwhile to ask how the U.S. has the confidence to make this public. Is it because they detect that some people in Cuban society are willing to collaborate openly with the U.S.? The U.S. is targeting this sector that now sees its role as promoters of the idealized U.S. policy while, of course, "keeping a check" on the U.S., which they consider, nevertheless, to be on the right track. Does blindly accepting the promise of "sovereignty," "rejection of regime change" and "transparency" mean that a few individuals are willing to be co-opted into the execution of subversive democracy promotion programs? Does this mean that some Cubans will go so far as to act on behalf of the U.S. against their own people under the pretext that they have been "consulted"? The U.S. has a great deal of experience in this. This transparency manoeuvre should perhaps be seen as a red flag.

This idealized presentation of U.S. Cuba policy has reached its full embodiment since the Trump upset. The outlook defends the Obama policy even more openly by further obscuring its negative features, such as subversion and intrusive U.S.-style democracy promotion. Dangerously concealed under the cover of the Trump-pretext, this mindset emerges as open promotion of the now so "politically correct" Obama policy, but sanitized of its subversive program.

This silence on subversion and democracy promotion as a principal feature of the Obama policy is linked to the explicit foundation of the new approach: Obama decided to change the tactics, which had *not worked* to subvert the Cuban Revolution and sovereignty, to others that he hopes *will work* to attain this. Since 17D, this has been largely overlooked by the pro-Obama tendency inside and outside Cuba. However, since the materialization of Trump as president, the silence on this basic rationale of the new Cuba policy is deafening. Between November 8 and the end of November 2016, Trump did not say anything about this sophisticated Obama policy of changing tactics. As mentioned in Chapter 4, his previous comments touched only on the pro-blockade code words in the Miami setting. In other contexts he gave the nod to the Obama opening with the proviso, of course, that he would have obtained a better deal. The Trump Cuba policy will merge into the Obama approach as far as tactics and goals are concerned, likewise aided and abetted by subversion and democracy promotion. Obama claims that his directive makes his new orientation irreversible toward what he defines as imminent normalization. However, Obama has in fact made *democracy promotion* and *subversive programs* irreversible. Trump is unlikely to oppose these programs. However, his acquiescence can be somewhat passive, as he is far less ideologically inclined than other establishment politicians from both main parties at all levels of government, not to mention his fellow business people. In any case, there can be no normalization while the pursuit of subversion and democracy promotion programs is in play.

The October 14 announcements constitute an escalation of the *offensive* against the Cuban socialist culture, independence and dignity. While reference was made previously in this book to the U.S. employing *leverage* to force Cuba to change, with the October 14 directive, the U.S. comes forth with the *stick* to use against Cuba. It uses "sovereignty," "transparency" and the "rejection of regime change" as the carrot behind which it disguises this intensification of pressure against Cuba. The Obama edict on October 14 zeroing in on the private sector, democracy and human rights represents an update of the long-standing democracy promotion programs under all the previous U.S. presidents. However, it now has a cool Obama look. It is ironic, yet cruel, that while the blockade may be lifted in the future along with its enabling legislation, Obama has codified subversive intents through democracy promotion and a private-sector Trojan horse as *permanent features* of U.S. Cuba policy. Trump will see no problem in cloaking himself in Obama's hipster Cuba orientation, a legacy handed to him on a silver platter.

While there were some positive aspects to the October ordinance, the private sector and democracy promotion clauses far outweigh the few positive ones. In fact, they are relatively meaningless. For example, the new cigar and rum importation directive for travellers still excludes the right for Cuba to export these products to the U.S. This would provide a big boost to Cuba's economy, given the weight that these two sectors hold in the Cuban economic system. Instead, Americans have to travel to Cuba to buy them, as opposed to making regular shopping visits to local outlets in the U.S. to purchase these products without any limits.

Moreover, Obama did not use the spotlight on the October 14 directive to boldly direct international financial institutions and companies to freely deal with Cuba in U.S. dollars. With regard to the new regulation on importing pharmaceutical and biotechnical products to the U.S., there are still restrictions on establishing Cuba–U.S. joint ventures on the island to increase research, production and marketing. It is a one-way relationship. For example, there have been no amendments allowing Cuba to access U.S. markets for medicines, medical instruments and supplies, or spare parts for diagnostic and treatment equipment, all necessary for the functioning of related sectors. In most cases, these products have to be acquired in geographically distant markets, which is more onerous, since Cuba must resort to intermediaries. This has repercussions in terms of delays in treatment for patients. In many cases, the alternative products are of lower quality, and this also has serious effects on treatment ("Cuba's Report on Resolution 70/5" 2016).

Regarding the waiving of "the restriction prohibiting foreign vessels from entering a U.S. port for purposes of loading or unloading freight for 180 days after calling on a Cuban port for trade purposes," this also is of limited benefit. The complete wording can be found under the heading "Treasury and Commerce Announce Further Amendments to Cuba

Sanctions Regulations." It includes a rider pertaining to whether "the items the vessel carried to Cuba would, if subject to the EAR, be designated as EAR99 or controlled on the Commerce Control List for anti-terrorism reasons only" (U.S. Department of Treasury 2016a). The exceptions are listed in several hundred pages (U.S. Department of Commerce 2016). Sorting through these alone could pour cold water on any vessel captain, ocean transport or other company that otherwise might be interested in taking a direct Cuba–U.S. route.

While the October 14 statements are disproportionate in appealing to small owners, the Obama Administration did not responded to the statement by Cuba's small coffee producers cited above in the section titled "The Blockade: What Is Brewing?" They want to export coffee to the U.S. but in conjunction with the Cuban state and society. They evidently do not fit into the U.S. plans for building a Trojan horse in Cuba.

Cuba has been striving to normalize relations since 17D, yet the U.S. is underhandedly refusing to do so. It has been covering this up with the illusion about some secondary concessions on the blockade and now, above all, with supposed opposition to regime change and respect for Cuba's sovereignty, which Trump has inherited if he chooses to take this path. This offensive is exacerbated by the conciliatory trend within and outside of Cuba that is indirectly providing this interference policy with credibility.

It did not take long for confirmation that the October 14 directive represents, not only an increase in subversion, but also its institutionalization as a permanent feature of U.S. Cuba policy. The ink was barely dry when, on October 19, the U.S. State Department (2016a) issued the following: "Bureau of Democracy, Human Rights and Labor Request for Statements of Interest: Programs Fostering Civil, Political, and Labor Rights in Cuba." The deadline to apply for a cut of the total US$5.6 million earmarked for successful applicants to the program was November 18, 2016. After providing a long list of supposed human rights violations in Cuba, it states:

> DRL's [Bureau of Democracy, Human Rights and Labor] programmatic emphasis aligns with the U.S. government policy to promote human rights in Cuba. Specifically, DRL programs in Cuba aim to strengthen the capacity of on-island, independent civil society to further the rights and interests of Cuban citizens, and to overcome the limitations imposed by the Cuban government on citizens' civil, political, labor, and religious rights. DRL strives to ensure its projects inter alia advance the rights and uphold the dignity of the most vulnerable, marginalized or at-risk populations.

Compare Obama's pretensions about the "recognition of Cuban sovereignty" and "rejection of regime change" with the above program.

There have been many reactions within Cuba to the October 14 presidential directive. Let us begin with Carlos Alzugaray, the Havana resident who describes himself as a retired diplomat and independent political analyst (2016a). We recall that it is not a question of personalities, but an outlook of thought as exemplified by Alzugaray. The goal of this analysis is to deepen awareness with regard to certain ideological and political anomalies. It is my hope that this analysis will result in a fertile and frank mutual exchange through our respective social media. His view, published on the website Cuba Posible[2] on October 17, provides some information, such as the fact that the directive must have come about as a result of a long process of consultation with all the bodies in the Executive Branch and the Pentagon, Department of Homeland Security and even the National Director of Intelligence. Thus, while the directive can in theory be revoked by Trump, he must also deal with the military, homeland security and the intelligence community, and stepping on those toes is not highly recommended. Despite this, illusions about Obama's policy is the main feature of Alzugaray's essay, which provides at least five such examples.

In the first example, he accepts U.S. recognition of Cuba's sovereignty and renunciation of regime change and says "regrettably" that the U.S. also has plans to interfere in Cuba's affairs. The dilemma viewed as a regrettable mistake naively denies the U.S. imperialist policy of employing a carrot on the one hand, in the form of diplomatic recognition and regime change renunciation, and ignores, on the other hand, the U.S. waving the stick of aggressive and highly funded democracy promotion subversion strategy. The outlook is blind to the fact that the U.S. has replaced the tactic of aggression with seduction. While Cuba's Ministry of Foreign Affairs does not, of course bring the U.S. to task for its positive steps by also aggressively throwing the negative ones in the American face, they are, however, the diplomats involved in negotiations. But does this mean that the entire Cuban polity must keep its mouth shut and censor itself? If this were to happen, Cuba would perhaps have already fallen under the U.S. sphere of influence. Even then, let's remember what Cuba's minister of foreign affairs Bruno Rodríguez Parrilla said in 2016: "We will not allow for the return of the *carrot and the stick* and I repeat that no one can beguile Cuba" (AVN 2016, emphasis added).

Second, Alzugaray states that there is "nothing illegitimate or interfering about American political leaders and diplomats holding a dialogue with all sectors of Cuban society in order to better understand our reality." Even though he says it is not right that these activities have as an objective to push forward changes, he makes two questionable points. What does he mean by "all sectors of society"? Is he referring to the dissident circles? This may be the case, as the website (Cuba Posible) he wrote this essay for is linked to dissidents in Cuba and the U.S. And when he assumes that the U.S. wants "to better understand" Cuban reality, is it by developing its links to those they hope will participate in subversive activity? "Understanding Cuban reality" is not even among the stated U.S. goals, which seek only American-style democracy promotion in Cuba. Potential subversive links constitute the only "Cuban reality" that interests Washington. This is examined in Chapter 4 in the section above titled "Cuban Participatory Democracy in 2016: Where Were the Obama Administration and the U.S. Media?"

Third, Alzugaray lends to the democracy promotion programs the supposedly positive notion that ultimately they cannot be carried out "without the consultation and consent of our [Cuban] authorities." This shift of U.S. policy toward "transparency" is perhaps encouraged by this very viewpoint existing in Cuba, which Obama detected and incorporated into his directive. Perhaps Obama felt that it is now possible to recruit some Cuban experts to assist, or partner with, the U.S. in administering its State Department programs, such as World Learning. After all, as cited below, Alzugaray saw nothing subversive in this program and even castigated the students for opposing it. This mindset is negligible at present. However, if allowed to flourish with the help of the U.S., how far can it extend into the Cuban political culture? The greatest assistance that the U.S. is providing, unintentionally, to this outlook is Trump. His rise to power is a godsend to this marginal section, which perhaps grows as it conceals itself in what could be seen as a Trump red herring.

Fourth, Alzugaray applauds what he sees as the U.S. acceptance of the Cuban government as the "primary interlocutor in its relation with Cuba." Does the "primary" qualifier leave the door open for others, which could include those who oppose the government either overtly or covertly? It must be recalled that in Cuba, there is only *one* interlocutor: the Councils of State and Ministers and all the ministries responsible to the National Assembly of People's Power and this body itself.

Fifth, Alzugaray concludes that, "based on all of the above, one can affirm that the directive confirms that, under Barack Obama, the U.S. policy toward Cuba is of historic significance." What is historic? Is it the diplomatic "recognition and the repudiation of regime change," or the unprecedented elaboration of subversion, or the masterful manipulation of the carrot-and-stick policy? Or is it the fact that Obama has succeeded in transforming his Cuba policy into an irreversible and a permanent feature of the U.S. state foreign policy? If it is the latter, do the facts not also illustrate that subversion aimed at regime change is also irreversible?

What have the other reactions in Cuba been? Cuba's Foreign Minister, Bruno Rodríguez, while calling the presidential directive a "positive sign," also noted:

> Regarding the recent Presidential Directive on U.S. policy toward Cuba, issued October 14 [2016], ... that while the U.S. government recognizes the Cuban government, it makes no effort to disguise its goal of altering the country's constitutional order and promoting changes to its political, economic, and social system. Nor does it hide plans for interventionist programs. (*Granma* 2016b)

In addition, far from seeing October 14 as another tempest in a teapot, on October 24,

> youth across the country joined women and workers in denouncing the interventionist nature of President Obama's recent policy directive and demanding an end to the blockade.... Jesús García, worker at Radio 26, noted that the measures are well thought-out, not to benefit the Cuban people, but rather U.S. interests. The presidential directive, he emphasized, continues to insist on regime change in Cuba, asking, "Who said that changes here are their business?" (ACN 2016)

A report in *Granma* was headlined: "Cuban women denounce U.S. blockade and intervention" (Merencio 2016b). *Granma* international editor Sergio Gómez titled his report on the latest U.S. program of incursion "Bureau of Democracy, Human Rights and Labor democracy promotion program: U.S. subversion against Cuba continues." He wrote: "Cuba recently denounced the true intentions behind the World Learning program, offering surreptitious summer scholarships to Cuban youth and organized outside of the state apparatus, which aim to create an alternative leadership movement to promote regime change on the island" (2016a).

The pivotal September 2016 Cuban opposition to the World Learning program is dealt with in Chapter 4 in the section titled "U.S. Democracy Promotion in Cuba: As American as Apple Pie." As analyzed there, Alzugaray somewhat astonishingly opposed resistance to the latest State Department USAID program in the following way: "In my opinion, it would be counterproductive to stir up a tempest in a teapot, which may *complicate diplomatic work*" (Alzugaray 2016b, emphasis added). The resistance seems to be building up beyond the youth. On October 25, 2016, it was reported that neighbourhood debates were initiated across the country in 18,000 zones of the Comités de Defensa de la Revolución (CDR), and would continue through March 2017:

> Orestes Yánez Mestre, national CDR deputy coordinator ... stressed that today, imperialism is changing its methods but not its objective to destroy the Revolution, thus we must think of Martí when he said that if the war we are undertaking is one of thought then we must prepare ourselves to win it by thought; also citing Che, when he said that imperialism cannot be trusted, not even one iota. (Merencio 2016a)

Thus, Cuba is in the throes of a major debate, which is largely not known about outside of Cuba. These differing outlooks constitute one of the main features with regard to understanding Cuba–U.S. relations. The conciliatory mindset is based on refusing to place in the very *foreground* of analysis the U.S. policy's determining characteristic, namely that it is a change of tactics to achieve the same historical goal. Making matters more precarious, this perspective rejects the notion that the U.S. is carrying out a cultural war against Cuba, turning a blind eye to the carrot-and-stick approach and how belligerence is being replaced by seduction. This conciliatory viewpoint is *objectively* merging into this cultural war against Cuba. As Howard Zinn wrote, "You can't be neutral on a moving train."

THE POWERFUL ANTI-BLOCKADE FORCES: WHAT WILL TRUMP DO?

Powerful bipartisan forces among politicians and business people at the national, state and municipal levels had their own movement developing on the Cuba issue long before Trump's win. Not only do they favour Obama's change in tactics, they also demand to go further by extending the legal possibilities for trade and travel through legislation and executive orders. Moreover, many of these individuals and associations champion the full lifting of the blockade by Congress. Pedro Freyre, an international lawyer based in Miami, told the conservative *Miami Herald* that Trump "won big in the Midwest farm states that want to sell agricultural products to Cuba and are pushing to have a financing prohibition lifted so their products will be more competitive" (Whitefield 2016). These anti-blockade lobbyists include the American Farm Bureau, the American Feed Industry Association and USA Rice. They are active in, among other states, three that Trump won: Idaho, Alabama and Georgia.

Charlie Serrano, managing director of Chicago-based Antilles Strategy Group, which has taken Congressional leaders and business executives to Cuba, said: "What I hope as a Republican and as someone who has been involved with Cuba for 24 years is that Trump would look at the potential for business with Cuba *and fast-track things*" (Whitefield 2016, emphasis added). James Williams, president of the Engage Cuba advocacy group based in Washington, D.C., is involved in bringing dozens of delegations of politicians and business people from Washington and the state levels to Cuba. His organization declared: "In the November 2016 Congressional elections the pro-engagement forces picked up four senators and over 10 pro-engagement members in the House." Williams highlighted an important feature of the new Congressional composition, its bipartisan and anti-blockade nature: "Even more pro-engagement Republican and Democratic Members of Congress [were elected], advancing the legislative path forward *to lift the embargo*'" (Engage Cuba Coalition 2016b, emphasis added).

Perhaps most indicative of the hard choice the Trump presidency is facing is that it will have to take into account examples such as the following from Texas. A conference call took place immediately after November 8, 2016, by Engage Cuba and the Engage Cuba Texas State Council. The latter's membership comprises more than fifty bipartisan politicians, business people and academics (Engage Cuba Coalition n.d.). Engage Cuba reported:

> The President of Engage Cuba James Williams started-off the call by noting that given Texas' strong agriculture industry, world-class ports and proximity to Cuba, the Lone Star State is uniquely positioned to be an international leader in exports to our island neighbor. Williams then turned it over to [Republican] Congressman [Ted] Poe, who optimistically discussed the growing Congressional support for establishing agricultural trade between the U.S. and Cuba and his hope that diplomatic ties between the U.S. and Cuba will be continued under a Trump Administration. "Mr. Trump is a businessman, and I hope that he can see the business and economic opportunity that Cuba presents for the United States," said Congressman Poe.
>
> "If Mr. Trump is building an 'America First' policy agenda, he will recognize that trading with Cuba is a step forward for American jobs, particularly with agricultural trade" said Congressman Poe. (2016a)

In addition, one can keep in mind that no less a personage than Texan Republican Governor Greg Abbott led a delegation from that state to Cuba for trade discussions and negotiations. Barely a day goes by without important business people voicing their concerns about Trump's possible rollback, a preoccupation that is given voice by powerful media. For example, *USA Today* reported:

> Dozens of major American companies that have started or expanded operations in Cuba under Obama's policy will try to persuade Trump to ignore the political side of his brain and listen to the business side. That will be the ultimate test for Obama's Cuba strategy of creating so many business opportunities that his successor would face the full weight of the U.S. Chamber of Commerce and a long list of businesses pushing to maintain the new links to the communist government that controls the country. (Gomez [A.] 2016a)

The newspaper goes on to highlight that a "powerful coalition of U.S. companies is preparing to appeal to President-elect Donald Trump's business instincts and drop his vow to reverse one of President Obama's signature achievements: renewed relations with Cuba." One of the many examples put forward of this ongoing spike in U.S.–Cuba business is Airbnb being used by 8,000 Cubans to rent their rooms.

I participated with others in advocacy meetings on Capitol Hill in Washington, D.C., with Congressional representatives on two occasions during the second Obama mandate. They were organized by the U.S.-based International Committee for Peace, Justice and Dignity to the Peoples. The goal was to exchange with Republican and Democratic Congressional members' staff of both the House and the Senate in order to win them over to end the blockade. An objective also consisted in encouraging broader support for three pieces of legislation already in the works at the time: first, more freedom to travel to Cuba; second, allowing private businesses to trade unrestrictedly with Cuba; and third, allowing the use of credits by Cuba for U.S. agricultural exports to Cuba. At latest count, these three proposed acts together had the support of 136 Democrats and 51 Republicans. However, I and other advocates on Capitol Hill noticed that there was an increasingly open-minded attitude by Republicans. In addition, as Engage Cuba analyzed above, the pro-Engage Cuba members of Congress gained forces from both sides of the aisle resulting from the November 2016 elections.

CONCLUDING REMARKS ON THE BLOCKADE:
"HUNGER," PRIVILEGE AND DEMOCRACY PROMOTION

The U.S. blockade against Cuba is not only the longest-lasting but the most complicated and aggressive set of laws and policies in the history of modern international relations. One can never forget that the initial explicit goal, on which the extraterritorial blockade is still based, aims to "starve" Cubans into submission.

However, with the new Obama policy, which Trump will most likely follow with perhaps his own brand of rhetoric, the U.S. seeks to seduce the more than 500,000 Cubans working in the private sector with direct economic assistance from the state and business and/or Cuban-American families living in the U.S. Instead of "starvation," they are being offered privilege and, with it, relative wealth. With or without the blockade (if it is eventually lifted), this U.S. policy has enormous potentially negative repercussions for the collective society based on equality, which the Cuban government is striving to preserve with taxes and other means to spread this wealth. Despite all U.S. attempts, Cubans are far from starving, but life is austere. For most Cubans, virtually every meal entails a collective family effort to procure and prepare it.

The Washington tactic poses a challenge to the Cuban socialist culture as the consensus on which the society is built. Unfortunately, as long as the U.S. exists as an Empire with world ambitions, Cuba will always be the subject of subversion, which can only be resisted by the people's own socialist culture, patriotism and anti-imperialism.

Notes

1   For the full Kerry quote, see my article "Cuba–U.S. Relations and the Perspicacity of Fidel Castro's Thinking" (August 2015b) in Chapter 2.
2   Editorial note: This is the correct Spanish spelling.

Chapter 6

FIDEL AND THE U.S.-LED CULTURAL BLITZKRIEG ON "DICTATORSHIP"

Fidel Castro represented in words and deeds Cuba's socialist culture, patriotism and anti-imperialism. Immediately after his passing on November 25, 2016, there was an establishment media onslaught in the U.S., Canada, the U.K. and other Western countries against Fidel as a "dictator," with Cuba being portrayed as a "dictatorship." The attack, while somewhat subdued since then, continues as these lines are written. This cultural onslaught, in the large sense of the term "culture," which includes ideology and politics and not merely the arts, is not new. It has been occurring to different degrees since 1959. However, never before has it consisted of such ferocious and concentrated international corporate media coverage. The death of Fidel catapulted his persona and the Cuban Revolution to the international centre stage for at least ten days. This was not the desire of Fidel or the Cuban government. It happened because friends naturally, while many foes forced by history, recognized that he was the most outstanding political figure of the twentieth century and into this century.

The U.S.-led media chorus strived to occupy this hitherto unavailable massive international stage of public opinion focused on Fidel to impose its completely unsubstantiated vocabulary of buzzwords against him and the Cuban Revolution. The negative monopoly narrative, dramatic TV clips, misinformed news and documentary/montage images were spiced up by gossip/interviews with the always-willing pro-U.S. dissidents in Cuba.

All of this carefully crafted scenario will fester in the minds of many in the West for a long period through no fault of their own. They are the victims of this media war regarding the Cuban domestic situation and its international relations. This circumstance is not the result of a conspiracy. The carefully selected journalists are well aware of how to not only maintain their highly lucrative jobs, but also increase their standings and commensurate salaries.

(For example, CNN's Anderson Cooper's net worth is $100 million.) Fidel leaves no room for neutrality. The mainstream journalists, aside from very few exceptions, all knew where to go.

WHAT IS THE PURPOSE?

The U.S. still vigorously pursues its main objective to subvert the Cuban Revolution and sovereignty by changing only the tactics in the hope of finally achieving this goal. In this context, what is the underlying narrative that accompanies the "dictator" code word? A close examination of the U.S. media and statements made by many establishment politicians leads us to the following. They concern domestic and international Cuban policies.

On the domestic front, the myth has been created through disinformation, shamelessly devoid of facts, that Fidel was against the current changes going on in Cuba led by Raúl. Fidel was, according to this fantasy, holding back the advances. There are many facts that tear this misapprehension to shreds. However, let us consider only five.

First is the September 8, 2010, issue of the American magazine *The Atlantic*, which reported on a personal interview and a series of exchanges that one of its editors, Jeffrey Goldberg, held that year with Fidel in Havana. The American was accompanied by Julia E. Sweig, Director for Latin America Studies at the Council on Foreign Relations (CFR). Goldberg wrote:

> I asked him [Fidel] if he believed the Cuban model was still something worth exporting.
> "The Cuban model doesn't even work for us anymore," he said.
> I asked Julia to interpret this stunning statement for me. She said, "He wasn't rejecting the ideas of the Revolution. I took it to be an acknowledgment that under 'the Cuban model' the state has much too big a role in the economic life of the country."
> Julia pointed out that one effect of such a sentiment might be to create space for his brother, Raúl, who is now president, to enact the necessary reforms.

Second, Fidel appeared at the watershed 2011 Congress of the PCC that was completely devoted to considering economic and social changes. His attendance was interpreted as showing approval.

Third, it is well known in Cuban political circles that Raúl and the other leaders regularly consulted with Fidel on important issues.

Fourth, Fidel, who regularly penned columns in the state media, never once wrote anything negative about the domestic "update of the Cuban socialist system," as it is known in Cuba. If he was against it or harboured any serious concern, he would have undoubtedly let his opinion be known, as he had always done.

And, fifth, it is argued that "Fidelistas" sprinkled inside the Cuban political apparatus purposely hold back procedures, such as granting licences to aspiring small business owners. This and other conscious manifestations of bureaucracy lead to corruption. For example, paying bribes to "get the paper work done" *does* exist in Cuba. However, this cancer still festering in Cuban society has nothing to do with Fidel, his politics or his ideology, and even less so is based on "loyalty" to him. On the contrary, Fidel was a continuous thorn in the side of bureaucracy and corruption. He acted on and expressed this on many occasions. To provide just one example, in his 2005 talk to university students, when dealing with the issue of corruption and bureaucracy in society, Fidel said, "This country can self-destruct; this Revolution can destroy itself, but they [the U.S.] can never destroy us; we can destroy ourselves, and it would be our fault." This had a profound impact on Cuban culture.

Nevertheless, the fiction regarding Fidel is inspired by one principal insistence: now that Fidel is gone, the Cuban government no longer has a "pretext." It is presumed that the government will thus quickly enact more "radical" domestic reforms, but now in the direction of capitalism and a U.S.-style multi-party system — in reality, a two-party one. This Cuba, crafted in the image of the U.S., can only come about by accepting the U.S. as the guiding economic and political force to nudge the island in that direction. This American aspiration for Cuba is directly linked to Cuba giving up its sovereignty and independence.

We now turn to the realm of international Cuba–U.S. relations. We can see from the above that this area is not at all separable from U.S. intentions for Cuba's internal situation. The figment of Washington's imagination consists simply in the unfounded assertion that Fidel was against the re-establishment of relations between the two neighbours and a process of normalization. There exist many refutations of this. Let us look at three.

First, several volumes have been written by Cuban and American scholars that clearly document how Fidel personally, in his capacity as prime minister and president, sent out diplomatic overtures to virtually all American presidents since 1959. Every U.S. president since Eisenhower participated in discussions with Cuba, in the main at the behest of Fidel (LeoGrande and Kornbluh 2014).

Second, even as we fast-forward to the current situation since 17D, when there are so many controversies, the facts are other than what the White House presupposes. Just barely a month after 17D, on January 26, 2015, Fidel made this statement to the Federation of University Students (FEU), apparently urging them to be cautious: "I do not trust the policy of the United States, nor have I exchanged one word with them, though this does not in any way signify a rejection of a peaceful solution to conflicts or threats of war." He expressed that he was leery about long-term American policies; however, in the very same sentence, he confirmed his support for negotiations with the neighbour to the North. Just to make sure there was no room for speculation, he wrote in that very same message that the "President of Cuba [Raúl] has taken pertinent steps in accordance with his prerogatives and faculties conceded by the National Assembly and the Communist Party of Cuba."

The third example is the most controversial of all his writings related to 17D. His piece "Brother Obama," written immediately following the outgoing U.S. president's 2016 visit to Havana, criticized many of Obama's statements and speeches made when he was afforded the opportunity to address the Cuban people. Fidel wrote about some aspects of his refutation of Obama's assertions: "I wouldn't even talk about this, if I didn't have the elemental duty to respond to Obama's speech in Havana's Alicia Alonso Grand Theater" (2016b). This is a most interesting comment and one that is often overlooked. Obama provoked Fidel to speak out. However, Fidel's piece was a word of caution to the Cuban people; it did not in any manner comprise a directive to reorient Cuba's U.S. policy. My discussions and correspondence with colleagues in Havana make it very clear that, even before Fidel wrote his letter, many Cubans on their own had raised similar rebuttals to Obama. Revolutionary bloggers and other journalists were active on that polemic the very next day after Obama's now notorious speech to the Cuban people from the Grand Theater. The comments from the grassroots to these blogs posted online reflected outrage at many of Obama's remarks. Fidel's "Brother Obama" did not drop from the sky; it was linked with what the majority of Cubans were thinking, as also indicated by the five interviewees' responses in Chapter 3. Fidel simply felt that it was his "elemental duty to respond."

The false conceptions promoted by the U.S. with regard to Fidel's views on Cuba–U.S. relations serve one main intention: now that Fidel has gone, the narrative states, all the impediments to develop this "thaw" have disappeared. Once again, Cuba no longer has an excuse. The bottom line of this depiction is that Cuba, not the U.S., must make concessions. At long last, Cuba must no longer be constrained by principles. According to this yarn, "normalization" can now take place. If Cuba wishes, détente is in the making. By putting this onus on Cuba on both the domestic and international fronts, the U.S. cultural war has been significantly stepped up since the passing of Fidel.

IS THIS WHAT DICTATORSHIP LOOKS LIKE?

The monopoly media in the U.S. and the most of West is the principal vehicle for the "dictatorship" barrage and its accompanying illusion of Fidel holding back domestic changes and the Cuba–U.S. "thaw." Consider our ongoing study of CNN since Chapter 2. CNN had its regular Havana correspondent cover the Fidel funeral ceremonies. A few examples are instructive to discover how the journalist tried to juggle "dictatorship" when faced with Cuban reality.

On November 27, regarding the long queues of people paying homage to Fidel, he tweeted: "Many visiting memorial to Castro ordered to come, many others appear to feel very real grief." Many ordered? How many? Who ordered them to come? Were there another few thousand, in addition to the thousands present, who wandered around Havana to order others to come? The CNN reporter is not sure if they were grieving, and certainly doubtful if it was "real grief." CNN will say anything in order to give the impression that the people are compelled by a "dictatorship."

However, even CNN had to face reality the very same evening. On the CNN TV live broadcast from the huge Plaza de la Revolución, the appropriate roll-overs and sound-overs were flashed, such as Fidel being a "patriarch" and a "dictator" who "jailed critics." However, CNN's Havana correspondent Patrick Oppman posted:

> With me is Patrick Oppman, CNN's Havana bureau chief. And we've been trying to assess how many people are here. And there are hundreds of thousands.
>
> Patrick Oppman, CNN correspondent: We know it is absolute capacity. This square can fit a million people. In the beginning days of the revolution you would have close to a million people here hanging on every word Fidel Castro said. I covered three papal visits here, when they brought Che Guevara's body back. This seems as full if not more full than those events. Most of Havana's is probably here tonight. (CNN 2016a)

The inherent contradiction of his reporting did not seem to faze him, as was the case with most mass media Western reporters. It did not dawn on this reporter to ask if Cuba really was a dictatorship. Why was there a record number of people (according to his *own* testimony) participating in an homage to Fidel? Is this what dictatorship looks like? In the U.S., when people take to the streets in the thousands protesting the elite's policies and their repressive state apparatus, this is the most popular chant in referring to their own movement in contrast to American democracy: "This Is What Democracy Looks Like!" When I was in Havana among the more than one million Cubans, and reflecting on one of the main themes of my writing, I thought to myself, "This is what democracy looks like!" Democracy and dictatorship, respectively, are in the eyes of the beholder. The overwhelming majority of Cubans at the grassroots implicitly perceived the nine-day mourning and homage as their way of participating in their own Revolution; and Fidel represents this Revolution for the vast majority of Cubans.

"Dictatorship" and "democracy" are manipulated by the U.S. in order to launch a new offensive: Cuba had better "change." Thus, the image of dictatorship had to be fostered at all costs. Undaunted by reality, the next morning the same correspondent reported on huge numbers of people lining the streets. They were assembled to bid a final farewell to their leader as the "Caravan of Freedom" passed through the streets of Havana carrying Fidel's ashes. The reporter wrote:

> Crowds of people, some of them bused in by the government, lined the streets as they waited for his funeral cortege to pass.… Political oppression under Fidel Castro's rule undermined his achievements, such as improved access to health and education, according to Amnesty International and Human Rights Watch, which issued two reports following Castro's death on human rights in Cuba. (Smith-Spark and Oppmann 2016)

Bused in? In Havana's Vedado neighbourhood, the thirty-minute (or so) brisk walk early in the morning of November 30 to the closest street where the caravan would pass is similar to what thousands of people did in that area alone. I did not see one bus. The caravan only passed through some of the main streets and avenues. As in similar areas in Havana, the people streamed by foot to the closest main avenues and boulevards and the Malecón. In fact, some people mentioned they had arrived at 5 a.m., a full two hours before the scheduled passing, to make sure that they were well-positioned in the approximate ten-people-deep crowds. Now, since the caravan did not transit all areas, it is only normal that residents living, say, ten to fifteen kilometres (five to ten miles) away from the central areas were afforded bus transportation by the local government.

Furthermore, we notice that any other pretext is fabricated, such as human rights violations, with the sole proof being the mention of two organizations linked to Western interests. "Human rights" is the standard buzzword applied to Cuba. This is propagated in order to impose on the American public an ingrained notion of one-man tyrannical rule embodied in Fidel, who is no longer there to hold back Cuba's move toward the U.S. political and economic model.

In Chapter 4, we also asked where Obama and the CNN correspondent were when the mass participatory exercise in democracy took place in Cuba from June 15 to September 20, 2016. We can likewise now challenge, based on its coverage after November 25, why CNN did not recognize Cuba's democratic grassroots participation instead of pointing a finger once again at Fidel Castro as the cause of retrogression and human rights violations. This explicit singling out of Fidel is what the same CNN correspondent did earlier in 2016, as indicated in Chapter 4, reporting on the Chanel fashion show, the *Adonia* cruise ship docking and the Rolling Stones concert.

The CNN reporting on Havana is so bent on portraying Fidel as the strong man holding back domestic and international change that it inadvertently showed that it is a non-partisan American policy favoured by both outgoing president Obama and Trump. For example, in a CNN TV broadcast on November 27, 2016, from Havana, a senior international correspondent read out the key positions of Trump's antagonistic and gruesome statement on the death of Fidel. This included the crude, undiplomatic slurs and political posturing about "dictatorship" and more. However, Trump also said that "our administration will do all it can to ensure the Cuban people can finally begin their journey toward prosperity and liberty." The CNN report concluded: "The President-elect's words may find some echo in the people here that perhaps the passing of Fidel Castro will begin to bring change that was not possible while he was still here" (Oppmann, Park and Smith-Spark 2016).[1]

Obama had also sent a similar message to the Cuban people on innumerable occasions in Washington and in Havana about his hopes for a Cuba endowed with prosperity and liberty. The Obama statement on the passing of Fidel can also be considered political posturing, but with diplomatic overtures replacing crudity. Even then, Obama's diplomatic approach to Fidel's passing was extremely limited. He did not attend the funeral of the person who, for fifty-six years, was prime minister and president of Cuba, with which the U.S. has diplomatic relations. Instead, Obama sent an explicit "non-delegation" consisting of Obama's national security advisor and speechwriter, Ben Rhodes, who of course joined the U.S. Embassy's representative in Havana already there. In contrast, earlier in 2016, Obama went to Israel to attend the funeral of *former* premier and president Shimon Perez (Michael 2016). In addition, the American Embassy was probably the only one not flying its flag at half-staff. The message is clear. Washington, whether Obama or Trump, each one based on different rhetoric, drives a clear wedge between the U.S. and Fidel Castro as part of this latest cultural offensive to pressure Cuba into "changing" now that the Fidel alibi is no longer there.

For the vast majority of Cubans, all the U.S. international media and political onslaught about "dictatorship," "democratic rights" and so on was like water off a duck's back. The millions of Cubans who participated in this memorial to Fidel will never forget those nine days on the streets, on rural country roads and plazas, or at home with families and friends riveted to their TV screens. Nonetheless, one cannot underestimate the challenge of this new and unprecedented stage of media and political aggression regarding Cuba–U.S. relations. However, perhaps a more dangerous threat to Cuba–U.S. relations, from the perspective of an ongoing positive outcome for the Cuban Revolution, is derived from its more subtle variety, which we deal with now.

THE AVATARS

Since the death of Fidel, Cuba–U.S. relations have become further complicated as the conciliatory trend on and off the island has largely succumbed to the U.S.-led media blitzkrieg. This outlook has just exchanged the term "dictatorship" for more politically correct and subtle buzzwords: independent press, freedom of speech, political parties, pluralism, civil liberties, repression, civil and political human rights, more democracy, ruthless with opponents and paranoia, to name a few. This false cryptography contributes to the U.S. narrative of dictatorship.

In the words of Ricardo Alarcón: "This book makes a contribution to a necessary discussion about our political system, and as such it is a useful tool that will help to refine this system, making it even more authentically democratic" (August 2014). Could this be written by someone who recommends making the Cuban system "even more authentically democratic," based on U.S. preconceived views? On the contrary, it is an excerpt from the foreword of my previous book, which takes up the issue of improving Cuban democracy from the standpoint of the *Cuban Revolution*, and *not* that of an American set of ideas and values. Since the death of Fidel, the media war is stoking a wildfire of supposedly transcendental political terms as listed above. It is a Western incursion striving to force the Cuban socialist culture into renouncing its revolutionary tradition, supposedly now outdated with the passing of Fidel. This latest amplified verbal belligerency has and will have a major impact on Cuba–U.S. relations.

The buzzwords mentioned above, such as "democracy," hang in the air with no explanation or facts at all, as if they are commonly understood by everyone in the same way, that is, the U.S.-centric outlook. To contrast this narrow view, American historical social scientist Immanuel Wallerstein wrote in 1996 about Eurocentrism (and by extension U.S.-centrism) being based, among other features, on "universalism [which] is the view that there exist scientific truths that are valid across all of time and space.... It has been argued that these allegedly universal theories are not in fact universal, but rather a presentation of the Western historical pattern as though it were universal."

The complication arises when the mindset that may superficially reject this outlook still falls prey to it. No serious progressive academic today, especially the pro-Cuban ones, would adhere to the notion that the U.S. model is applicable to all, especially to Cuba. However, when push comes to shove, the bias of the "non-biased" rears its head. This is why Wallerstein titled his classic essay "Eurocentrism and Its Avatars." The "anti-Eurocentrism" becomes an incarnation of another form of Eurocentrism that is ostensibly against the West's one-sided outlook but is in reality its apologist. Thus, despite its avowed progressive outlook, abstract terms such as "democracy," "independent press" and so forth are unleashed even though, as Samir Amin (another outstanding authority on Eurocentrism) writes, they put forward "expressions of the Eurocentric construct without being embarrassed by the incoherence of the overall vision that results" (2009: 186).

One such avatar is Carlos Alzugaray, who, as our ongoing case study shows, is representative of the conciliatory strand of thinking consistent with U.S. goals. In an interview after Fidel's death published in the right-wing Spanish/Catalonian newspaper La Vanguardia, Alzugaray even further developed the U.S.-led mantra on Fidel and change: "Many changes have been postponed out of respect for a figure who can be seen as the respected patriarch of a family that knows it has to change, but does not want to displease the founder while living." He goes on in the interview to make the macabre claim (for a Cuban person living in Havana) by saying that "'the old guard' in the Cuban leadership 'may have been shielded with the physical presence of Fidel to avoid the most daring changes,' but 'now he is no longer there'" (Cantó 2016). Thus, he once again flashes a signal to the West that he is at their service.

When it would seem that the rhetoric had reached its apex, it has morphed even further into providing uncritical support for the Obama policy (including its glaring hostile features) under the pretext of opposing the devil Trump. For example, the bilingual media based in Havana, Cuba Posible, to which Alzugaray is a regular contributor, published a piece by Ted Piccone on the second anniversary of December 17, 2014. Piccone, a senior fellow at the Brookings Institution, wrote the definitive Memorandum to Obama on January 17, 2013, titled "Opening to Havana," on which Obama largely acted and based his new Cuba policy. Piccone's anniversary piece could have been written by Obama himself as it so lavishly praised his policy (2016). It illustrates the extent to which the U.S. Cuba policy is operating *inside* Cuba. Coupled with this, Cuba is now obliged to resist the latest phase of the cultural war, the assertion that Fidel was an obstacle to "change." This is sustained by the new wave of U.S.-centric notions of democracy and its subordinates, all of which are being increasingly taken up by the conciliatory trend, as indicated by the Alzugaray archetype.

FIDEL'S PASSING HAS VITALIZED THE REVOLUTION

Throughout the island, the nine days of mourning and the following week of tributes and intense reflections together comprised an unprecedented experience. My mingling and conversing among the thousands of people in Havana's Plaza de la Revolución and in the streets, my stay at a colleague's family home and sharing this intimate period by watching on TV what we could not directly experience, as well as my exchange of views in a special meeting with Cuban journalists, allow me to make a tentative conclusion.

While the overwhelming majority of Cubans were expecting Fidel's passing, no one could have imagined the effect it would have on Cuban political culture. Before November 25, 2016, the Cuban Revolution was not stagnating; however, it was not gathering momentum either. This status quo predicament started to change immediately after his death. The once-in-a-lifetime circumstance seems to have awakened most Cubans to the stark reality that it is now up to each individual as part of the collective to carry on the Revolution and thereby safeguard Cuba's sovereignty and dignity. Of course, they were conscious of this before November 25, partly because Fidel and the rest of the leadership have always called on the people, especially the youth, to take up their responsibilities. However, the actual death of the figure that shaped the Revolution, rather than the apprehension of his passing, is not the same.

In the streets of Havana, the slogan "I am Fidel!" ("¡Yo soy Fidel!") erupted as a spontaneous cultural expression and spread from one end of the island to the other. No one handed out any list of official slogans, nor did the Cuban media prompt it, although once it became part of the political landscape, the Cuban media gave echo to it. Contrary to what has been said by those trying to denigrate Cubans, the outpouring of "I am Fidel!" and other demonstrations of commitment were not — and are not — a simplistic emotional reaction. Any serious long-term foreign observer from the *inside* of Cuban reality knows that Cuban socialist culture is not only rational, but highly sophisticated, even when confronting the impassioned reality of Fidel's passing.

In fact, Cuban culture is far more refined and worldly than all the proponents of U.S.-centric notions of democracy and its derivatives combined. After having read articles influenced by U.S.-centric prejudice from outside Cuba, and even from the island, one cannot help but wonder: how is it possible that the vast majority of Cuban students, workers, intellectuals, journalists, farmers, pensioners and householders do not have this problem with democracy aside from how to improve it *within* Cuba's parameters rather than being dictated to by U.S. one-sided views? The Cuban reality clashes with the preconceived notions propagated in the North. We are talking about two different — even opposing — worlds.

THE JURY IS STILL OUT: WHAT WILL THE CUBAN PEOPLE'S VERDICT BE?

The issues addressed in Chapters 4, 5 and 6 were still unfolding as I attempted to foresee their evolution. The U.S.-led cultural offensive after the death of Fidel is perhaps one of the most bellicose since 1959 and certainly since 17D. The Trump transition period is in flux. In forging a conclusion, the following points warrant attention.

Obama long claimed, even before his March 2016 visit to Cuba and especially since then, that, along with the Iran nuclear deal, Cuba is the most important feature of his foreign policy legacy. Leaving aside the controversies swirling around Iran, it is true that Cuba became the hallmark of Obama's foreign policy and was, in fact, the only example in the eyes of most Americans. Moreover, the Cuba–U.S. "thaw" itself — now perhaps a permanent feature of U.S. policy toward Cuba — can be considered a foreign policy of the U.S. and not so much a partisan political issue, thanks to Obama.

Multitudes of business people, members of Congress, politicians at the state and municipal levels, academics, cultural figures and ordinary American people will have visited Cuba before the end of Obama's mandate. In many ways, some of them will become further involved and will continue their commitment to improving Cuba–U.S. relations. The eventual lifting of the blockade may be only a matter of time, even if it does not seem imminent. It will, of course, assist Cuba–U.S. trade and commerce. Trump will benefit politically from the derivative effect of this foreign policy, including the eventual lifting of the blockade. However, as important, given its extraterritorial nature, it will contribute to bringing Cuba into the international economic arena beyond the U.S.

While this Obama-initiated foreign policy includes positive steps, it also continues its pursuit to undermine the Cuban Revolution, now also carried out from within Cuba. The tactics have changed from physical or military aggression to seduction. The hazard is highlighted throughout the book, including by the Cuban interviewees. The main feature is the cultural war against the Cuban socialist system and its sovereignty. The "dictatorship" assault against Cuba that erupted in the U.S. and much of the West since the death of Fidel brought the verbal animosity to an entirely new level. It cannot be discounted, especially as it now expands its influence even further from the inside, that is, through the pro-Obama outlook. Equally important is the Cuban resistance to this type of aggression, which, in the wake of Fidel's passing, has raised its cultural consciousness and determination to a new level. It is unquestionably a life-and-death struggle.

In order to reach a conclusion as to which side is winning at this time and is the most likely to emerge victorious in the future, another factor must be considered. As indicated in some of the articles I wrote in 2015–16 (reprinted in Chapter 2), the following question arises: Despite the precarious international and domestic conditions prevailing from the 1959 to the 17D period, can contemporary circumstances nevertheless be considered more complex and difficult? My conclusion is yes, mainly because of the dissimulated cultural war, more overt since the passing of Cuba's leader, which many analysts outside of Cuba (and even some in Cuba) are not inclined to examine. The relative complexity of the current situation in Cuba is only bound to become greater under the Trump presidency.

Since 17D, U.S. Cuba policy is being implemented for the first time since January 1, 1959, *within* Cuba (and not only from the outside), as symbolized by Obama's visit to Havana. This change of tactics was exemplified once again by Obama's October 14, 2016, plan for future administrations, including the unexpected Trump mandate. Its Trojan horse policy and democracy promotion programs are imperceptible to a mindset that believes the superficial rhetoric about the U.S. recognizing Cuba's sovereignty and renouncing efforts at regime change. Such a credulous orientation is seemingly oblivious to the pressures of the establishment media on democracy. However, this latest manipulation of intentions by American elites marks another step in a shift to sabotage the Revolution from the inside with the aid of a naive or purposely collaborative marginal section of Cuban society.

One must always keep in mind that while the U.S. has changed its tactics, its objective remains the same — to subvert the Revolution and Cuba's independence. This is a determining factor. It must be inserted into the equation of Cuba–U.S. relations at all times. However, this is not always applied. Whether the U.S. or Cuba will win the cultural war is yet to be decided. The jury is still out and will be for the foreseeable future. It would be misleading to suggest that the Cuban Revolution is hanging by a thread, but it would also be overly optimistic to suggest that the preservation of Cuba's revolutionary heritage is not at risk. One thing is certain: it will require the Cuban people's resistance to the cultural aggression in order to render the verdict in Cuba's favour.

Note

1   Notes taken by the author from the video.

REFERENCES

ABC Color. March 21, 2011. "Samba, capoeira y fútbol para Obama en la Ciudad de Dios." <abc.com.py/nota/samba-capoeira-y-futbol-para-obama-en -la-ciudad-de-dios>.

Acheson, Dean. March 25, 1952. "Memorandum for the President, Subject: Continuation of Diplomatic Relations with Cuba." *Latin American Studies.* <latinamericanstudies.org/embassy/R39-Memo-3-17-1952.pdf>.

ACN. October 25, 2016. "Youth Across the Country Insist: Cuba Is Ours." *Granma.* <en.granma.cu/cuba-vs-blockade/2016-10-25/ youth-across-the-country-insist-cuba-is-ours>.

Adams, John Quincy. April 28, 1823. John Quincy Adams to Hugh Nelson, U.S. Congress, House of Representatives, 32nd Congress, 1st Session, House Doc. No. 121, Ser. 648.

Alarcón de Quesada, Ricardo. 2003. "La Inocencia Perdida." La Jiribilla. (Quotes translated by Arnold August.) <epoca2.lajiribilla.cu/2003/n101_04/ paraimprimir/101_03_imp.html>.

Alzugaray, Carlos. October 17, 2016a. "La Directiva Política Presidencial 43 y la política hacia Cuba." Cuba Posible. (Alzugarary quotes translated by Arnold August.) <cubaposible.com/la-directiva-politica-presidencial-43-la-politica-hacia-cuba>.

———. September 29, 2016b. "Distinto tratamiento del tema de World Learning por el MINREX, Granma y Cubadebate." Medium. (Alzugarary quotes translated by Arnold August.) <medium.com/@Zuky43/distinto-tratamiento-del-tema-de-world-leaning-por-el-minrex-granma-y-cubadebate-70ff3663bb04>.

———. September 19, 2016c. "Profundizar las reformas en Cuba: hacia dónde y cómo." Cuba Posible. (Alzugarary quotes translated by Arnold August.) <cubaposible.com/profundizar-las-reformas-en-cuba-hacia-donde-y-como-dialogo-con-carlos-alzugaray>.

Amin, Samir. 2009. *Eurocentrism: Modernity, Religion and Democracy.* New York: Monthly Review Press.

Arias-Polo, Arturo. December 13, 2016. "Cantante cubano Issac Delgado: 'La política no es mi tema.'" *El Nuevo Herald.* <elnuevoherald.com/entretenimiento/musica/ article120672453.html>.

August, Arnold. n.d. *Democracy in the U.S.* <democracyintheus.com>.

———. April 25, 2016a. "Thoughts on Cuban Resistance to US Ideological/ Political War." *CounterPunch.* <counterpunch.org/2016/04/25/ some-thoughts-on-cuban-resistance-to-us-ideologicalpolitical-war>.

———. March 26, 2016b. "Obama in Cuba: How Political Prisoners Hit the

Corporate International Media Headlines." *The Citizen* (India). <thecitizen.in/index.php/NewsDetail/index/1/7236/Obama-in-Cuba-How-Political-Prisoners-Hit-the-Corporate-International-Media-Headlines>.

———. March 13, 2016c. "Obama in Cuba: Will the Visit Advance the US Cultural War Against Cubans?" *Global Research.* <globalresearch.ca/obama-in-cuba-will-the-visit-advance-the-us-cultural-war-against-cubans/5513854>.

———. March 5, 2016d. "Obama's Visit to Cuba and Human Rights." *Global Research.* <globalresearch.ca/obamas-visit-to-cuba-and-human-rights/5512021>.

———. February 25, 2016e. "Why Doesn't Obama Use His Executive Power to Close Guantánamo? *Global Research.* <globalresearch.ca/why-doesnt-obama-use-his-executive-power-to-close-guantanamo/5510166>.

———. February 23, 2016f. "The White House National Security Agenda for Obama's Visit to Cuba." *Global Research.* <globalresearch.ca/the-white-house-national-security-agenda-for-obamas-visit-to-cuba/5509755>.

———. January 20, 2016g. "What Obama Really Said About Cuba, Foreign Affairs and the US." *CounterPunch.* <counterpunch.org/2016/01/20/what-obama-really-said-about-cuba-foreign-affairs-and-the-us>.

———. December 26, 2015a. "The Hand of Washington in the 'Election Coups' in Venezuela." <globalresearch.ca/the-hand-of-washington-in-the-election-coups-in-venezuela/5497953>.

———. November 13, 2015b. "Cuba–US Relations and the Perspicacity of Fidel Castro's Thinking." *CubaSí.* <cubasi.com/specials/item/5859-cuba-us-relations-and-the-perspicacity-of-fidel-castro-s-thinking>.

———. September 9, 2015c. "Cuba–US Relations and Freedom of the Press." *Global Research.* <globalresearch.ca/cuba-us-relations-and-freedom-of-the-press/5474897>.

———. July 18, 2015d. "Democracy and the Restoration of Cuba–US Diplomatic Relations: Embassies in Havana and Washington on July 20." *Global Research.* <globalresearch.ca/democracy-and-the-restoration-of-cuba-us-diplomatic-relations/5463081>.

———. January 7, 2015e. "Whither Cuba–US Relations? Part 2 of 2: Interview with Author Arnold August." *Dissident Voice.* <dissidentvoice.org/2015/01/whither-cuba-us-relations>.

———. 2014. *Cuba y sus vecinos: Democracia en movimiento.* (Quotes translated by Arnold August.) Ciencias Sociales: La Habana.

———. 2013. *Cuba and Its Neighbours: Democracy in Motion.* Nova Scotia: Fernwood Publishing.

———. April 2012a. "Dissidents in the Nomination Process as Part of U.S. Democracy Promotion." Chap. 7, *Democracy in the U.S.* <democracyintheus.com/Dissidents_in_the_Nomination_Process_as_Part_of_U.S._Democracy_Promotion.pdf>.

———. April 2012b. "Imperialism and Democracy in Cuba." Chap. 4, *Democracy in the U.S.* <democracyintheus.com/Imperialism_and_Democracy_in_Cuba.pdf>.

———. April 2012c. "The Origins and Development of U.S. Democracy Promotion." Chap. 2, *Democracy in the U.S.* <democracyintheus.com/The_Origins_and_Development_of_U.S._Democracy_Promotion.pdf>.

———. April 2012d. "Two Visions of Democracy: U.S. vs. Fidel Castro." Chap. 4, *Democracy in the U.S.* <democracyintheus.com/Two_Visions_of_ Democracy_U.S._vs._Fidel_Castro.pdf>.

———. March 2012e. "Appropriating U.S.-Centrism for Itself." Chap. 2, *Democracy in the U.S.* <democracyintheus.com/Appropriating_U.S.-Centrism_for_Itself. pdf>.

———. October 2011a. "Brazil: Democracy, Libya, Selective History and the African-American President." Chap. 2, *Democracy in the U.S.* <democracyintheus.com/ Brazil_Democracy_Libya_Selective_History_and_the_African-American_ President.pdf>.

———. October 2011b. "The Manifest Destiny of the U.S. and Beyond to World War II." Chap. 2, *Democracy in the U.S.* <democracyintheus.com/ The_Manifest_Destiny_of_the_U.S._and_Beyond_to_World_War_II.pdf>.

———. October 2011c. "Obama in Chile: Pinochet and Cuba." Chap. 2, *Democracy in the U.S.* <democracyintheus.com/Obama_in_Chile_Pinochet_and_Cuba.pdf>.

———. June 6, 2011d. "Ravsberg, BBC, Shakespeare y Cuba." *Rebelión.* <rebelion. org/noticia.php?id=129797>.

AVN. June 10, 2016. "Cuba Calls for Strengthening Strategies to Confront Imperialist Intervention in the Region." *Granma.* <en.granma.cu/mundo/2016-06-10/ cuba-calls-for-strengthening-strategies-to-confront-imperialist-intervention-in-the-region>.

Balan, Matthew. March 21, 2016. "CNN's Cuomo Wears Shirt from Fidel Castro as He Covers Obama's Cuba Visit." *MRC News Busters.* <newsbusters.org/blogs/nb/matthew-balan/2016/03/21/ cnns-cuomo-wears-shirt-fidel-he-covers-obamas-cuba-visit>.

Blinken, Antony J. March 2, 2016. "National Statement at the Human Rights Council." U.S. Department of State. <state.gov/s/d/2016d/253899.htm>.

Bloomberg. n.d. "Executive Profile: Antonio J. Gracias, J.D." <bloomberg.com/ research/stocks/private/person.asp?personId=23717025&privcapId=606015 6&previousCapId=6521013&previousTitle=Museum%20of%20Science%20 and%20Industry>.

Borón, Atilio. December 31, 2014. "Cuba y Estados Unidos: ¡ni un tantico así!" *Cubadebate.* <cubadebate.cu/especiales/2014/12/31/ cuba-y-estados-unidos-ni-un-tantico-asi>.

Bowden, Brett. 2009. *The Empire of Civilization: The Evolution of an Imperial Idea.* Chicago: University of Chicago Press.

Brzezinski, Zbigniew. 2007. *Second Chance: Three Presidents and the Crisis of American Superpower.* New York: Basic Books.

Business News. March 27, 2014. "Factbox: What's New in Cuba's Proposed Foreign Investment Law." Reuters. <reuters.com/article/ us-cuba-investment-factbox-idUSBREA2Q1I820140327>.

Business Wire. March 19, 2016. "Starwood Hotels and Resorts Announces Groundbreaking Expansion to Cuba." <businesswire.com/news/home/20160319005015/en/ Starwood-Hotels-Resorts-Announces-Groundbreaking-Expansion-Cuba>.

Cabral, Paulo. March 21, 2011. "Obama Woos Brazil in Bid to Build Better Ties." *BBC News,* Rio de Janeiro. <bbc.co.uk/news/world-latin-america-12802978>.

Cantó, Lorena. December 4, 2016. "Murió Fidel Castro. Y ahora, ¿qué?" *La Vanguardia.* (Quotes translated by Arnold August.) <lavanguardia.com/politica/20161204/412403121505/murio-fidel-castro-y-ahora-que.html>.

Caputo, Marc. September 16, 2016. "In Miami, Trump Morphs Back into a Cuba Hardliner." *Politico Magazine.* <politico.com/story/2016/09/donald-trump-miami-cuba-hardliner-228314>.

Carlisle, Rodney P., and J. Geoffrey Golson (eds.). 2007. *Manifest Destiny and the Expansion of America.* Santa Barbara: ABC-CLIO.

Carter, Jimmy. May 21, 2002. "President Carter's Cuba Trip Report." The Carter Center. <cartercenter.org/news/documents/doc528.html>.

Castro Ruz, Fidel. April 20, 2016a. "Fidel Castro: The Cuban People Will Overcome." *Granma.* <en.granma.cu/cuba/2016-04-20/fidel-castro-the-cuban-people-will-overcome>.

———. March 29, 2016b. "Brother Obama: In the Footprints of the Conquistadores." *CounterPunch.* <counterpunch.org/2016/03/29/brother-obama-in-the-footprints-of-the-conquistadores>.

———. January 27, 2015. "For My Federation of University Students Classmates." *Granma.* <en.granma.cu/cuba/2015-01-27/for-my-federation-of-university-students-classmates>.

———. November 17, 2005. "Speech delivered by Dr. Fidel Castro Ruz, President of the Republic of Cuba, at the Commemoration of the 60th Anniversary of his admission to University of Havana, in the Aula Magna of the University of Havana, on November 17, 2005." Gobierno de Cuba. <cuba.cu/gobierno/discursos/2005/ing/f171105i.html>.

———. 1972. "Al Tribunal de Urgencia." Brief presented on March 24, 1952, to the Court of Appeals of Havana. *Granma* (July 26, 1966). Translated and reprinted in Rolando E. Bonachea and Nelson P. Valdés, *Revolutionary Struggle 1947–58: Selected Works of Fidel Castro (Vol. 1).* Cambridge: The MIT Press.

———. January 8, 1959. "Discurso pronunciado por el comandante Fidel Castro Ruz, a su llegada a La Habana, en Ciudad Libertad, el 8 de enero de 1959." Gobierno de Cuba. (Quotes translated by Arnold August.) <cuba.cu/gobierno/discursos/1959/esp/f080159e.html>.

Castro Ruz, Raúl. April 18, 2016. "The Development of the National Economy, Along with the Struggle for Peace, and Our Ideological Resolve, Constitute the Party's Principal Missions." *Granma.* <en.granma.cu/cuba/2016-04-18/the-development-of-the-national-economy-along-with-the-struggle-for-peace-and-our-ideological-resolve-constitute-the-partys-principal-missions>.

———. December 23, 2014a. "The Unwavering Confidence in Victory Which Fidel Instilled in Us Will Continue to Guide Our People." *Granma.* <en.granma.cu/cuba/2014-12-23/the-unwavering-confidence-in-victory-which-fidel-instilled-in-us-will-continue-to-guide-our-people>.

———. December 20, 2014b. "Statement by Army General Raúl Castro Ruz." Gobierno de Cuba. <cuba.cu/gobierno/rauldiscursos/2014/ing/r201214i.html>.

————. December 17, 2014c. "Statement by the Cuban President." Gobierno de Cuba. <cuba.cu/gobierno/rauldiscursos/2014/ing/r171214i.html>.

Center for Democracy in the Americas. October 14, 2016. "Obama's Imprint on Cuba Policy: Historic. More than Rum & Cigars. More Left to Do." <cubacentral. wordpress.com/2016/10/14/obamas-imprint-on-cuba-policy-historic-more-than-rum-cigars-more-left-to-do>.

Chomsky, Noam. 2003. *Hegemony or Survival: America's Quest for Global Dominance.* New York: Metropolitan Books.

Chomsky, Noam, and Edward S. Herman. 2002. *Manufacturing Consent: The Political Economy of the Mass Media.* New York: Pantheon Books.

CNN. November 30, 2016a. "Brazil Mourns for Three Days; Bill That Could Silence Prayers; Havana Bids Farewell to Fidel Castro; Unending Bombings in Syria; Tennessee Wildfires; Modern-Day Slavery in Greece." <transcripts.cnn.com/ TRANSCRIPTS/1611/30/cnr.20.html>.

————. March 21, 2016b. "The Final Five: Interview with Donald Trump; Interview with Hillary Clinton." <cnn.com/transcripts/1603/21/se.02.html>.

————. July 24, 2007. "Part I: CNN/YouTube Democratic Presidential Debate Transcript." <cnn.com/2007/POLITICS/07/23/debate.transcript>.

Coatsworth, John H. 2005. "United States Interventions: What For?" *ReVista: Harvard Review of Latin America* IV, 2 (Spring/Summer).

Cockcroft, James D. 1996. *Latin America: History, Politics, and U.S. Policy* (2nd ed.). Chicago: Nelson-Hall Publishers.

Communist Party of Cuba. n.d. "Estatutos del Partido Comunista de Cuba." <www. pcc.cu/pdf/documentos/estatutos/estatutos6c.pdf>.

Consejo de Estado. August 15, 2015a. "En conferencia de prensa conjunta Bruno Rodríguez Parrilla y John Kerry." *Granma.* <granma.cu/relaciones-diplomaticas-cuba-eeuu/2015-08-15/ en-conferencia-de-prensa-conjunta-bruno-rodriguez-parrilla-y-john-kerry>.

————. August 15, 2015b. "Es el momento de acercarnos como dos pueblos que ya no son enemigos ni rivales, sino vecinos." *Granma.* <granma.cu/ relaciones-diplomaticas-cuba-eeuu/2015-08-15/es-el-momento-de-acercarnos-como-dos-pueblos-que-ya-no-son-enemigos-ni-rivales-sino-vecinos>.

Council on Foreign Relations. November 21, 2008. "Transition 2008: Advising America's Next President: The Future American Leadership." <cfr.org/us-strategy-and-politics/transition-2008-advising-americas-next-presidentfuture-american-leadership-video/ p17834>.

Craig, Gregory B., and Cliff Sloan. November 6, 2015. "The President Doesn't Need Congress's Permission to Close Guantanamo." *The Washington Post.* <washingtonpost.com/opinions/the-president-doesnt-need-congresss-permission-to-close-guantanamo/2015/11/06/4cc9d2ac-83f5-11e5-a7ca-6ab6ec20f839_story.html>.

Cremata Ferrán, Mario. October 18, 2016. "El problema ahora no es Platt, sino los plattistas." *Juventud Rebelde.* <juventudrebelde.cu/cuba/2016-10-18/ el-problema-ahora-no-es-platt-sino-los-plattistas>.

Cruz Ramos, Rafael. October 6, 2015. Blog Turquinauta. "Periodismo de Barrio en alemán." *CubaSí.* <cubasi.cu/cubasi-noticias-cuba-mundo-ultima-hora/item/43887-periodismo-de-barrio-en-aleman>.

Cubadebate. May 5, 2016. "Statement by the ANAP Regarding U.S. Government Measure." <en.cubadebate.cu/news/2016/05/05/statement-by-anap-regarding-us-government-measure>.

"Cuba's Report on Resolution 70/5 of the United Nations General Assembly Entitled 'Necessity of Ending the Economic, Commercial and Financial Blockade Imposed by the United States of America Against Cuba,' June 2016." June 2016. <www.cubavsbloqueo.cu/sites/default/files/InformeBloqueo2016EN.pdf>.

de Moura, Helena. March 20, 2011. "Obama Charms Brazilians During Two-Day Visit, Observers Say." CNN. <edition.cnn.com/2011/WORLD/americas/03/20/brazil..obama>.

Documentos para la historia de Cuba [Documents for the History of Cuba], II. 1969. Ed. Hortensia Pichardo. La Habana: Ciencias Sociales.

Domínguez, Jorge I. 1978. *Cuba: Order and Revolution.* Cambridge: The Belknap Press, Harvard University Press.

Eichenwald, Kurt. September 29, 2016. "How Donald Trump's Company Violated the United States Embargo Against Cuba." *Newsweek.* <newsweek.com/2016/10/14/donald-trump-cuban-embargo-castro-violated-florida-504059.html>.

Elizalde, Rosa Miriam. February 23, 2016. "Tom Wilner: No está claro si Obama utilizará su poder ejecutivo para cerrar la prisión en Guantánamo." *Cubadebate.* <cubadebate.cu/noticias/2016/02/23/tom-wilner-no-esta-claro-si-obama-utilizar-su-poder-ejecutivo-para-cerrar-guantanamo>.

Elizalde, Rosa Miriam, and Ismael Francisco. July 21, 2015. "Cuba-EEUU: Lo difícil viene ahora." *Cubadebate.* <cubadebate.cu/noticias/2015/07/21/cuba-eeuu-lo-dificil-viene-ahora>.

Ellis, Keith. 1983. *Nicolás Guillén: Poetry and Ideology.* University of Toronto Press.

Engage Cuba Coalition. n.d. "Texas." *Engage Cuba.* <engagecuba.org/texas>.

———. November 17, 2016a. "Engage Cuba Hosts Call with Congressman Ted Poe." *Engage Cuba.* <engagecuba.org/press-releases/2016/11/17/engage-cuba-hosts-call-with-congressman-ted-poe>.

———. November 9, 2016b. "2016 Election Results Advance Legislative Path to Lift Cuba Embargo." *Engage Cuba.* <engagecuba.org/press-releases/2016/11/9/2016-election-results-advance-legislative-path-forward-to-lift-cuba-embargo>.

Etcheverry Vázquez, Pedro, and Andrés Zaldívar Diéguez. September 16, 2016. "The U.S. Blockade of Cuba Remains in Full Force." *Granma.* <en.granma.cu/cuba/2016-09-16/the-us-blockade-of-cuba-remains-in-full-force>.

Fonticoba Gener, Onaisys. May 10, 2016. "Rápido y furioso, tras su paso por La Habana." *Juventud Rebelde.* (Quotes translated by Arnold August.) <juventudrebelde.cu/cultura/2016-05-10/rapido-y-furioso-tras-su-paso-por-la-habana>.

Frank, Marc. October 18, 2016. "Havana Suspends New Licenses for Private Restaurants, Owners Fret." Reuters. <reuters.com/article/us-cuba-reform-idUSKBN12H1RI>.

Franklin, Jane. 1997. *Cuba and the United States: A Chronological History.*

Melbourne: Ocean Press.

Galeano, Eduardo. 1997. *Open Veins of Latin America: Five Centuries of the Pillage of a Continent.* New York: Monthly Review Press.

Global Entrepreneurship Summit 2016. June 24, 2016a. "Remarks by President Obama and Conversation with Mark Zuckerberg and Entrepreneurs at GES 2016." <ges2016.org/press-releases/2016/6/24/remarks-by-president-obama-and-conversation-with-mark-zuckerberg-and-entrepreneurs-at-the-global-entrepreneurship-summit>.

———. June 21, 2016b. "GES Featured Speakers Announced." <ges2016.org/press-releases/2016/6/21/global-entrepreneurship-summit-featured-speakers-announced>.

Globovisión. March 20, 2011. "Obama juega fútbol en Ciudad de Dios." <globovision.com/news.php?nid=181704>.

Gobierno Nacional de la República del Ecuador. August 29, 2016. "Nine Latin American Countries Sign Letter Urging the United States to Review Its Policy on Cuban Immigration." Ministerio de Relaciones Exteriores y Movilidad Humana. <cancilleria.gob.ec/en/nine-latin-american-countries-sign-letter-urging-the-united-states-to-review-its-policy-on-cuban-immigration>.

Goldberg, Jeffrey. September 8, 2010. "Fidel: 'Cuban Model Doesn't Even Work for Us Anymore.'" *The Atlantic.* <theatlantic.com/international/archive/2010/09/fidel-cuban-model-doesnt-even-work-for-us-anymore/62602>.

Gomez, Alan. November 20, 2016a. "U.S. Businesses to Pressure Trump to Keep Ties to Cuba." *USA TODAY.* <usatoday.com/story/news/world/2016/11/20/cuba-donald-trump-barack-obama-diplomatic-opening/93956270>.

———. June 21, 2016b. "First Cuban Product to Be Sold in U.S.: Coffee — Sorry No Cigar." *USA TODAY.* <usatoday.com/section/global/elections-2016>.

———. June 16, 2016c. "Cuban TV Programming to Be Broadcast in U.S." *USA TODAY.* <usatoday.com/story/news/world/2016/06/16/cuban-television-broadcast-us-dish-network/85956642>.

Gómez, Sergio Alejandro. October 24, 2016a. "U.S. Subversion Against Cuba Continues." *Granma.* <en.granma.cu/cuba-vs-blockade/2016-10-24/us-subversion-against-cuba-continues>.

———. May 4, 2016b. "Chanel no tiene problemas políticos." Medium. (Quotes translated by Arnold August.) <medium.com/@sergioalejandrogmezgallo/chanel-no-tiene-problemas-pol%C3%ADticos-d87fb56be131#.699dethqs>.

Gorgoy Crespo, Jorge. June 28, 2016. "Sesionó VI Pleno Ampliado del Comité Nacional de la Upec." Cubaperiodistas.cu. <www.cubaperiodistas.cu/index.php/2016/06/sesiono-vi-pleno-ampliado-del-comite-nacional-de-la-upec>.

Granma. October 26, 2016a. "The World Against the Blockade." <en.granma.cu/mundo/2016-10-26/the-world-supports-cubavsbloqueo>.

———. October 25, 2016b. "Cuba Hopes U.S. Vote in the United Nations Is Reflected in Reality." <en.granma.cu/cuba-vs-blockade/2016-10-26/cuba-hopes-us-vote-in-the-united-nations-is-reflected-in-reality>.

———. March 9, 2016c. "President Barack Obama's Visit to Cuba." <en.granma.cu/cuba/2016-03-09/president-barack-obamas-visit-to-cuba>.

Granma International News. August 18, 2015. "Bruno Rodríguez and John Kerry Hold Joint Press Conference." *Granma.* <en.granma.cu/cuba/2015-08-18/ bruno-rodriguez-and-john-kerry-hold-joint-press-conference>.

Grant, Will. November 12, 2016. "What Does a Trump Presidency Mean for Cuba–US Relations?" *BBC World News.* <bbc.com/news/world-latin-america-37949743>.

Guillén, Nicolás. 1985. "Se acabó." *Tengo* [1964]. *Obra Poética,* La Habana: Editorial Letras Cubanas.

Hernández, Michel. September 13, 2016. "UNEAC: Incrementar la proyección en la sociedad." *Granma.* (Quotes translated by Arnold August.) <www.granma.cu/cultura/2016-09-13/ incrementar-la-proyeccion-en-la-sociedad-13-09-2016-23-09-07>.

Hevia, Aixa. August 19, 2016. "Verde con puntas es 'Guanábana.'" *La pupila insomne.* (Quotes translated by Arnold August.) <lapupilainsomne.wordpress. com/2016/08/19/verde-con-puntas-es-guanabana-por-aixa-hevia>.

Hoovers. 2016. "The Trump Organization Inc.: Competition." <hoovers. com/company-information/cs/competition.the_trump_organization_ inc.5de03b41824ce5ab.html>.

Izquierdo Canosa, Raúl. 1998. *Las prefecturas mambisas (1868–1898).* Havana: Ediciones Verde Olivo.

Jefferson, Thomas. 1975. "First Inaugural Address." In Merrill D. Peterson (ed.), *The Portable Thomas Jefferson.* New York: Penguin Books.

Kerry, John. August 14, 2015. "Remarks at Flag Raising Ceremony." U.S. Department of State. <state.gov/secretary/remarks/2015/08/246121.htm>.

Labacena Romero, Yuniel. July 1, 2016. "Los ejes de una verdad compartida." *Juventud Rebelde* 51, 218. (Quotes translated by Arnold August.)

Lambie, George. 2010. *The Cuban Revolution in the 21st Century.* New York: Pluto Press.

Latin American Studies. March 22, 1952. "Memorandum of Conversation, by the Ambassador in Cuba (Beaulac)." <latinamericanstudies.org/cable/cable-3-22-52.htm>.

Lazzaro, Sage. February 16, 2016. "Uber's 10 Worst Actions — Threats, Lies, Sexism & Shady Business Deals." *Observer.* <observer.com/2016/02/ ubers-10-worst-actions-threats-lies-sexism-shady-business-deals>.

Leip, Dave. 2011. "Dave Leip's Atlas of U.S. Presidential Elections." <uselectionatlas. org>.

LeoGrande, William M. May 24, 2016. "Despite Loosened Embargo, Bankers' Fears Block U.S. Commerce with Cuba." *World Politics Review.* <worldpoliticsreview.com/articles/18866/ despite-loosened-embargo-bankers-fears-block-u-s-commerce-with-cuba>.

LeoGrande, William M., and Peter Kornbluh. 2014. *Back Channel to Cuba: The Hidden History of Negotiations between Washington and Havana.* Chapel Hill: University of North Carolina Press.

Lindsay, Reed. Dec. 3, 2013. "Paraguay's Forgotten Coup." *Al Jazeera.com.* <aljazeera.com/programmes/peopleandpower/2013/12/paraguay-forgotten-coup-2013122585659847327.html>.

LoBianco, Tom. November 22, 2016. "Donald Trump Outlines Policy Plan for First 100 Days." CNN Politics. <cnn.com/2016/11/21/politics/donald-trump-outlines-policy-plan-for-first-100-days/index.html>.

Machado Rodríguez, Darío. July 9, 2016a. "Palos porque bogas … " Cubadebate. (All quotes translated by Arnold August.) <cubadebate.cu/opinion/2016/07/09/palos-porque-bogas>.

———. June 10, 2016b. "Es imprescindible un ambiente de discusión y creatividad." Cubadebate. <cubadebate.cu/opinion/2016/06/10/es-imprescindible-un-ambiente-de-discusion-y-creatividad#.V4QH8fkrJMw>.

Maier, Charles S. July/August 2010. "Empire Without End: Imperial Achievements and Ideologies." Foreign Affairs 89, 4.

Manzaneda, José. May 5, 2016. "La extraña lista de 'presos políticos' en Cuba." La pupila insomne. <lapupilainsomne.wordpress.com/2016/05/05/la-extrana-lista-de-presos-politicos-en-cuba-por-jose-manzaneda>.

Marrón González, Karina, and Jesús Jank Curbelo. September 9, 2016. "El intercambio fértil." Granma. <www.granma.cu/cuba/2016-09-09/el-intercambio-fertil-09-09-2016-22-09-23>.

Martí, José. 1979. "Congreso Internacional de Washington: Su historia, sus elementos y sus tendencias." [1889] Obras escogidas en tres tomos. I. La Habana: Editora Política.

Mason, Jeff. June 13, 2016. "Exclusive: Obama Administration Not Pursuing Executive Order to Shut Guantanamo — Sources." Reuters. <reuters.com/article/us-usa-guantanamo-idUSKCN0YZ11V>.

McCallum, Jack. 2006. Leonard Wood: Rough Rider, Surgeon, Architect of American Imperialism. New York and London: New York University Press.

Merencio, Jorge Luis. October 25, 2016a. "Neighborhood Debates Kick Off in Guantánamo." Granma. <en.granma.cu/cuba/2016-10-25/neighborhood-debates-kick-off-in-guantanamo>.

———. October 24, 2016b. "Cuban Women Denounce U.S. Blockade and Intervention." Granma. <en.granma.cu/cuba-vs-blockade/2016-10-24/cuban-women-denounce-us-blockade-and-intervention>.

Michael, Tom. September 30, 2016. "Laid to Rest: Prince Charles, Obama and Boris join 70 World Leaders for State Funeral of Former Israeli PM Shimon Peres in Jerusalem as Terror Attack Fears Spark Massive Security Operation." The Sun (U.K. Edition). <thesun.co.uk/news/1884123/prince-charles-obama-boris-world-leaders-funeral-shimon-peres>.

Ministry of Foreign Affairs of Cuba. January 31, 2003. "The Text of the Constitution of the Republic of Cuba." Official Gazette of the Republic of Cuba. Special Edition No. 3. <anterior.cubaminrex.cu/English/LookCuba/Articles/AboutCuba/Constitution/inicio.html>.

Monroe, John. December 2, 1823. "State of the Union Address." U.S. National Archives and Records Administration. <ourdocuments.gov/doc.php?doc=23&page=transcript>.

Muse, Robert L. n.d. Law Offices of Robert L. Muse. <robertmuse.com>.

National Constitution Center. n.d. "Article II: Executive Branch." <constitutioncenter.

org/interactive-constitution/articles/article-ii>.

New York Times. January 13, 2017. "Ending a Misguided Cuban Migration Policy." <www.nytimes.com/2017/01/13/opinion/ending-a-misguided-cuban-migration-policy.html>.

Obama, Barack. October 14, 2016a. "Presidential Policy Directive—United States–Cuba Normalization." White House. <whitehouse.gov/the-press-office/2016/10/14/presidential-policy-directive-united-states-cuba-normalization>.

———. September 13, 2016b. "Presidential Determination — Continuation of the Exercise of Certain Authorities Under the Trading with the Enemy Act." <whitehouse.gov/the-press-office/2016/09/13/presidential-determination-continuation-exercise-certain-authorities>.

———. March 22, 2016c. "Remarks by President Obama to the People of Cuba." <whitehouse.gov/the-press-office/2016/03/22/remarks-president-obama-people-cuba>.

———. March 21, 2016d. "Remarks by President Obama and President Raul Castro of Cuba in a Joint Press Conference." White House. <whitehouse.gov/the-press-office/2016/03/21/remarks-president-obama-and-president-raul-castro-cuba-joint-press>.

———. March 21, 2016e. "Remarks by President Obama at an Entrepreneurship and Opportunity Event — Havana, Cuba." <whitehouse.gov/the-press-office/2016/03/21/remarks-president-obama-entrepreneurship-and-opportunity-event-havana>.

———. February 23, 2016f. "Remarks by the President on Plan to Close the Prison at Guantanamo Bay." White House. <whitehouse.gov/the-press-office/2016/02/23/remarks-president-plan-close-prison-guantanamo-bay>.

———. February 18, 2016g. "Press Briefing by Press Secretary Josh Earnest and Deputy National Security Advisor Ben Rhodes." White House. <whitehouse.gov/the-press-office/2016/02/18/press-briefing-press-secretary-josh-earnest-and-deputy-national-security>.

———. January 13, 2016h. "Remarks of President Barack Obama — State of the Union Address As Delivered." White House. <whitehouse.gov/the-press-office/2016/01/12/remarks-president-barack-obama-%E2%80%93-prepared-delivery-state-union-address>.

———. September 28, 2015a. "Remarks by President Obama to the United Nations General Assembly." White House. <whitehouse.gov/the-press-office/2015/09/28/remarks-president-obama-united-nations-general-assembly>.

———. April 11, 2015b. "Remarks by the President in Press Conference after the Summit of the Americas." White House. <whitehouse.gov/the-press-office/2015/04/11/remarks-president-press-conference-after-summit-americas>.

———. December 19, 2014a. "Remarks by the President in Year-End Press Conference." The White House. <whitehouse.gov/the-press-office/2014/12/19/remarks-president-year-end-press-conference>.

———. December 17, 2014b. "Statement by the President on Cuba Policy Changes." White House. <whitehouse.gov/the-press-office/2014/12/17/statement-president-cuba-policy-changes-0>.

———. March 21, 2011a. "Remarks by President Obama and President Sebastian Piñera of Chile at Join[t] Press Conference." White House. <whitehouse.gov/the-press-office/2011/03/21/remarks-president-obama-and-president-sebastian-pinera-chile-join-press->.

———. March 21, 2011b. "Remarks by President Obama on Latin America in Santiago, Chile." White House. <whitehouse.gov/the-press-office/2011/03/21/remarks-president-obama-latin-america-santiago-chile>.

———. March 20, 2011c. "Remarks by the President to the People of Brazil in Rio de Janeiro, Brazil." White House. <whitehouse.gov/the-press-office/2011/03/20/remarks-president-people-brazil-rio-de-janeiro-brazil>.

———. March 19, 2011d. "Remarks by President Obama and President Rousseff of Brazil in Brasilia, Brazil." White House. <whitehouse.gov/the-press-office/2011/03/19/remarks-president-obama-and-president-rousseff-brazil-brasilia-brazil>.

———. March 19, 2011e. "White House." <whitehouse.gov/the-press-office/2011/03/19/remarks-president-libya>.

———. 2009. "A More Perfect Union: 'The Race Speech,' March 18, 2008." In Jaclyn Easton (ed.), *Inspire a Nation: Barack Obama's Most Electrifying Speeches from Day One of His Campaign Through His Inauguration*. Lexington, KY: Publishing 180.

———. 2006. *The Audacity of Hope: Thoughts on Reclaiming the American Dream*. New York: Vintage.

———. 2004. *Dreams from My Father: A Story of Race and Inheritance*. New York: Random House, Inc.

Oppmann, Patrick, Madison Park and Laura Smith-Spark. December 1, 2016. "In Cuba, Days of Mourning for Fidel Castro." CNN. <cnn.com/2016/11/26/world/fidel-castro-death-reaction>.

Padrón Cueto, Claudia. July 3, 2016. "CubaMax TV: Cuban TV in the USA." *On Cuba*. <oncubamagazine.com/culture/cubamax-tv-cuban-tv-in-the-usa>.

Parenti, Michael. 2008. *Democracy for the Few* (8th ed.). Boston: Thomson Wadsworth.

Pérez, Louis A., Jr. 1995. *Cuba: Between Reform and Revolution*. New York: Oxford University Press.

Pérez Santana, Amarilys. December 16, 2008. President, Comisión de Candidaturas Nacional (CCN), 2007–08; member, National Secretariat, Central de Trabajadores de Cuba (CTC). Personal interview with Arnold August. Havana.

Piccone, Ted. December 4, 2016. "U.S.-Cuba Normalizations: A Balance Sheet." Cuba Posible. <cubaposible.com/u-s-cuba-normalizations-balance-sheet>.

———. January 17, 2013. Memorandum to President Obama. Brookings. <brookings.edu/wp-content/uploads/2016/06/opening-to-havana.pdf>.

Pogolotti, Graziella. May 7, 2016a. "Moriré de cara al sol." *Juventud Rebelde*. (Quotes translated by Arnold August.) <juventudrebelde.cu/opinion/2016-05-07/morire-de-cara-al-sol>.

———. May 11, 2016b. "Moriré de cara al sol." *Granma* 52, 113.

"Press Release by the Cuban Mission 'Obama Has Fined 49 Companies for Violating the Embargo Against Cuba.'" October 8, 2016. Cuba Ontime. <cubaontime. com/press-release-by-the-cuban-mission-obama-has-fined-49-companies-for-violating-the-embargo-against-cuba>.

Ramírez Cañedo, Elier. February 24, 2016. "Estados Unidos-Cuba: ocho mitos de una confrontación histórica." *Cubadebate.* (Quotes translated by Arnold August.) <cubadebate.cu/opinion/2016/02/24/estados-unidos-cuba-ocho-mitos-de-una-confrontacion-historica-tercera-parte-y-final>.

———. February 7, 2015. "La 'nueva política' de los Estados Unidos hacia Cuba (ii y final)." *Cubadebate.* (Quotes translated by Arnold August.) <cubadebate.cu/opinion/2015/02/07/la-nueva-politica-de-los-estados-unidos-hacia-cuba-ii-y-final>.

Ravsberg, Fernando. August 16, 2016. "Expulsan a periodista cubano." Cartas Desde Cuba. <cartasdesdecuba.com/expulsan-a-periodista-cubano>.

Recio, Milena. June 27, 2016. "ges 2016: Cuban Entrepreneurs in Stanford." *OnCuba.* <oncubamagazine.com/society/ges-2016-cuban-entrepreneurs-in-stanford>.

Redacción Internacional. March 2, 2016. "Cuba responde a Estados Unidos en el Consejo de Derechos Humanos de la onu." *Granma.* <granma.cu/relaciones-diplomaticas-cuba-eeuu/2016-03-02/cuba-responde-a-estados-unidos-en-el-consejo-de-derechos-humanos-de-la-onu-02-03-2016-22-03-12>.

Reuters. June 20, 2016. "Cuban Coffee Returning to U.S. but Only for Nespresso Brewers." <reuters.com/article/us-cuba-coffee-nestle-idUSKCN0Z61E3>.

Rice, Susan. October 14, 2016a. "54 Years Later, We're Marking a New Day in America's Relationship with Cuba." DipNote U.S. Department of State Official Blog. <blogs.state.gov/stories/2016/10/14/54-years-later-we-re-marking-new-day-america-s-relationship-cuba>.

———. October 14, 2016b. "A New Day Between the United States and Cuba." The Wilson Center, Washington, D.C. <wilsoncenter.org/event/new-presidential-action-cuba-conversation-national-security-advisor-susan-e-rice>.

Robinson, Lisa. November 2015. "Rihanna in Cuba: The Cover Story." *Vanity Fair.* <vanityfair.com/hollywood/2015/10/rihanna-cover-cuba-annie-leibovitz>.

Robles, Frances. November 15, 2016. "Business or Politics? What Trump Means for Cuba." *New York Times.* <nytimes.com/2016/11/16/world/americas/cuba-donald-trump.html>.

Rolling Stones, The. July 28, 2016. "Havana Moon in Cinemas for One Night Only." <rollingstones.com/2016/07/28/the-rolling-stones-in-cuba-concert-film-havana-moon-to-be-premiered-in-cinemas-for-one-night-only>.

Roosevelt, Franklin D. December 29, 1940. "The Great Arsenal of Democracy." *American Rhetoric.* <americanrhetoric.com/speeches/PDFFiles/FDR%20-%20 Arsenal%20of%20Democracy.pdf>.

Rousseau, Jean-Jacques. 2007. In Victor Gourevitch (ed.), *Rousseau: The Social Contract and Other Later Political Writings.* Cambridge: Cambridge University Press.

———. 2004. *Discourse on the Origin of Inequality.* Mineola, New York: Dover.

Sánchez, Iroel. June 21, 2016. "Inti Illimani clandestino en Cuba." *La pupila insomne.* (Quotes translated by Arnold August.) <lapupilainsomne.wordpress.

com/2016/06/21/inti-illimani-clandestino-en-cuba-por-iroel-sanchez>.

Sánchez Espinosa, Iroel. April 2012. *Sospechas y disidencias: Una mirada cubana en la red*. Havana: Casa Editorial.

Sánchez Serra, Oscar. September 29, 2016. "What Normalization of Relations Are We Talking About? *Granma*. <en.granma.cu/cuba/2016-09-29/what-normalization-of-relations-are-we-talking-about>.

Smith-Spark, Laura, and Patrick Oppmann. December 1, 2016. "Fidel Castro's Ashes Start Journey Across Cuba." CNN. <cnn.com/2016/11/30/americas/cuba-fidel-castro-ashes-funeral/index.html>.

The Sun (U.K. Edition). September 16, 2016. "The Rolling Stones in Cuba: Mick Jagger Talks Fidel Castro, Learning Spanish and Staying Match-Fit Aged 73." <thesun.co.uk/tvandshowbiz/1792996/mick-jagger-talks-fidel-castro-learning-spanish-and-staying-match-fit-aged-73>.

Taggart, Frankie, and Carlos Batista. June 18, 2016. "US Film Industry Says 'Hola' to Havanawood." *Yahoo! News*. <yahoo.com/news/us-film-industry-says-hola-havanawood-052956111.html>.

Tapper, Jake. August 14, 2015a. "New Era Begins in U.S.–Cuba Relations." *The Lead with Jake Tapper*. <transcripts.cnn.com/transcripts/1508/14/cg.02.html>.

———. August 14, 2015b. "Stars and Stripes Over Cuba." *The Lead with Jake Tapper*. <transcripts.cnn.com/transcripts/1508/14/cg.01.html>.

———. August 14, 2015c. "American Embassy Opened in Havana." *Anderson Cooper 360 Degrees*. <transcripts.cnn.com/transcripts/1508/14/acd.01.html>.

———. August 14, 2015d. "U.S. Embassy Reopens in Cuba." *The Situation Room*. <transcripts.cnn.com/transcripts/1508/14/sitroom.01.html>.

Taylor, Guy. March 22, 2011. "What's Driving Obama's Latin America Trip." *World Politics Review*. <worldpoliticsreview.com/trend-lines/8275/whats-driving-obamas-latin-america-trip>.

Time. April 21, 1952. "Cuba: Dictator with the People." <time.com/time/magazine/article/0,9171,889465,00.html>.

Tracy, James F. December 15, 2015. "The CIA and the Media: 50 Facts the World Needs to Know." *Global Research*. <globalresearch.ca/the-cia-and-the-media-50-facts-the-world-needs-to-know/5471956>.

Trujillo, Mario. August 16, 2015. "Cable Networks Could Cash in on Republican Debate Ratings." *The Hill*. <thehill.com/policy/technology/251162-fox-ratings-could-boost-debate-ad-costs>.

Ubieta Gómez, Enrique. September 27, 2016. "Being a Revolutionary in Cuba Today." *Granma*. <en.granma.cu/cuba/2016-09-27/being-a-revolutionary-in-cuba-today>.

UNEAC. May 10, 2016. "Declaración de la Comisión Permanente de Cultura, Turismo y Espacios Públicos de la UNEAC." (Quotes translated by Arnold August.) <uneac.org.cu/noticias/declaracion-de-la-comision-permanente-de-cultura-turismo-y-espacios-publicos-de-la-uneac>.

USAID (U.S. Agency for International Development). "Who We Are." <usaid.gov/who-we-are>.

U.S. Congress. 1975. "House Committee on Foreign Relations. Background

Information of the Use of Force of U.S. Armed Forces in Foreign Countries, 1975 Revision." Committee Print, 94th Congress, 1st Session.

U.S. Department of Commerce. October 17, 2016. "License Exceptions." Export Administration Regulations, Bureau of Industry and Security. <bis.doc.gov/index.php/forms-documents/doc_view/986-740>.

———. May 12, 2015. "Antonio J. Gracias." <commerce.gov/directory/antoniojgracias>.

U.S. Department of State. n.d. "Congressional Budget Justification: Foreign Operations; Appendix 3, Fiscal Year 2016." <www.state.gov/documents/organization/238222.pdf>.

———. October 19, 2016a. "Bureau of Democracy, Human Rights and Labor Request for Statements of Interest: Programs Fostering Civil, Political, and Labor Rights in Cuba." <state.gov/j/drl/p/263310.htm>.

———. August 30, 2016b. "State Department Announces Inaugural Class of Fellows for the Young Leaders of the Americas Initiative Exchange Program." <state.gov/r/pa/prs/ps/2016/08/261377.htm>.

———. June 3, 2016c. Daily Press Briefing. <state.gov/r/pa/prs/dpb/2016/06/258027.htm>.

———. April 22, 2016d. "Updates to the List of Eligible Imports Produced by Independent Cuban Entrepreneurs." <state.gov/r/pa/prs/ps/2016/04/256514.htm>.

———. October 2, 2015a. "Interview with Amaro Gomez-Pablos of Television Nacional de Chile." <state.gov/secretary/remarks/2015/10/247853.htm>.

———. August 14, 2015b. "Press Availability with Cuban Foreign Minister Bruno Eduardo Rodriguez Parrilla." <state.gov/secretary/remarks/2015/08/246133.htm>.

———. April 13, 2012. "Women's Entrepreneurship in the Americas (WEAmericas)." <state.gov/r/pa/prs/ps/2012/04/187904.htm>.

———. April 6, 1960. "499. Memorandum from the Deputy Assistant Secretary of State for Inter-American Affairs (Mallory) to the Assistant Secretary of State for Inter-American Affairs (Rubottom)." Office of the Historian. <history.state.gov/historicaldocuments/frus1958-60v06/d499>.

U.S. Department of Treasury. October 14, 2016a. "Treasury and Commerce Announce Further Amendments to Cuba Sanctions Regulations." <treasury.gov/press-center/press-releases/Pages/jl0581.aspx>.

———. March 15, 2016b. "Treasury and Commerce Announce Significant Amendments to the Cuba Sanctions Regulations Ahead of President Obama's Historic Trip to Cuba." <treasury.gov/resource-center/sanctions/Programs/Documents/cuba_fact_sheet_03152016.pdf>.

———. Government. March 12, 1996. "Cuban Liberty and Democratic Solidarity (Libertad) Act of 1996." <treasury.gov/resource-center/sanctions/Documents/libertad.pdf>.

———. October 23, 1992. "Cuban Democracy Act ('CDA')." <treasury.gov/resource-center/sanctions/Documents/cda.pdf>.

U.S. House of Representatives Committees on Appropriations. June 2015. Report

114. <appropriations.house.gov/uploadedfiles/hrpt-114-hr-fy2016-stateforop.
pdf>.

U.S. Office of the Secretary of the Senate. n.d. "Constitution of the United States."
United States Senate. <senate.gov/civics/constitution_item/constitution.htm>.

Van Alstyne, Richard W. 1960. *The Rising American Empire: A Provocative Analysis
of the Origins of the United States as a Nation State*. New York: Norton and
Company.

Vargas, Andrew S. May 3, 2016. "'Fast and Furious 8' Shoot in Havana Pays Extras
More in One Day Than Most Cubans Make in a Month." *Remezcla*. <remezcla.com/
film/fast-furious-8-shoot-havana-pays-extras-one-day-cubans-make-month>.

Vásquez, Carlos Chirinos. April 19, 2009. "ee.uu Se
Siente Bienvenido." *bbc Mundo*. <bbc.co.uk/mundo/
america_latina/2009/04/090418_0349_entrevista_restrepo_gm.shtml>.

Voz de América. March 20, 2011. "Los Obama Visitan el Cristo Redentor." <voanews.
com/spanish/news/latin-america/rio-janeiro-Obama-rousseff-gira-118312809.
html>.

Wallerstein, Immanuel. 1996. "Eurocentrism and Its Avatars: The Dilemmas
of Social Science." Website. Keynote address at the isa East Asian
Regional Colloquium, "The Future of Sociology in East Asia," November
22–23, 1996, Seoul, Korea, co-sponsored by the Korean Sociological
Association and International Sociological Association. <iwallerstein.com/
eurocentrism-and-its-avatars-the-dilemmas-of-social-science/>.

Weisbrot, Mark. April 22, 2016. "Washington's Dog-Whistle Diplomacy Supports
Attempted Coup in Brazil." *The World Post*. <huffingtonpost.com/mark-
weisbrot/washingtons-dog-whistle-d_b_9757652.html>.

Weiss, Rusty. n.d. "Jeb Bush: My Father Is the Greatest Man Alive." Headline Politics.
<headlinepolitics.com/jeb-bush-father-greatest-man-alive>.

Whipp, Lindsay. June 20, 2016. "us Coffee Drinkers to Get Taste of Cuba."
Financial Times. <ft.com/cms/s/0/92cf2c14-36fd-11e6-9a05-82a9b15a8ee7.
html#axzz4DCAvAr76>.

Whitefield, Mimi. November 10, 2016. "A Trump Attempt to Reverse Obama's Cuba
Policies Could Be Complicated and Costly." *Miami Herald*. <miamiherald.com/
news/nation-world/world/americas/cuba/article114076713.html>.

White House, U.S. Government. n.d.-a. "Charting a New Course on Cuba: The
Progress We've Made Since 2014." <whitehouse.gov/issues/foreign-policy/cuba>.

———. n.d.-b. "The Presidents." <whitehouse.gov/1600/Presidents>.

———. May 20, 2016. "How the Real Obama Met the Real Pánfilo." Medium.
<medium.com/the-white-house/how-the-real-obama-met-the-real-pánfilo-
aa35e93577e6#.m2wt50xd4>.

Wikipedia. n.d. "Ugly American (pejorative)." <en.wikipedia.org/wiki/
Ugly_American_(pejorative)>.

———. n.d. "Mick Jagger." <en.wikipedia.org/wiki/Mick_Jagger>.

———. "Dog-whistle politics." <en.wikipedia.org/wiki/Dog-whistle_politics>.

Williams, Emily. July 7, 2016. "Cuba Making It Difficult for Farmers to Export Coffee
to the U.S." *In Cuba Today*. <incubatoday.com/news/article88165802.html>.

Williams, James. November 17, 2016. "Florida Waits to See What President Trump Does with Cuba." *Newstalk Florida.* <newstalkflorida.com/featured/florida-waits-see-president-trump-cuba/>.

World Learning. n.d.-a. "Civil Society and Governance." <worldlearning.org/our-approach/civil-society-and-governance>.

———. n.d.-b. Home page. <worldlearning.org>.

———. n.d.-c. "Donald Steinberg." <worldlearning.org/who-we-are/bios/donald-steinberg>.

———. n.d.-d. "Programa de Verano para Jóvenes Cubanos, Julio/Agosto 2016." <regonline.com/builder/site/default.aspx?EventID=1686856>.

———. n.d.-e. "Trading Places: Partner's Perspective USAID Forward and Global Development." <worldlearning.org/media/press-room/speeches/trading-places-a-partner-s-perspective-usaid-forward-and-global-development>.

———. n.d.-f. "USAID Diversity and Inclusion." <worldlearning.org/media/press-room/speeches/usaid-diversity-and-inclusion>.

Zacharia, Janine. August 24, 2007. "Brzezinski Embraces Obama Over Clinton for President." Bloomberg. <scam.com/showthread.php?30633-Obama-s-Foreign-Policy-Superior-To-Clinton-s-Brzezinski-Sounds-Off>.

INDEX